Multireligious Reflections on Friendship

RELIGION AND BORDERS

Series Editor: Alexander Y. Hwang, Holy Family University, PA

Traditional borders and boundaries are challenged, tested, defended, and redefined in unprecedented ways. Our current crises can be seen as a consequence of conflicting interpretations of the meaning and purpose of borders and boundaries—tribal, political, national, theological, religious, social, familial, sexual, gender, and psychological, among others. The crises of immigration, refugees, famine, disease, poverty, wars, misogyny, sexism, and the environment originate from reified misunderstandings of borders and boundaries. Borders and boundaries define who we are and are not; they divide those who suffer and perish from those who flourish and survive. Religion, itself based on "holiness," or separateness, plays a vital role—both as object and subject—in better understanding borders and boundaries. Religion and Borders interrogates and reconceptualizes the nature and function of borders and the role that religion plays in enforcing or overturning barriers. This series welcomes different scholarly approaches that examine the connection between religion and borders/boundaries, broadly defined. It aims to illuminate how religion—as a socio-cultural phenomenon and a discipline—constitutes itself on the premise of borders, while containing within itself the resources, instincts, and practices to resist boundaries and enclosures.

Volumes in the series explore the methodological and theoretical dimensions of the discipline, but will engage with salient social and political issues, particularly the various crises that are deeply embedded in religious discourse (e.g., migration, environment, public health, sexuality, poverty, war/violence). Projects that engage and draw upon comparative theology, comparative religion, multi-religious sources, interreligious engagement, and interdisciplinary perspectives are especially welcome.

Titles in the Series

Multireligious Reflections on Friendship: Becoming Ourselves in Community edited by Anne-Marie Ellithorpe, Hussam S. Timani, and Laura Duhan-Kaplan
Moved by the Spirit: Religion and the Movement for Black Lives edited by Christophe D. Ringer, Teresa L. Smallwood, and Emilie M. Townes
Process Thought and Roman Catholicism: Challenges and Promises edited by Marc A. Pugliese and John Becker
Indigenous and Christian Perspectives in Dialogue: Kairotic Place and Borders by Allen G. Jorgeson

Multireligious Reflections on Friendship

Becoming Ourselves in Community

Edited by

Anne-Marie Ellithorpe
Laura Duhan-Kaplan
Hussam S. Timani

LEXINGTON BOOKS
Lanham • Boulder • New York • London

Published by Lexington Books
An imprint of The Rowman & Littlefield Publishing Group, Inc.
4501 Forbes Boulevard, Suite 200, Lanham, Maryland 20706
www.rowman.com

86-90 Paul Street, London EC2A 4NE, United Kingdom

British Library Cataloguing in Publication Information Available

Library of Congress Cataloging-in-Publication Data Available

ISBN 978-1-66691-735-2 (cloth : alk. paper) | ISBN 978-1-66691-736-9 (ebook)

♾™ The paper used in this publication meets the minimum requirements of American National Standard for Information Sciences—Permanence of Paper for Printed Library Materials, ANSI/NISO Z39.48-1992.

*To becoming good ancestors
as we recognize our kinship
and become ourselves
in friendship and in community*

Contents

Acknowledgments

We are grateful for the diverse relationships that have sustained us as co-editors throughout the development of this volume. This includes the friendships that have been developed through this collective project, the sustenance of the lands on which we live, and our families. We are especially indebted to our spouses for their encouragement, support, patience, and endurance from the conception to the completion of this project.

We are thankful to each contributor for the thoughtful, creative, and interdisciplinary ways in which they have engaged with the interrelationship of friendship, religion, and spirituality through various texts and traditions. The Religious Reflections on Friendship Seminar Unit of the American Academy of Religion has provided an invaluable forum for collaboratively exploring the interrelationship of friendship and religion. A number of these chapters have been enriched through discussions in this context.

Last, but by no means least, our thanks go to Megan White and her editorial team at Lexington Books for their diligence in bringing this project to completion.

Introduction

Laura Duhan-Kaplan, Hussam S. Timani, and Anne-Marie Ellithorpe

Friendship, like religion and spirituality, helps us find meaning in life. Friendships form us, socially, ethically, and spiritually. They motivate us to overcome prejudice, understand what a truly common good can be, and work together for justice. Friendships draw us out of loneliness and alienation. Often, friendships bring us joy. But they also have seasons of tension, so they help us learn how to navigate conflict. Thus, friendship has tremendous potential for uniting people across profound differences. Both ancient and modern spiritual traditions value friendship highly. In this volume, fifteen interdisciplinary scholars explore teachings about friendship in six different global traditions. Drawing on ancient teachings, they argue for the power of friendship to help people connect in our times. This introductory section places their arguments in the context of friendship studies, religious and spiritual teachings about friendship, and the line of thinking this book presents.

FRIENDSHIP STUDIES

Friendship studies, though important, have not been systematically developed. Until the late twentieth century, anthropologists focused their attention on kinship. Sociologists focused on family and community organization,[1] regarding friendship as a private relationship and a playful form of sociability, less important than other life issues such as family and work.[2] Modern philosophers, aware that ancient philosophers identified friendship as a school of virtue integral to living the best life possible, have nonetheless been "largely silent about friendship."[3] Some theologians grappled with the relationship

1

between friendship and the love of neighbor, but others dismissed friendship as unworthy of academic study.

In recent years, however, scholars have turned more attention to friendship. American anthropologist John Terrell, for example, asserts that friendship is innate to what it means to be human.[4] British sociologists Liz Spencer and Ray Pahl argue that friendship has become increasingly important as "social glue" within personal communities (i.e., "the microsocial world of significant others for any given individual").[5] North American feminist and ecological theologian Sallie McFague explores *friend* as a non-authoritarian, non-familial, non-gender-related metaphor for God.[6] Catholic theologian James L. Fredericks advocates for the recognition of interreligious friend-ships as a theological virtue and an example of a human excellence.[7] Several political philosophers and theologians have sought to recover the classical concept of "friends as fellow-citizens," and of "fellow-citizens as friends."[8] Others have pointed towards friendship's decolonizing potential.[9] But the transformative potential of friendship-focused research has yet to be realized. In this volume, we draw on global religious and spiritual traditions to develop friendship studies.

FOUNDATIONAL TRADITIONS

Many Indigenous traditions see friendship as foundational to community. Friends are understood as extended family. For example, many nations indigenous to what is now known as North America see treaty as a process of "making relatives." Treaty ceremonies welcome new kin and affirm their commitment to cooperation and mutual respect.[10] Half a globe away, in the islands now often referred to as Aotearoa New Zealand, the traditional Māori concept of *whanaungatanga* (kin and kin-like relationships) has some paral-lels to the classical Greek notion of civic friendship.[11]

In the western intellectual traditions, friendship studies also begin with this notion. In philosophical discussions of friendship emerging from Aristotle's analysis of *philia*, loving a friend may be fostered through relationships of mutual pleasure, utility, or virtue. Love promotes concern for the other for their sake and not for our own. The perfect form of friendship, as described in Aristotle's *Nicomachean Ethics*, is the friendship between "good men who are alike in excellence or virtue. . . . Those who wish for their friends' good for their friends' sake are friends in the truest sense."[12] Shared concern for the good of others in community, or civic friendship, makes a democratic society possible.[13] We might reject Aristotle's gendered language and allusion to similarity, but still be moved by his emphasis on love for the sake of the other. Christian theologians often speak of friendship in ways that rely on, but go beyond, Aristotelian understandings of friendship. According to friendship scholar Liz Carmichael, the friendship of Christ "is not directed only toward those who are good"[14] but also towards sinners and strangers.[15] For many influential Christian thinkers, accepting and living into God's friendship includes sharing friendship with God's creatures.

Early Jewish thought draws on different traditions of story, poetry, and wisdom literature. In the Torah, Moses' face-to-face encounter with God (Exod. 33:7–11) symbolizes a friendship between Moses and God that "offers a model of covenant faithfulness for the whole people of God."[16] Prophetic visions point towards the possibility of developing peace through friendship.[17] Both the Talmud, a foundational collection of Jewish law and lore, and the Zohar, an early collection of mystical writings, describe friendship as essential to learning and spiritual development. Islam shares similar theological understandings of friendship. The Qur'an says that "Allah chose Abraham as a close friend" (4:125). Because Abraham submitted to monotheism, God established an intimate friendship with him. Abraham's encounter with God was foundational and necessary to establish God's intimate friendship with Muslims and their commitment to monotheism (*tawhid*). Over time, each Islamic movement developed a particular understanding of the nature of that friendship.

Eastern traditions present friendship as a key that unlocks the spiritual path. In the Hindu tradition, for example, the medieval Sanskrit text *Bhakti-rasamrita-sindhu* (Ocean of the Nectar of Divine Love) presents friendship as one of a spiritual seeker's five joys. Within this emotional flavor of joy, a seeker can meet Lord Krishna as an "equal friend."[18] In Buddhist traditions, friendship is also seen as an excellent container for spiritual work. The Buddha, for instance, told Ananda, his chief attendant, that friendship is not half, but the whole of the spiritual life.[19] He told Meghiya, another attendant, that one way to release awareness is to develop friendships with "admirable people." Through those friendships, monks learn virtue, listening, persistence, and discernment "relating to arising and passing away."[20]

As these snippets from global traditions show, people come together in friendship to cooperate, accomplish tasks, help one another, create communities, make peace between communities, find joy, and learn interpersonal virtues. In friendship, we encounter one another as complex living beings, not as abstractions. Often, we learn about religious traditions as abstractions— either generously through sacred texts or pejoratively through propaganda. But, for friends from different traditions, "the religious Other is present not as an abstraction on paper but as an embodied truth in all its historical ambiguity."[21] Interreligious friends welcome, delight, challenge, and learn from one another. We invite you to join us as interreligious friends as you read this book.

MULTIRELIGIOUS REFLECTIONS:
A GUIDE TO THIS BOOK

Each of the chapters in this book is grounded in a particular religious or spiritual tradition. Most also reach beyond that tradition to discuss interreligious friendship. Some of the chapters were shaped in friendly conversation, as authors presented early versions at annual meetings of the American Academy of Religion Seminar Unit, Religious Reflections on Friendship. As other authors responded to an open call for papers, our circle of scholars collaborating on friendship studies grew. The interests of the authors represent the diversity of interests within the American Academy of Religion: half of the chapters explore non-Christian traditions, and half explore Christian traditions.

The book begins with a most ancient tradition, and a discussion that opens onto the themes of the book. In "Friendship, Treaty, and Family: Indigenous Insights," friends Raymond C. Aldred and Allen G. Jorgenson engage in a dialogue about friendship as the "making of relatives." Many Indigenous traditions say that people are related to family, to friends, to land, and to the Creator. Treaties draw these diverse beings into intentional relationship. Thus, conversations between friends always cross boundaries, and bring diversity into a community. Aldred and Jorgenson's chapter touches on themes that recur throughout the book: friendship across difference, with the land and its creatures, with the divine, towards creating community, and for the sake of accomplishing shared goals.

Jeffery Long takes up the theme of diversity in "Friendships of Equality: Mitratva, Hindu Traditions, and Interfaith Possibilities." Long begins with Swami Vivekananda's teaching about friendship of equality, which is rooted in Hindu teachings about *maitri* (i.e., benevolence, loving-kindness, and friendliness). Friendships of equality, Long argues, are often established in everyday relationships, where people engage multiple facets of their identities. To develop this argument, Long draws on the work of Lori Beaman on everyday pluralism and Amin Maalouf on the relational nature of identity.

In "Civic Friendship and Reciprocity: Ancient Biblical Exhortations, Contemporary Opportunities," Anne-Marie Ellithorpe shows how shared everyday life on the land requires a practice of friendship. Drawing on historical studies of the Hebrew Bible, Ellithorpe focuses on duties of reciprocity in Iron Age agrarian societies. Reciprocity involves both general neighborly duties and fairness in economic exchange. The Book of Deuteronomy teaches that God, who cares for the vulnerable, loves justice, and hates bribery, insists on reciprocity. The prophet Amos critiques the breakdown of reciprocity. These ancient perspectives, Ellithorpe concludes, also speak urgently into our time.

It is important, John Thompson writes, to invest in becoming a person who is a good friend; that is the first step in building a good community of friends. In "Becoming a Friend to the World: Śāntideva on 'Bodhisattva Friendship,'" Thompson explores this teaching in classical and contemporary Buddhist sources. Śāntideva's poetic treatise on the bodhisattva path says that, through friendship, seekers have the opportunity to refine themselves. Learning to truly become friends with all beings is a key practice on the path to Awakening. Contemporary Buddhist teachers who speak to global audiences, such as the fourteenth Dalai Lama and the Zen teacher Thich Nhat Hanh, emphasize that the path of friendship is open to all.

In "Sacred Fellowship Among Learners: A Kabbalistic Pedagogy for Our Times," Laura Duhan-Kaplan describes her work helping a diverse group of university students in the United States travel the path of friendship. In the months following September 11, 2001, these students shared personal stories of challenge and wonder through structured listening activities. Together, they built a community like the circle of spiritual friends described in the *Zohar*, a classic text of Jewish mysticism. Like the *Zohar*'s friends, together this group of students traversed worlds of consciousness, modeled unity in diversity, learned about the power of ritual, and became a kind of family.

Hussam S. Timani's chapter, "God, Prophecy, and Friendship in Islam," circles back to the theme of friendship with the Creator. Within Islamic thought, Timani asks, who can be friends of God? Sunni teachings say that the Prophet Muhammad is the last person to be taken by God as a friend. Shi'ism teaches that the Prophet's family were also friends of God. Sufi Islam adds that spiritually evolved saints can become friends of God. Timani, however, argues that the friendship of God is available to all who assert the *Shahada* (testimony). This declaration, that "There is no god but God and Muhammad is the Messenger of God," affirms the connection between God and an entire community of believers.

Dorothy Dean explores an aspect of friendship with the land and its creatures in the chapter "Ineffable Accompaniment: Towards a Theology of Friendship and The Human Animal." Dean argues that both friendship and spirituality are grounded in embodied affective experience. Humans, along with many other species, experience affect. Thus, we may experience cross-species friendships. And we may learn from our friends to live into broader experiences of spirituality. Dean supports this theological perspective using a broad interdisciplinary lens, drawing from psychology, biology, and film, as well as theology.

Liz Carmichael's chapter begins a section of the book exploring explicitly Christian perspectives on friendship. In these perspectives, God's loving presence becomes a model for human relationships. In "I Have Called You Friends: Friendship in the New Testament and Early Christianity," Carmichael reviews the development of ideas of friendship in early Christian theology, beginning with influential motifs in classical Greek and ancient Jewish thought. The New Testament describes God's friendship as a love that reaches out to all people in an open offer of friendship. Early Christian writers developed this theology of friendship in ways that continue to influence Christian compassion, humanitarian outreach, and peacemaking.

In "Seeking God Together in Christ—Friendship in the Christian Life," Paul Wadell takes a more detailed look at the work of three great early Christian writers: Augustine of Hippo, Aelred of Rievaulx, and Thomas Aquinas. Like the Buddhist poet Śāntideva, these three Christian thinkers understand friendship as a path of spiritual flourishing. Augustine, adapting classical views of friendship, describes friends who aim to realize the love of God together. Aelred of Rievaulx distinguishes these spiritual friendships from relationships that are morally and spiritually corrupting. Aquinas defines "charity" as a life of friendship with God that unfolds in an ever-expanding love and friendship for others.

In "Love, Friendship, and Solidarity: A Christian Theology of Friendship," Marcus Mescher discusses some challenges of living into this vision of charity. Aquinas seems to call Christians into two competing activities. On the one hand, Christians are called to express *agape* (divine love) towards God and neighbor. On the other hand, they are also called to express *philia* (particular human love) by fulfilling duties to family, friends, and neighbors. Mescher resolves the tension by articulating a vision of particular friendships that also express *agape*. He acknowledges that this integration is not a simple matter. For example, people of relative privilege who wish to practice charity through friendship may need to learn how to participate respectfully in an inclusive solidarity.

In "A Path Through the Hell of War Trauma: Pavel Florensky's Theology of Friendship," Adam Tietje focuses on particular friendship. Writing out of his experience as a military chaplain, Tietje says, "there is a path through the hell of trauma and it is best walked with a friend." Through the writings of Orthodox Christian theologian Florensky, Tietje explores the power of a friendship of spiritual accompaniment. Florensky describes post-traumatic stress as an existential hell, freezing a person in the past, and hiding the presence of God. But, through the care of an intimate friend, Florensky returns to the present, and finds himself in God's presence. In intimate friendship, Florensky writes, the dance between friends' inner selves is a kind of *perichoresis,* the mutual interbeing of the aspects of God's trinitarian nature.

Brandy Daniels and Shelly Penton also speak about this dance of friendship in their chapter, "The Project of Friendship: Biblical, Butlerian, and

Beer-Brewing Reflections." Daniels and Penton reflect creatively on what they call the "project" of their friendship. They articulate two dimensions of the project. Existentially, friendship itself is a project, as friends develop their selves in a relational partnership. Friends also engage in shared public action when they work on a project together. Finally, Daniels and Penton tell the story of starting a microbrew beer company, navigating the ups and downs of working together as friends. Their experience brings them to a deeper understanding of Jesus' teaching, "No one has greater love than this, to lay down one's life for one's friends" (John 15:13, NRSV).

The book's final chapter, by Sara Ann Bixler, ties together its wide-ranging discussions of spiritual friendship. Bixler observes that forming a network of friends is integral to the human experience of religion. In "Religion Has No Bo(u)nds? Expanding the Dimensions of Religion for the Attachment of Spiritual Friendship," Bixler draws connections between the psychosocial study of attachment theory and Christian theology. Early attachment theory (c. 1960) focused on isolated pairs of relatives and friends, but later critiques broadened the focus to broader networks and multiple dimensions of attachment. Similarly, Cistercian monk Aelred of Rievaulx (1110–1167) describes a network of friendship, situated in the context of a religious community. Bixler's discussion brings the book to a close by offering yet another vocabulary for exploring the book's opening idea: friendship can be seen as the "making of relatives." As you read, we hope you feel welcomed into relationship with a global community of thinkers, seekers, and friends.

NOTES

1. Graham Allan and Rebecca G. Adams, "The Sociology of Friendship," in *21st Century Sociology: A Reference Handbook*, ed. Clifton D. Bryant and Dennis L. Peck (Thousand Oaks, CA: Sage, 2007), 123.

2. Ray Pahl, *On Friendship* (Malden: Blackwell, 2000), 36. See also Alice P. Julier, *Eating Together: Food, Friendship, and Inequality* (Urbana: University of Illinois Press, 2013), 2.

3. Michael Pakaluk, ed., *Other Selves: Philosophers on Friendship* (Indianapolis: Hackett, 1991), vii.

4. John Terrell, *A Talent for Friendship: Rediscovery of a Remarkable Trait* (Oxford: Oxford University Press, 2014), 5, 17.

5. Ray Pahl and Liz Spencer, "Family, Friends, and Personal Communities: Changing Models-in-the-Mind," *Journal of Family Theory & Review* 2, no. 3 (2010): 197.

6. Sallie McFague, *Metaphorical Theology: Models of God in Religious Language* (Philadelphia: Fortress, 1982); Sallie McFague, *Models of God: Theology for an Ecological, Nuclear Age* (Philadelphia: Fortress, 1987).

7. James L. Fredericks, "Interreligious Friendship: A New Theological Virtue," *Journal of Ecumenical Studies* 35, no. 2 (Spring 1998).

8. Guido de Graaff, *Politics in Friendship: A Theological Account* (London: T&T Clark, 2014), 4.

9. Astrid H.M. Nordin, "Decolonising Friendship," *AMITY: The Journal of Friendship Studies* 6, no. 1 (2020). See also Heather Devere et al., "Friendship and Decolonising Cross-Cultural Peace Research in Aotearoa New Zealand," *AMITY* 6, no. 1 (2020).

10. Black Elk, "Hunkapi: The Making of Relatives" in Joseph Epes, in *The Sacred Pipe: Black Elk's Account of the Rites of the Oglala Sioux* (Norman, OK: University of Oklahoma Press, 2012), 101–115.

11. Anne-Marie Ellithorpe, *Towards Friendship-Shaped Communities: A Practical Theology of Friendship* (Oxford: Wiley Blackwell, 2022), 4. See also Māmari Stephens, "'He Rangi tā Matawhāiti, he Rangi tā Matawhānui': Looking towards 2040," in *Indigenous Peoples and the State: International Perspectives on the Treaty of Waitangi*, ed. Mark Hickford and Carwyn Jones (London: Routledge, 2018), 193.

12. Aristotle, *Nicomachean Ethics*, trans. Martin Ostwald (Indianapolis: Bobbs-Merrill Educational Publishing, 1962), 219.

13. Robert Mayhew, "Aristotle on Civic Friendship," *The Society for Ancient Greek Philosophy Newsletter* 197 (1966). https://orb.binghamton.edu/sagp/197.

14. Liz Carmichael, "Friendship and Dialogue," *Journal of World Christianity* 7, 1 (2017): 29.

15. See, for example, Matt. 11:19 and Luke 7:34.

16. Jacqueline E. Lapsley, "Friends with God? Moses and the Possibility of Covenantal Friendship," *Interpretation* 58, 2 (April 2004): 117.

17. Laura Duhan-Kaplan, *Mouth of the Donkey: Re-imagining Biblical Animals* (Eugene, OR: Cascade, 2021), 70.

18. David L. Haberman, "A Selection from the *Bhaktirasamritasindhu* of Rupa Gosvamin: *The Foundational Emotions (Sthayi-bhavas)*," in *Krishna,* edited by Edwin F. Bryant (Oxford: Oxford University Press, 2007), 416.

19. *Samyutta Nikaya* 45.2, trans. by Bhikkhu Bodhi, in *The Connected Discourses of the Buddha: A New Translation of the Samyutta Nikaya* (Wisdom Publications: Boston, 2000), 1524.

20. "Meghiya Sutta: About Meghiya." Trans. Thanissaro Bhikkhu, 2012. https://www.accesstoinsight.org/tipitaka/kn/ud/ud.4.01.than.html.

21. Fredericks, "Interreligious Friendship."

BIBLIOGRAPHY

Allan, Graham, and Rebecca G. Adams. "The Sociology of Friendship." In *21st Century Sociology: A Reference Handbook*, edited by Clifton D. Bryant and Dennis L. Peck, 123–32. Thousand Oaks, CA: Sage, 2007.

Aristotle. *Nicomachean Ethics.* Translated by Martin Ostwald. Indianapolis: Bobbs-Merrill, 1962.

Black Elk, "Hunkapi: The Making of Relatives" in Joseph Epes. in *The Sacred Pipe: Black Elk's Account of the Rites of the Oglala Sioux.* Norman, OK: University of Oklahoma Press, 2012, 101–115.

Carmichael, Liz. "Friendship and Dialogue." *Journal of World Christianity* 7, no. 1 (2017): 28–46.

de Graaff, Guido. *Politics in Friendship: A Theological Account.* London: T&T Clark, 2014.

Devere, Heather, Kelli Te Maihāroa, Maui Solomon, and Maata Wharehoka. "Friendship and Decolonising Cross-Cultural Peace Research in Aotearoa New Zealand." AMITY 6, no. 1 (2020): 53–87.

Duhan-Kaplan, Laura. *Mouth of the Donkey: Re-Imagining Biblical Animals.* Eugene, OR: Cascade, 2021.

Ellithorpe, Anne-Marie. *Towards Friendship-Shaped Communities: A Practical Theology of Friendship.* Oxford: Wiley Blackwell, 2022.

Fredericks, James L. "Interreligious Friendship: A New Theological Virtue." *Journal of Ecumenical Studies* 35, no. 2 (Spring 1998): 159–74.

Haberman, David. "A Selection from the *Bhaktirasamritasindhu* of Rupa Gosvamin: The Foundational Emotions (Sthayi-bhavas)." In *Krishna*, edited by Edwin F. Bryant, 409–40. Oxford: Oxford University Press, 2007.

Julier, Alice P. *Eating Together: Food, Friendship, and Inequality.* Urbana: University of Illinois Press, 2013.

Lapsley, Jacqueline E. "Friends with God? Moses and the Possibility of Covenantal Friendship." *Interpretation* 58, no. 2 (2004): 117–29.

Mayhew, Robert. "Aristotle on Civic Friendship." *The Society for Ancient Greek Philosophy Newsletter* 197 (1996). https://orb.binghamton.edu/sagp/197.

"Meghiya Sutta: About Meghiya." Translated by Thanissaro Bhikkhu, 2012. https://www.accesstoinsight.org/tipitaka/kn/ud/ud.4.01.than.html.

Nordin, Astrid H.M. "Decolonising Friendship." *AMITY: The Journal of Friendship Studies* 6, no. 1 (2020): 88–114.

Pahl, Ray. *On Friendship.* Malden: Blackwell, 2000.

Pakaluk, Michael, ed. *Other Selves: Philosophers on Friendship.* Indianapolis: Hackett, 1991.

Stephens, Māmari. "'He Rangi Tā Matawhāiti, He Rangi Tā Matawhānui': Looking Towards 2040." Chap. 10 in *Indigenous Peoples and the State: International Perspectives on the Treaty of Waitangi*, edited by Mark Hickford and Carwyn Jones. London: Routledge, 2018.

"Samyutta Nikaya" 45.2. Translated by Bhikkhu Bodhi. In *The Connected Discourses of the Buddha: A New Translation of the Samyutta Nikaya.* Boston: Wisdom Publications, 2000.

Terrell, John. *A Talent for Friendship: Rediscovery of a Remarkable Trait.* Oxford: Oxford University Press, 2014.

Chapter 1

Friendship, Treaty, and Family

Indigenous Insights

Raymond C. Aldred and Allen G. Jorgenson

In keeping with the dialogical spirit of this volume, we have opted to construct this chapter by way of conversation. Conversation is at the heart of relationships: between God and humans, between human persons, and between human and nonhuman persons, as the First Peoples of Turtle Island/ North America remind us. The biblical affirmation "In the beginning was the Word, and the Word was God" (John 1:1) could well be translated as "In the beginning was Conversation, and the Conversation was God." Conversation, then, is participation in a divine way of being and so revelatory. Both authors hope that readers experience our conversation, recorded here, as revelatory in some way as we imagine how the Indigenous practice of making treaty might inform interreligious friendships or even friendship between the religions. These kinds of friendship are both enticing and frightening in that they invite us to cross boundaries as we reach out in relationship.

Anantanand Rambachan speaks of the power of relationships that cross boundaries, noting that they open conversations that allow us to explore identity, difference, and so ethics.[1] Friendships that cross cultures, religions, worldviews, and more enable us to attend to our responsibilities as human beings to advance the flourishing of creation. In the context of Turtle Island, no conversation is so critical as that between the First Peoples of this land and those settlers who have found themselves here for various reasons and in various ways. That settling took shape as a colonialism that is etched across the land, and it is given to us to speak the truth of this tragedy in service of reconciliation and reparation. One of the greatest tragedies of this history is the ongoing breaking of treaties that were developed between people indigenous to this land and those new to it. The practice of making treaty predated the arrival of settlers, and was a tool used by First Nations to establish relationships. In what follows we explore the phenomenon of treaty making as a resource for understanding human relationships in many guises.

CONVERSATION

Allen: Family and friends are two big pieces of our human life together. I'd be interested for you to talk about some Indigenous worldviews around these two phenomena of family and friends. What does it mean to be family, and friends, from an Indigenous perspective and how might they relate?

Ray: Alright, well immediately I think about Indigenous psychologist and theologian Martin Brokenleg in a chapter for a book called *Coming Full Circle*. He's talking about the church when it comes to the Lakota, the Dakota people. He makes an interesting comment regarding the significance of the term *wotakuye*, or "relative" from a phrase that's translated into English as "all my relatives."[2] He notes that someone who is not a relative in this worldview is of no consequences. They're not acknowledged as part of the community. So then, because of that, you make relatives of all so that everybody's your relative. Friendship, I think, was what that means in many instances. In many ways family and friendship are almost synonymous.

A: Right. So maybe, maybe, the category of friend may be included in the idea of a relative in an Indigenous worldview.

R: There's a variety of terms in Cree to talk about kinship that don't translate well in English, because it only has a few rather than several words for cousin, for instance. I suppose you say in English your second cousin, or a cousin twice removed.

So, of course, a treaty, especially in the northern plains was all about making relatives. And I do know that how some folk from that region think about treaty might be a little different than how other folk think about it, even in Indigenous circles.

A: That makes sense. In *Treaty Elders of Saskatchewan*, Harold Cardinal and Walter Hildebrant gave one definition of the Cree word for treaties as "agreements or arrangements establishing and organizing good relations, or relations of friendship between sovereigns."[3] I notice that this references both relationship between friends and relationship between relatives as if they're synonymous.

R: This understanding of treaty comes with a view that when you look at the world you see all the movements and that everything is related and interrelated: How could we not be relatives?

A: And of course, that phrase "all my relations" points to more than just humans: it includes nonhuman persons for most Indigenous worldview is as I understand it.[4]

R: Yes. This phrase "all my relations" presumes a whole cosmology that says it's a good world. This is the starting point: it's a good world. And so, as we observe this world, we embrace it. I know that there's an ethnography on the Cree from Waskaganish (Moose Factory), by Richard Preston called *A Cree Narrative*.[5] He writes that the Cree abhor any violence directed towards another person—because you just don't do that.[6] That's just not something you do. And I know of teachings among the Blackfoot that they have no enemies. The Blackfoot have no enemies, that doesn't mean they're not in competition with others, but they have no enemies. And the way you overcome supposed enmity is by making relatives.

A: And that's what treaty is? Making kin?

R: That's what treaty is. Yes, likewise, among the Lakota making relatives was how you overcome enmity and difficulties: you come together. And the land teaches you that too.

A: The land teaches you that too. That's a good point. Let's talk a bit about the land. I mean, "all my relations" includes everything, and the land I know sometimes is described as our first Mother or Mother, which is a pretty significant and powerful image I think for most of us to really sit with. What does that mean from an Indigenous perspective: to say that the land is your Mother?

R: The land provides clothing, and food, and shelter. And like with a mother you don't have to wonder if she's going to take care of you. She will. She will take care of you. So then there's a mutual respect. Of course, with your own mother you know you shift from her caring for you to you caring for her.

It's about the task of growing up. And then, of course, I always found Irenaeus' observation powerful when he says, as Adam came forth from the virgin soil, so Christ came forth from a virgin.[7] He's saying that to refute the idea that the earth is somehow substandard. This is clearly already the case for Indigenous folk, who didn't read Irenaeus! But they had the understanding that—especially for the Lakota or Dakota—humanity came out of a cave in the ground. For many Indigenous groups their origins narratives include them coming out of a pit in the ground or from the earth. Since they come out into the land everybody's connected to the land. And so we are all spiritually connected.

A: I was just going to ask: could we talk about land as friend too, or would that devalue our relationship with the land?

R: I think in considering treaty, for now, I'm not going to differentiate between friendship and kinship. But I think that with our modern society, one of the things that happens is you don't need anybody. Your survival is guaranteed by conveniences. But maybe we need to take a look at the land. The land teaches us about reciprocity. Even though we say we understand that the land cares for us still there's a part for us in thanksgiving in ceremony; our part is to maintain the harmony that's founded in creation and we are to try to live into that and to learn from that. It's interesting, my family includes the land and nonhuman persons.

So, for instance, it seems like we have this relationship with ravens in a certain part of the land. When we were hunting for moose in Northern Alberta, and couldn't find them, we would look for ravens to see where the moose were. And then we would go to where they were, and oftentimes there was a moose. After harvesting the moose, our part of the deal was that we would leave the heart for the ravens. I don't recall where we learned to do this. My brothers and I would leave the heart for the ravens. I know some people like to eat the heart. Lots of Indigenous people do, and that's fine but we would leave the heart on a live tree for the ravens. That way we would ensure that we would have good hunting. I don't know if that's friendship, but it was a relationship.

A: Yes, a relationship, and with a relationship, there's a reciprocity. Aristotle said virtuous friendships include enjoying one another's company, helping one another and a shared moral vision.[8] In some ways that sort of reflects the hunt you just described, doesn't it?

R: Yes. Now some folks might say well that's just superstition. We weren't really being superstitious. In our mind we weren't doing it as some kind of quasi sympathetic magic that we were performing. We were practicing reciprocity.

Now I do know I have seen studies that crows at least can remember people who are good to them and people who aren't good to them and so I thought, well, maybe the ravens understand. The Indigenous people believe that in the hunt animals give themselves to you, because they feel sorry for you; they recognize your need and meet it. And in thanksgiving we acknowledge that and the mutual relationship of things. Being in treaty is being attentive to all of our relations.

Part of the idea of treaty was that it was to be renewed every year to remind people that they were in this relationship. The Hudson Bay Company picked up on that and practiced a yearly renewal. And that whole process is part of the treaty; regularly returning to it.

A: Returning to treaty, and clarifying, and renewing it so that the relationship is made fresh. That way we recall that we are connected to one another; that we no longer see ourselves as separated.

R: There's that famous poem called "Mending Fences" by Robert Frost where he mocks fences; mocking the platitude that good fences make good neighbors. And it has the following line: "Before I built a wall I'd ask to know / What I was walling in or walling out, / And to whom I was like to give offense."[9] He asks: "Are you really saying good fences make good neighbors?"

In some ways it resonates with the parable in Luke 11:5–13, wherein Jesus tells a tale about a friend who comes and says "Hey I need something!" And because they're friends, the one who was sleeping says "No! Come on. What are you doing?" But then because the friend in need is persistent, he acquiesces.

One of the best things about friendship and kinship is that you're a little freer to say "not now, not now" and you're also free to push back.

A: If it's a real relationship there is freedom to be both persistent and resistant. Is that what you're getting at?

R: Yes, I think there's the idea that we're not trying to absorb the other. You know we're not trying to absorb another into what we're doing. I was thinking about my experiences on the west coast and I was thinking about a paper by Patricia Vickers in which she said "Respect is an energy outside of self that one enters into that guides one to right action."[10] The ideal is that there is that space or place. And related to that is the category of "our group," which I address in my doctoral dissertation.[11] In Cree, this category is so important: the "our" or the collective. Interestingly, this is the communal idea that has informed Canadian identity: you are related to everybody in the nation—that was the idea. And that's a little different from the modern notion of the state, in which the individual has priority.

A: So, within any given First Nation everybody within it would see themselves as related. And what about the nation-to-nation relationships? Would that still be family, or would that be something different?

R: That's family. At least that is how we have it on the Northern Plains. There is the story of a chief who sees himself as the son-in-law to the Queen.[12] And so he says to an official representing the Crown: "How's my brother-in-law today?" This chief is a son of the Queen via the treaty since the queen was like a mother. And this other fellow was related to the Queen by merits of his position so that the chief thought they were brothers-in-law by virtue of the treaty. But this didn't mean that there wasn't a proper way to respect one another. This goes all the way down to personal relationships, which Rupert Ross writes about when he says that there's this ethic of noninterference in Indigenous cultures. No one has the right to tell anyone else what to do.[13] And even though the community is noncentralized it doesn't devolve into chaos because everybody's committed to using their freedom for the good of everyone else—not just to get their own way.

So that's a little different than what we see sometimes in Ottawa and other places. Wolfhart Pannenberg talks about that too: the whole rights space thing seems to be devoid of any concern for the collective.[14] It's highly individualistic. When this individualism is seen in the church, it doesn't seem to flow from a very good ecclesiology.

A: That's an important piece to remember: how do we construe rights in our worldview and how does friendship and family—making friends, making family, making treaty—how does that impact our understanding of rights and duties and obligations? A healthy individual identity, it seems, is contingent on a healthy collective. I recall your saying that the Cree start with the "we."

R: Also, related to all of this is the idea that you would be friends with the Creator. That was a good thing that seemed helpful for Indigenous People's lives too. I know there was one person up north when I talked about a theology of Mother Earth, who said to me after the talk, "You taught me something today— about the whole mother thing. Because I had the impression that to be a good Christian, I couldn't love the earth; there wasn't a place for that."

A: Western Christianity has been kind of hostile to land, I think.

R: Probably because Western Christians were scared of the land, maybe. Or scared of themselves. I know that there's this irrational fear that you might accidentally, you know, create an idol of the land, or its nonhuman inhabitants. I say that because I'm aware that people are always accusing Indigenous people of worshipping the earth itself.

A: Do you think it's kind of connected with Christians' difficulty with the idea that there are nonhuman persons for Indigenous people?

R: I think you're right.

A: And so when Indigenous people refer to being in conversation with the tree or raven or whatever then automatically the traditional Christian go to is "This is completely upsetting my worldview." So their response is some sort of a "there's an idolatrous movement or moment here." In a way, the point is that the western Christians weren't sure what to do with Indigenous people because their worldview is so different. And that includes an Indigenous understanding of family and friends.

R: Another thing that Martin Brokenleg says regarding the Lakota, is that a family is about 250 people, when you talk about a family you're talking about 250 people, which includes multiple generations.[15] But in the colonizing need to break people away from land and from one another so that they'll be more easily able to be shipped around different places to work, then, it seems like kinship is seen as sort of something to be overcome.

So then, for Indigenous folks they might see kinship and friendship really as synonymous. Some might raise kinship above family, but it seems that in modern society friendship is elevated even above the family that it holds up.

A: I suppose one thing that's quite different between friendship and family is you choose your friends while you don't choose your family. Although that does sort of break apart when you talk about treaty as making relations, right. So, the default Western view is that my family is the people I'm stuck with, and my friends are the people I really want to be with. So, you value one more than the other for that reason, I think.

R: Both are prone to dysfunction.

A: Both are prone to dysfunction; people can have dysfunctional friendships and dysfunctional families both. I think there is an interesting corrective that treaty making can provide: when you make treaty with somebody, you're not allowed this "I can dump you when you become inconvenient" attitude, which sometimes is a part of modern friendships.

R: Right.

A: So, I think one of the things interesting for me in terms of this volume is what might be the nature of interreligious friendships, either in terms of friendships between people of different religions, or the religions themselves—if we can imagine that. So, then you might ask the question in discussing friendship in interreligious contexts: "Okay, that's great but what kind of friendship are we talking about? Treaty friendship? Or are we talking about modern Western friendship where, you know, as long as we're on the same page we're going to be friends but as soon as we're not the deal's done." Can we imagine interreligious friendship as informed by treaty and by Indigenous spiritualities?

R: Indigenous spirituality is highly individual without becoming individualistic. In fact, it's pluralistic in that you're not trying to tell someone else how to be even while there are conventions that you follow because you learn things; you learn ceremonies. There's a way to do ceremonies. Ceremonies inform everything, including making treaty. And so, I heard this from Isaiah Beardy, Bishop Isaiah Beardy, from Northern Manitoba: The elders thought they could make treaty with these newcomers because they prayed, they saw them praying. They particularly noticed them taking the Lord's Day off from treaty negotiations. The elders saw this and they thought "These people pray, and we pray, we can be in relationship with these people." By virtue of that they were seen as spiritual people.

A: In *Treaty Elders of Saskatchewan,* it is noted that the first mark of a treaty is its spiritual character: a treaty is made before the Creator, who is a witness to the treaty.[16] So this idea is that your relationship of family or friendship, or whatever you want to call what the treaty creates, the commitment to being family and friends is done in the presence of the Creator. So, it's a spiritual relationship.

R: Yes, so then you help one another to be better. I think that's what George Lindbeck's trying to get at in *The Nature of Doctrine.* In another one of his writings, he asks "What if instead of trying to convert one another, you just try to help one another be better; to learn from each other?"[17] So then Indigenous spirituality, because it is decentralized is more open to what you can learn from one another and how we can help one another to be better. But above all it's always about connection to the land.

A: So if we imagine a friendship or a treaty relationship between the religions— if that's one of the principal questions of the volume—then those lessons are pretty transferable: how can Muslims help Hindus, for example, better connect to the land, to grow etc.

Another thing I was thinking about from my context is that the Haudenosaunee have the Friendship Wampum. And in this treaty illustrated in beads on a belt, there is an image of two people linked by a chain: one represents the Haudenosaunee and the other represents the settlers. They are connected to each other by a silver chain. The chain itself has also been described as being composed of respect, trust, and friendship.[18] Does that ring true for you at all:

that respect, trust, and friendship somehow hold together? Together, these three constitute a good relationship as a treaty relationship?

R: I think that that's right. To me making treaty was always a way to overcome enmity, to deal with difficult feelings. To make friends you need to deal with this interloper of enmity between human beings. And this enmity, it's not natural. It's not natural. Friendship is this tool that is used to overcome this unnatural way of being and also to trust in that. It brings to mind what I learned from my homiletics professor, who also taught me pastoral methods. He used to say "I just assume people are committed." That was his approach to ministry. I think Indigenous people just assume in a treaty relationship that everybody's committed. You need to assume that everybody's committed; that they're committed to try to work towards a society that values children and our grandchildren, and we're trying to leave the world a better place than we found it. Maybe people would say "You're naive Ray" but I don't know of any other way that we can move together and try to accentuate harmony. We need to trust: so, respect and trust do hold together with friendship.

Now friendship requires—for the Haudenosaunee too—befriending the stranger as we see in the condolence ceremony.[19] When you see the stranger at the wood's edge, and you see they're suffering, then you go to them, and you take care of them. That is what you do. You care. You go with a good mind, in peace. That way, you'll do what people do and that way you'll take care of each other.

A: The phrase "all my relations" really does mean, I'm related to everything and everybody. So in a way, treaty making as making friends, or family, is simply acknowledging what's already true. Would that be the case?

R: Yes. I recall sitting with Stan Beardy in Thunder Bay and talking to him about treaty, because I had these inklings that treaty was a resource that we had that was underused in Canada. We don't use it, for example, in the way that it helps to form and inform relationships within the New Zealand context. And I know that in Australia they're trying to introduce treaty even though it's a foreign concept, in order to have better relationships between the Indigenous and Settler peoples. Historically, they don't have the resource of treaty to help them. And the three things that Stan Beardy said about treaty was that treaty was above all else the privilege of a peaceful existence; an inherent right if you want to call it, for peaceful existence. The second thing was access to the land, and you can't own the land. Arthur Noskey would say, you can only own what you can carry. That's why you can't own the land, because you can't carry the land. If anything, the land carries you. So then, access to the land was the second, and it flows into the third one which is the privilege or the right to live off the bounty of Mother Earth. The treaties afford all who live in Canada on the land this right. This is the way that creation is and this flows out of creation. And then Mark McDonald added one: the right to be who the Creator made you to be.[20] And not all groups are exactly the same.

A: All four of those points could actually be powerful in terms of reframing how the religions relate to one another.

R: I think so too.

A: This understanding of treaty relationship can inform what it means to be together on Turtle Island. We're in this pluralistic society with all these different people. How are we going to be together because we are in relationship? What's the nature of our relationship? Can we come together in treaty?

R: For Indigenous people, treaty making wasn't about trying to get more. It was about making sure everyone had enough—everybody.

A: Making sure everyone has enough—what a great way to imagine all our relationships: shaped by that concern that all have enough. This is contrary to our colonial mindset that pits one person against another.

R: So, you see that the Cree and other Indigenous people abhor violence towards other human beings, this is not normal. If that has to happen that's not because things are normal, there's something abnormal that's happening. And a piece of this treaty worldview includes access to the land because this is what it is to be human: to be in relationship with creation. Being human is to be fed from Mother Earth, which comes from access to the land. This speaks to homelessness. Homelessness is such a tragedy; that anyone should be homeless is especially tragic because there should always be access to the land. Even nomadic people aren't homeless, they're moving in their home, fed from the bounty of Mother Earth. This underscores why hunger should never happen, and if it does, then we need to share.[21] So treaty was all about how we respected one another, and our groups, so that everybody did well. It wasn't about eliminating anybody; it is about sharing the space where we find ourselves. And beyond that, making treaty is about maintaining collaboration, which Sophie McCall discussed in "What the Map Cuts Up, the Story Cuts Across," where she notes that the space between us is the opportunity for collaboration and that's what we're doing in making treaty.[22]

A: The space between us as the opportunity for collaboration: that's very potent. There are some great possibilities for the religions to imagine that the spaces, the differences that constitute them also are the possibilities for them to creatively engage the world.

R: We can do something together; something that we can't do on our own.

A: Yes, something that we can't do on our own is now possible because we each bring something to the table that's a bit different; something that illuminates possibilities that I can't see by myself.

R: I like that.

A: Interreligious cooperation makes possible what's not possible by monocultures. Monocultures are very unhealthy things, right?

R: Yes, this was the problem with the model of the Catholic Church whenever it saw itself as an institution in no need of the outside world, because it was sufficient within itself. Well, God's not even like that. I was reading an essay by Christina Conroy in which she makes the case that some people take the idea of *creatio ex nihilo* to demonstrate that God doesn't need anybody else.[23] But isn't that a little speculative in the sense that everything that God does is always about relationship? Karl Barth says there is no basis for an idea of human-less God, a God aside from humanity or creation.[24] If such a God exists, there's nothing in revelation to reveal that picture of God.

A: Right, and at the core of the Christian scriptures is the affirmation that God chooses to be in need. God chooses to be needy; God chooses to need others in the incarnation, because needing others is at the core of being in relationship, whether it's family or friends or both really. That's the message of the incarnation: God chooses to be needy.

R: Applied to the religions, the message is you need others.

A: No one religion by itself is enough for the cosmos. It's kind of a radical way to reframe things, but it's at the core of treaty making, isn't it? We need one another.

CONCLUSION

In this chapter we have explored the practice of making treaty, wondering about its possibilities for interreligious friendship. Dana Robert, in considering the nature of cross-culture friendship in the context of an equally colonized society—India—makes the following observation regarding collaborative friendships between those identified with colonizers and the colonized:

> The higher purpose of these collaborative friendships was to counteract the racism and superiority complex of Westerners toward persons of other cultures and faiths, thereby standing together in solidarity as witnesses to the kingdom of God.[25]

Friendships that cross boundaries have profound potential to speak truthfully in service of reconciliation and reparation. In the context of Turtle Island, we believe that this project is well served when such a friendship is construed and/or constructed under the paradigm of treaty. Reflecting together after our conversation, it calls attention to potent learnings from the Elders of the region called Saskatchewan by settlers. They outline the nature of treaty as marked by the following points:

- Presupposing fidelity to the Creator
- Including an irrevocable commitment to peace

- Committing to a perpetual familiar relationship
- Committing to survival of each via mutual sharing
- Promising a continuing right to a mean of making a living[26]

All of these presuppose that those making treaty on the land are sovereign nations. Such an identity, however, is one of interdependence by virtue of the treaty. If treaty is to inform interreligious friendships, the space between the religions or the friends of different religious persuasions is a space of creative tension enabling honor, respect, and collaboration. We believe that such a notion of friendship implies three interweaving themes: friendship is dialectically related to family; friendship is dialectically related to strangeness; and friendship is located in between the Creator and the land.

As noted above, the Indigenous attention to "all my relations" circumscribes treaty making and so the making of interreligious friendship. The phenomena of friendship and family are simply different poles of the same reality when interreligious friendship is made under the tutelage of treaty. The notion of the friend as someone who can be de-friended is lost when we make treaty friends. We are committed to one another: we have opened our hearts to one another in care for each other.[27] People who have approached interreligious friendships in this manner know that such friendships are life-giving and fulsome. Moreover, insofar as "all my relations" informs this friendship, we understand that treaty making reveals the deeper truth that we are utterly enmeshed in relation to all whom we encounter. Making treaty reveals this truth, and interreligious friendship informed by this makes possible work together that establishes a plural agency to the end that we can do together what we cannot do on our own.[28] But this plural agency does not result in our being subsumed into one another.

Interreligious friendship is also dialectically related to strangeness. As such, informed by treaty, it recognizes the sovereignty, or singularity, of each partner in such a friendship. James Fredericks names this well when he notes that "Friendships that are lasting never lose sight of the stranger within the friend."[29] There is a creative and generative tension in an interreligious friendship that secures the possibility of being persistent and resistant in relationships. The religions and religious practitioners are dependent because we are both born of one mother, and we are independent because religions are incommensurable at some level. The Indigenous ethic of noninterference speaks to the need for interreligious friendship to allow the religions and religious practitioners to develop under the vitality of each religious worldview, even while that energy is informed by interactions with the irreducible other.

Finally, interreligious friendship informed by treaty is located between the Creator and the land: treaty takes place before the Creator and on the land. The former may be considered commonsensical since we imagine the Creator to witness all, but the latter might demand revisioning what it means to be friends when our friendship is circumscribed by the treaty realization that we are all relations, including nonhuman persons. The earth, for interreligious friendship, is more than a site for our meeting but a partner in our friendship, as is the Creator. Every friendship, then, involves four partners: the Creator, the land, and two partners—all who have voice and whose voice needs to be heeded as we explore what it means to be together. Moreover, in the context of Turtle Island, knowing that the earth is our Mother means that our circle of friends and relations includes nonhuman persons, whose care ought to be our concern. At a fundamental level, the possibility of experiencing friendship as a location for growth of the religions and the religious means the flourishing of all creation to the joy of the Creator.

Interreligious friendship, then, informed by the practice of making treaty is holistic, inclusive, and respectful. It makes possible peaceful existence, provides access to the land, and gives each the right to live off the land, as well as the right to be whom the Creator makes each to be. Treaty formation can be a beacon on Turtle Island as others see that the path of colonization is not the only option for relating those indigenous to this land and those settling here from afar. Such a friendship can be a joy to all our relations and to the Creator whom we meet in each relationship.

NOTES

1. Anantanand Rambachan, "'Love Speaking to Love': Friendship across Religious Traditions," in *Friendship across Religions*, ed. Alon Goshen-Gottstein (Lanham: Lexington Books, 2015), 103.

2. Martin Brokenleg, "Church—Wocekiye Okolakiciye: A Lakota Experience of the Church," in *Coming Full Circle: Constructing Native Christian Theology*, ed. Steve Charleston and Elaine A. Robinson (Minneapolis: Fortress, 2015), 142.

3. Harold Cardinal and Walter Hildebrandt, *Treaty Elders of Saskatchewan: Our Dream Is That Our Peoples Will One Day Be Clearly Recognized as Nations* (Calgary: University of Calgary Press, 2000), 53.

4. Randy S. Woodley, *Shalom and the Community of Creation: An Indigenous Vision*, Prophetic Christianity, (Grand Rapids: Eerdmans, 2012), 81. Woodley describes "all my relations" as follows: "The idea that all people and things are related to each other includes all of humanity. This idea opens ups to the possibility of once again becoming the family we already are. By realizing the connectedness of humankind to all animal life, we become aware of new possibilities for learning and maintaining a concern for the preservation of all things."

5. Richard J. Preston, *Cree Narrative: Expressing the Personal Meaning of Events* (Montréal: McGill-Queen's University Press, 2014).

6. Preston, *Cree Narrative*, 78.

7. Saint Irenaeus, "Against the Heresies, Volume 1," in *Ante-Nicene Fathers*, ed. Alexander Roberts, James Donaldson, and Arthur Cleveland Coxe (Peabody, MS: Hendrickson, 1999), 3.18.7.

8. Harvey Cox, "Theology, Politics, and Friendship," *Christianity and Crisis* 46, 1 (February 3, 1986): 505, 13. Aristotle, *Nicomachean Ethics*, trans. H. Rackham (Cambridge, MA: Harvard University Press, 1999), 505, 513.

9. Robert Frost, "Mending Wall," Poetry Foundation, Accessed February 24, 2022, https://www.poetryfoundation.org/poems/44266/mending-wall.

10. Patricia J. Vickers, "Christ and Ayaawx (Ts'msyen ancestral law)," *Journal of North American Institute for Indigenous Theological Studies* 13 (2015): 26.

11. Raymond Clifford Aldred, "An Alternative Starting Place for an Indigenous Theology" (ThD diss., University of Toronto, 2020).

12. J. R. Miller, "Compact, Contract, Covenant: The Evolution of Indian Treaty-Making," in *New Histories for Old: Changing Perspectives on Canada's Native Pasts*, ed. Theodore Binnema and Susan Neylan (Vancouver: UBC Press, 2007), 84.

13. Rupert Ross, *Dancing with a Ghost: Exploring Indian Reality* (Toronto: Penguin, 2006), 48, 49.

14. Bradley Shingleton, "Recognition and Mutuality: Pannenberg's Theology of Law," *The Journal of Law and Religion* 28, no. 1 (2012): 225–52.

15. Brokenleg, "Church—Wocekiye Okolakiciye: A Lakota Experience of the Church," 143.

16. Cardinal and Hildebrandt, *Treaty Elders of Saskatchewan*, 31.

17. George A. Lindbeck, *The Future of Roman Catholic Theology; Vatican II—Catalyst for Change* (Philadelphia: Fortress, 1970), 50.

18. Richard W. Hill Sr. and Daniel Coleman, "The Two Row Wampum-Covenant Chain Tradition as a Guide for Indigenous-University Research Partnerships," *Cultural Studies, Critical Methodologies* 19, no. 5 (2019): 16. The trio of friendship, good minds, and peace has also been used (ibid).

19. Taiaiake Alfred, *Peace, Power, Righteousness: An Indigenous Manifesto*, 2nd ed. (Toronto: Oxford University Press, 2009), 17–20.

20. Personal communication with Ray Aldred, circa 2014.

21. For an account of the Canadian government's intentional disregard of the lessons of treaty in service of colonial ends see James W. Daschuk, *Clearing the Plains: Disease, Politics of Starvation, and the Loss of Aboriginal Life* (Regina: University of Regina Press, 2013).

22. Sophie McCall describes collaborative authorship in: Sophie McCall, "'What the Map Cuts Up, the Story Cuts Across': Translating Oral Traditions and Aboriginal Land Title," *Essays on Canadian Writing* 80 (Fall 2003): 324.

23. Christina Conroy, "Reconciliation and the Doctrine of Creation," *Critical Theology* 3, 2 (Winter 2021): 19–22.

24. Karl Barth, *Church Dogmatics II.2, The Doctrine of God*, ed. G.W. Bromiley and T.F. Torrance (Edinburgh: T&T Clark, 1957), 94–102.

25. Dana L. Robert, "Cross-Cultural Friendship in the Creation of Twentieth-Century World Christianity," *International Bulletin of Missionary Research* 35, no. 2 (April 2011): 105.

26. Cardinal and Hildebrandt, *Treaty Elders of Saskatchewan*, 31–35.

27. SimonMary Aihiokhai, "Locating the Place of Interreligious Friendship in Comparative Theology," *Buddhist-Christian Studies* 38, no. 1 (2018): 150.

28. Taraneh Wilkinson, "Drawing and Being Drawn: On Applying Friendship to Comparative Theology," *Journal of Ecumenical Studies* 83, no. 3 (Summer 2013): 312.

29. James L. Fredericks, "Interreligious Friendship: A New Theological Virtue," *Journal of Ecumenical Studies* 35, no. 2 (Spring 1998): 169.

BIBLIOGRAPHY

Aihiokhai, SimonMary. "Locating the Place of Interreligious Friendship in Comparative Theology." *Buddhist-Christian Studies* 38, no. 1 (2018): 149–52.

Aldred, Raymond Clifford. "An Alternative Starting Place for an Indigenous Theology." ThD diss., University of Toronto, 2020.

Alfred, Taiaiake. *Peace, Power, Righteousness: An Indigenous Manifesto.* 2nd ed. Toronto: Oxford University Press, 2009.

Aristotle. *Nicomachean Ethics.* Translated by H. Rackham. Cambridge, MA: Harvard University Press, 1999.

Barth, Karl. *Church Dogmatics II.2, the Doctrine of God.* Edited by G.W. Bromiley and T.F. Torrance. Edinburgh: T&T Clark, 1957.

Brokenleg, Martin. "Church—Wocekiye Okolakiciye: A Lakota Experience of the Church." In *Coming Full Circle: Constructing Native Christian Theology*, edited by Steve Charleston and Elaine A. Robinson, 133–49. Minneapolis: Fortress, 2015.

Cardinal, Harold, and Walter Hildebrandt. *Treaty Elders of Saskatchewan: Our Dream Is That Our Peoples Will One Day Be Clearly Recognized as Nations.* Calgary: University of Calgary Press, 2000.

Conroy, Christina. "Reconciliation and the Doctrine of Creation." *Critical Theology* 3, 2 (Winter 2021): 19–22.

Cox, Harvey. "Theology, Politics, and Friendship." *Christianity and Crisis* 46, 1 (February 3, 1986): 16–18.

Daschuk, James W. *Clearing the Plains: Disease, Politics of Starvation, and the Loss of Aboriginal Life.* Regina: University of Regina Press, 2013.

Fredericks, James L. "Interreligious Friendship: A New Theological Virtue." *Journal of Ecumenical Studies* 35, no. 2 (Spring 1998): 159–74.

Hill Sr., Richard W., and Daniel Coleman. "The Two Row Wampum-Covenant Chain Tradition as a Guide for Indigenous-University Research Partnerships." *Cultural Studies, Critical Methodologies* 19, no. 5 (2019): 339–59.

Irenaeus, Saint. "Against the Heresies, Volume 1." In *Ante-Nicene Fathers*, edited by Alexander Roberts, James Donaldson and Arthur Cleveland Coxe. Peabody, MS: Hendrickson, 1999.

Lindbeck, George A. *The Future of Roman Catholic Theology; Vatican II—Catalyst for Change.* Philadelphia: Fortress, 1970.

McCall, Sophie. "'What the Map Cuts up, the Story Cuts Across': Translating Oral Traditions and Aboriginal Land Title." *Essays on Canadian Writing* 80 (Fall 2003): 305–28.

Miller, J. R. "Compact, Contract, Covenant: The Evolution of Indian Treaty-Making." Chap. 4 In *New Histories for Old: Changing Perspectives on Canada's Native Pasts*, edited by Theodore Binnema and Susan Neylan. Vancouver: UBC Press, 2007.

Preston, Richard J. *Cree Narrative: Expressing the Personal Meaning of Events.* Montréal: McGill-Queen's University Press, 2014.

Rambachan, Anantanand. "'Love Speaking to Love': Friendship across Religious Traditions." In *Friendship across Religions*, edited by Alon Goshen-Gottstein, 97–115. Lanham: Lexington Books, 2015.

Robert, Dana L. "Cross-Cultural Friendship in the Creation of Twentieth-Century World Christianity." *International Bulletin of Missionary Research* 35, no. 2 (April 2011): 100–7.

Ross, Rupert. *Dancing with a Ghost: Exploring Indian Reality.* Toronto: Penguin, 2006.

Shingleton, Bradley. "Recognition and Mutuality: Pannenberg's Theology of Law." *The Journal of Law and Religion* 28, no. 1 (2012): 225–52.

Vickers, Patricia J. "Christ and Ayaawx (Ts'msyen Ancestral Law)." *Journal of North American Institute for Indigenous Theological Studies* 13 (2015): 25–33.

Woodley, Randy S. *Shalom and the Community of Creation: An Indigenous Vision.* Prophetic Christianity. Grand Rapids: Eerdmans, 2012.

Chapter 2

Friendships of Equality

Mitratva, Hindu Traditions, and Interfaith Possibilities

Jeffery D. Long

This chapter explores the ideal of friendship in the Hindu tradition. It begins with a specific focus on the teachings of Swami Vivekananda—a prominent modern Hindu teacher—and the story of Krishna and Sudama, widely seen within the tradition as a paradigmatic tale illustrative of the meaning of friendship. It then considers this ideal in relation to interfaith cooperation and understanding, bringing Hindu concepts of friendship into dialogue with the work of Lori Beaman on quotidian relationships as a key to greater pluralism, and Amin Maalouf on the relational nature of identity.

MITRATVA: FRIENDSHIP IN THE HINDU TRADITION

In a 2016 editorial in *The Hindu*, in the "Faith" section, the following reflections are offered on the nature of friendship from a Hindu perspective:

> Friendship is an ennobling relationship to be cherished and it can blossom between individuals only with God's grace. Friends belong to a different class and are a cut above all other human relationships. Relatives demand, but friends give. A Friend is selfless, informal, bound by love and kindness alone, and one who stands like a rock in times of calamity.[1]

In short, a friend, in the Hindu tradition, as in other traditions around the world, is one who loves unconditionally, and who associates with us purely because they enjoy our company, and not due to any external obligation or

⸺mpulsion. A friend is therefore a gift from God: a loved one who can be trusted with our deepest secrets and who will help us in any way possible in troubled times.

Mitratva, meaning *friendship*, is a Sanskrit term derived by combining the word *mitra*, or friend, with the suffix *-tva*, which roughly corresponds to the English suffix *-ness*, referring to the essence or essential quality of a thing. Given, however, that there is no such word as "friendness" in English, "friendship" would seem to be the best translation for this term. A *mitra*, or a friend, is a person characterized by the quality of *maitri*, which refers to benevolence, loving-kindness, and friendliness. In the Buddhist tradition, the next Buddha predicted to appear on the earth after our current era's Siddhārtha Gautama will be Maitreya, literally "the benevolent one," or "the friendly one," who is now a bodhisattva, or Buddha-to-be, residing in the Tuṣita heaven.

The modern Hindu teacher, Swami Vivekananda (who lived from 1853 to 1902), offers a number of reflections on friendship, emphasizing that, while we should display a friendly attitude towards all beings, we must be discerning about the persons we actually befriend, i.e., those to whom we become personally close. He also emphasizes the importance of friendship being a relationship between equals, not involving any power or coercion.

With regard to being discerning about whom one befriends, he says:

> It is the duty of the householder not to pay reverence to the wicked; because, if he reverences the wicked people of the world, he patronises wickedness; and it will be a great mistake if he disregards those who are worthy of respect, the good people. He must not be gushing in his friendship; he must not go out of the way making friends everywhere; he must watch the actions of the men he wants to make friends with, and their dealings with other men, reason upon them, and then make friends.[2]

On the other hand, he also says the following when commenting upon the *Yoga Sūtra* of Patañjali in his volume *Raja Yoga*:

> We must have friendship for all; we must be merciful towards those that are in misery; when people are happy, we ought to be happy; and to the wicked we must be indifferent.[3]

At first glance, Swami Vivekananda's statement that "We must have friendship for all" seems to contradict his earlier statement about not being "gushing" in friendships. The basic attitude of a spiritual aspirant, he appears to be saying, ought to be friendly: that is, open to the good in all, the divinity that exists within all, which is the basis of the Hindu greeting "Namaste," which literally means "I bow to the divinity within you." One must also practice discernment, however, in bestowing one's friendship by becoming truly close to another person.

One must also not hate those who do evil, but rather remain "indifferent" to them. As Swami Vivekananda goes on to explain, "Every reaction in the form of hatred or evil is so much loss to the mind," an expenditure of psychic energies which one needs to cultivate and concentrate so that one might achieve the goal of spiritual life.[4] Friendship and loving-kindness, on the other hand, enhance and increase our spiritual powers, and reflect the deeper nature of the soul. Qualities of this kind enable us to perceive our true nature and cultivating them is vital for spirituality.

In speaking of love for God, Swami Vivekananda explains that one form which such love often takes is the form of friendship:

> Just as a man opens his heart to his friend and knows that the friend will never chide him or his faults but will always try to help him, just as there is the idea of equality between him and his friend, so equal love flows in and out between the worshipper and his friendly God. Thus God becomes our friend, the friend who is near, the friend to whom we may freely tell all the tales of our lives. The innermost secrets of our hearts we may place before Him with the great assurance of safety and support. He is the friend whom the devotee accepts as an equal. God is viewed here as our playmate. We may well say that we are all playing in this universe. Just as children play their games, just as the most glorious kings and emperors play their own games, so is the Beloved Lord Himself in sport with this universe.[5]

When speaking of friendship between two human beings, however, Swami Vivekananda emphasizes that, "There cannot be friendship without equality, and there cannot be equality when one party is always the teacher and the other party sits always at his feet."[6] Elsewhere he says that, "friendship can only be expected between two equals. When one of the parties is a beggar, what friendship can there be?"[7]

One of the most famous stories of friendship in the Hindu tradition is the story of Krishna and Sudama. Krishna, depending upon which sources one consults, is either an *avatāra*, or avatar—an incarnation of the Supreme Being—or the Supreme Being himself, in the fullness of his divinity. Sudama, on the other hand, is a poor Brahmin villager. The story of Krishna and Sudama can be found in the *Bhāgavata Purāṇa*, one of the collections of "ancient lore" (*purāṇas*) of the Hindu tradition, and a particularly sacred text for the Vaiṣṇava traditions, which focus chiefly on devotion (*bhakti*) toward Krishna as the supreme path to liberation from the cycle of suffering and rebirth.

According to the *Bhāgavata Purāṇa*, in their childhoods Sudama and Krishna both studied together under the teacher Sāndīpani. The two became close friends during this period, once surviving being lost in the woods during a storm by refusing to let go of one another's hands. As the two friends grew older, however, the circumstances of their lives caused them to part company.

Krishna famously went on to become the king of Dvāraka. He first had to defeat his wicked uncle, Kaṃsa, an oppressive tyrant. Krishna also figures prominently in the events of one of the two great Hindu epics, the *Mahābhārata*, serving as a friend and ally to the Pāṇḍava brothers, who are the heroes of the epic, and to the brother Arjuna in particular, to whom he gives instruction on the eve of the climactic battle of the epic. This instruction is famously narrated in the *Bhagavad Gītā*, or "Song of God," a portion of the *Mahābhārata* which has become an important scriptural text in its own right. Along with the *Upaniṣads* and the *Brahma Sūtra*, the *Bhagavad Gītā* forms part of the *prasthāna traya*, or "triple foundation" of the Hindu philosophy of Vedānta. It is also an important Vaiṣṇava text, given Krishna's central role in it as a teacher.

Sudama, for his part, lives out his life as a poor Brahmin, residing in a village with his wife. At one point, Sudama is reminiscing about his childhood friend, Krishna, who now lives opulently as the lord of Dvāraka. Sudama harbors no resentment or ill will towards Krishna, only fondness and friendship. Sudama's wife encourages him to go to Krishna and ask for his help, given that Krishna is now fabulously wealthy, while Sudama suffers in poverty. Sudama is reluctant to ask his friend for help, thinking it presumptuous; but his wife finally persuades him that it is his duty as a householder to look after his family, and that if his friendship with Krishna enables him to do so more effectively, then he should at least make the attempt.

When the poor Brahmin shows up at Krishna's palace in Dvāraka, Krishna is overjoyed to see him. He allows the poor man to sit on his throne, and even washes his feet. He then playfully asks what gift Sudama has brought for him. Sudama has brought a very modest gift for Krishna—three small bags of puffed rice. It is not a gift fit for a king, but it is all that Sudama and his wife could afford. When he offers the gift to Krishna, Krishna exclaims that this is his favorite food, and offers Sudama anything he might ask in return. Sudama, however, is overwhelmed, and cannot bring himself to ask Krishna for anything. He returns home, only to find that his humble hut has been transformed into a palace, and his wife is now wearing expensive silks. It is a miracle wrought by Krishna for his childhood friend.

This story is greatly beloved as an illustration of friendship in the Hindu tradition. It speaks to the ideal of friendship as something that lasts for a lifetime, and which can cross boundaries such as class and wealth, as well as of the ideal that true friendship expresses itself in generosity. Sudama's modesty, too, and his hesitation to ask for help for the divine Krishna, is an expression of friendship as well. Sudama does not want to inconvenience his friend, even though Krishna has wealth and power almost beyond Sudama's comprehension. Clearly, not every friend is able to be as lavishly generous as Krishna: a great king who is also God, and is thus possessed of miraculous abilities. But a true friend would *want* to show such generosity, were it in their power to do so. A true friend also does not forget. When Sudama entered his palace, Krishna immediately recognized the small boy who was once his playmate and constant companion.

MITRATVA AND INTER-RELIGIOUS RELATIONS

What can Hindu ideals of friendship offer to the fraught topic of inter-religious relations? We have seen Swami Vivekananda enjoin an attitude of friendliness toward all beings. The basis of this friendliness is the inherent divinity of the soul, according to Vedānta philosophy. And we have seen Krishna and Sudama illustrate that true friendship crosses artificial social boundaries.

Theologians and philosophers of religion have, in the last few decades, spent a great deal of time and effort in developing theologies and philosophies of religious pluralism, arguing for the proposition that there are many true and salvifically efficacious paths, and that the world would be a more humane and habitable place if exclusivist doctrines were to be set aside in favor of ways of thinking that would enjoin mutual respect and appreciation. Major figures who have contributed to this conversation include John Hick, Wilfred Cantwell Smith, Paul F. Knitter, David Ray Griffin, and John B. Cobb, as well as, more recently, Mark Heim and Kenneth Rose. Much of my own work, too, in the philosophy of religion has been dedicated to precisely this same project. While I remain deeply committed to developing philosophical models conducive to greater inter-religious harmony, pursuing this work does sometimes raise the question, particularly in a world where intolerance seems to be increasing all the time, of how effective such philosophizing is in bringing about real change.

How might the good theoretical work of theologians and philosophers of religion, who have been seeking to develop pluralistic models in the name of improving interfaith relations, translate into practical outcomes? Lori Beaman's work—specifically, her book *Deep Equality in an Era of Religious Diversity*—suggests a focus on quotidian relationships across religious boundaries as a promising starting point. Seeing inter-religious friendships as an alternative to dominant concepts of "toleration" and "accommodation," with their underlying and inherent majoritarianism, Beaman proposes the idea of "deep equality," which approaches human beings as complex intersections of multiple identities, including, but not limited to, their religious affiliations: seeing others as whole people, just as a friend would see us. A similar conception of identity is also developed in Amin Maalouf's *In the Name of Identity: Violence and the Need to Belong*, with its proposal that we are all made up of numerous "allegiances." Both studies will be engaged here with the aim of beginning the process of developing a way to translate the theories of pluralism into practice.

We begin with Lori Beaman's *Deep Equality in an Era of Religious Diversity*. This hopeful study approaches the topic of religious diversity not as a problem to be solved, but as intrinsic to the broader web of daily human interaction which is experienced in increasingly diverse Western democracies. The author, a scholar with backgrounds in philosophy, law, and sociology, is in an excellent position to take up this complex issue, with previous publications that include *Defining Harm: Religious Freedom and the Limits of the Law* and *Shared Beliefs and Different Lives: Women's Identities in Evangelical Context*. In these works, she has already begun to explore questions such as the legal accommodations that have come to be required in a religiously diverse society, as well as the complexities of identity, which can rarely, if ever, be reduced simply to a matter of religious affiliation.

Beaman begins her study of deep equality with standard questions, "How shall we accommodate religious minorities? What are the limits of tolerance?"[8] However, she quickly moves beyond the obvious limitations of the approach to religious diversity that these questions reflect: the idea that there is a monolithic "we" that can be taken for granted, and that this "we" possesses a moral obligation to "tolerate" the difference in its midst. As pointed out long ago by Swami Vivekananda, there is an inherent violence in the concept of "tolerance." "Toleration means that I think that you are wrong and I am just allowing you to live."[9] Similarly, Beaman "questions the work done by the concepts of tolerance and accommodation as they circulate in various realms, effectively maintaining the status quo, preserving the hegemony of religious majorities and indeed of cultural majorities."[10] She acknowledges the ways in which the concepts of toleration and accommodation can "mask privilege."[11] Beaman continues:

> To be sure, the notion of tolerance has produced restraint, grudging sharing of resources, and a sense that there are moral "shoulds" underlying the negotiation of difference . . . But the balance of power, or more specifically, the veto power, lies predominantly with religious and cultural majorities.[12]

Beaman instead offers a far more positive approach. As an alternative to concepts of toleration and accommodation, with their underlying and inherent majoritarianism and implied violence, Beaman proposes the idea of "deep equality." Deep equality approaches human beings not as members of majority or minority communities, but as complex intersections of multiple identities. These identities include, but are by no means limited to, religious affiliation. These identities are fluid and are in a state of constant negotiation as people interact with one another on a daily basis. Some identities are relevant to some situations, while others are not. My religious identity may be deeply important to my own sense of self, but it is not likely to arise at all as I exchange pleasantries with the checkout person at the supermarket as I am buying my groceries.

Beaman turns her reader's attention not to communities or religions writ large—"religions" and "communities" being, in any case, abstractions from the more basic lived realities of human existence—but to the common interactions of ordinary people. Such interactions involve friendship, humor, and mutual respect. Viewed through this lens, religious difference is seen less as a problem to be solved and more as part of the regular fabric of daily human existence. Because you are my friend, I see you as a whole person, and not simply as a token of one of the many identities that go into making you the rich and complex being that you are.

Beaman's method is to attend to the stories of positive human interaction that subjects often narrate to sociologists, but whose deeper significance, Beaman maintains, is often lost due to the methodological lenses that sociologists apply to the data which they gather. She sees her work as being in continuity with that of Les Back, who "criticizes the failure of sociology to engage with stories and voices in a meaningful way," arguing "that sociology has lost the art of listening, of carefully attending to the detail of what people do and say in their day-to-day lives, and instead has 'been diverted by an enchanted obsession with the spectacular, namely, the loudest voices, the biggest controversy and the most acute social concern.'"[13] This emphasis of sociology loses sight of everyday phenomena, such as friendship, which really make up the fabric of most people's lives.

The stories Beaman narrates, drawing on the work of previous sociologists, but presenting their descriptions of varied human interactions in a new light, are of real people who are interacting in positive ways with religious difference. These stories are striking precisely because they are so mundane. Beaman mentions, for example, an account of an Indian Muslim in Delhi who is preparing to perform his daily prayer, or *namaaz*. He refers casually to his prayers as his *puja*. *Puja*, meaning "worship," is a term with deep associations with Hinduism. If one's work is focused on the fraught politics of Hindu-Muslim relations in India, this casual use of a Hindu term by a Muslim to refer to one of his most sacred daily obligations (for indeed, the injunction to perform *namaaz* five times daily is one of the five pillars of Islam), is quite striking indeed. It is particularly striking if one bears in mind that *puja* in a Hindu context specifically refers to a sacred exchange in which one offers such items as food and flowers to a deity through the medium of a *murti*, or image of that deity. If one imagines Muslims purely in terms of some abstract concept of what Islamic belief entails, one is likely to expect that a Muslim would object to using the term *puja* to refer to his *namaaz*; for one might expect that *puja* would be seen as idolatry from such an imagined Muslim perspective. Such a usage might thus be seen as anomalous . . . but for its commonplace nature.

A simple example of this kind is powerful, because it reveals a truth that religion scholars often take for granted, but that is all too rare in wider society, which is that one cannot simply deduce the behaviors, attitudes, words, or actions of religious people based simply on a textbook understanding of the teachings of their religion. People are complex beings, not walking stereotypes. This is only one of the many examples that Beaman brings to bear on the issue of religious diversity. Her point is that the more dramatic instances of religious *intolerance* which typically attract the attention of scholars occur against a mundane backdrop, not of mere tolerance, but of ongoing negotiation and integration of difference.

Indeed, this has been my own experience over the course of many years of fieldwork in India. A casual observer of India, drawing information about this country primarily from media sources, is likely to see Indian society as fraught with constant communal violence. And, to be sure, such violence does exist and is a social problem in urgent need of resolution. But it occurs against a background in which the "normal" state of affairs is one of mundane harmony.

It is this background of daily interaction that Beaman refers to as "deep equality." What she means by deep equality is a state of human flourishing that is characterized by the negotiation of difference "towards similarity and around sameness."[14] This characterization is, of course, bound to set off alarms in the minds of thoughtful readers. If "deep equality" involves a trend towards similarity and sameness, is it really proper to refer to it as equality, or is it really another form of majoritarianism in which dominant views, values, and ways of life still maintain their dominance through a process by which members of religious minority communities accommodate themselves to the dominant paradigm? This is certainly not what Beaman intends. It soon becomes apparent, by reading Beaman's examples, that by "similarity" and "sameness" she means "common ground": a social space in which members of diverse religious communities can co-exist, not in spite of, but with full awareness and appreciation of, their many differences. She is aware that she is describing an "amorphous and fragile reality,"[15] and dedicates her last chapter to the question of how we ought to go about sustaining and "getting to deep equality."[16]

Beaman's work is challenging precisely because it is so difficult to articulate what deep equality precisely means. It seems deep equality is better illustrated with examples than defined using the terms of philosophy or sociology. Part of the difficulty is also that Beaman is charting new ground and challenging us to break our habits of attending to problems rather than solutions. But her approach to diversity is a refreshing one, and certainly worthy of further exploration, especially as many of us become increasingly frustrated by the seeming lack of progress—and indeed, of much apparent movement in the opposite direction—when it comes to inter-religious relations. More than theoretical models of religious pluralism, it would seem that actual inter-religious friendships that occur in the concrete environment of quotidian human interaction might hold promise of pointing the way to a world in which inter-religious conflict, even if it is not wholly overcome, is at least mitigated.

Beaman's conception of identity as involving many facets in an ongoing and fluid process of negotiation echoes that of yet another author, the French-Lebanese, Arab-Christian novelist and essayist, Amin Maalouf. In a prescient essay published in the year 2000, entitled *In the Name of Identity: Violence and the Need to Belong*, Maalouf traces the connections between violence and identity. Intriguingly, although identity is widely seen as basic to why inter-religious and other kinds of communal violence takes place—hence the term "identity politics"—according to Maalouf, it is an impoverished concept of identity, rather than identity itself, that is the root of the problem.

Maalouf defines *identity* straightforwardly by saying, "My identity is what prevents me from being identical to anybody else."[17] He elaborates by explaining that,

> Each individual's identity is made up of a number of elements . . . Of course, for the great majority these factors include allegiance to a religious tradition; to a nationality–sometimes two; to a profession, an institution, or a particular social milieu. But the list is much longer than that; it is virtually unlimited. A person may feel a more or less strong attachment to a province, a village, a neighbourhood, a clan, a professional team or one connected with sport, a group of friends, a union, a company, a parish, a community of people with the same passions, the same sexual preferences, the same physical handicaps, or who have to deal with the same kind of pollution or other nuisance. Of course, not all these allegiances are equally strong, at least at any given moment. But none is entirely insignificant, either. All are components of personality—we might almost call them "genes of the soul" so long as we remember that most of them are not innate. While each of these elements may be found separately in many individuals, the same combination of them is never encountered in different people, and it's this that gives every individual richness and value and makes each human being unique and irreplaceable.[18]

The root of violence, Maalouf argues, is not, as one might expect, an egotistical desire to assert or to protect our unique, special, individual identities. These he regards, as his language in the quotation just given suggests, as precious, as a source of "richness and value." Difference as such is not the problem. Maalouf's celebration of difference and uniqueness resonates well with a variety of philosophical positions, including that offered in the thought of Alfred North Whitehead, in which the *telos* of the universe is the generation of diverse and novel forms of experience. Difference, in such a worldview, is to be celebrated, not problematized.[19]

The problem, Maalouf says, arises when we define ourselves in terms of just one of our many allegiances, taking religious allegiance, for example, or ethnicity, to be our singular defining characteristic to the exclusion of all the other things that make us who we are. This seizing upon a single aspect of self as all-defining is a kind of violence to the self, in which we subvert the totality of our complex selves to just one defining allegiance. Maalouf's insight here would seem to be at one with Beaman's understanding that it is in the totality of our daily interactions, the sum total of what we are, in our actual, concrete reality, and not in some abstracted reification of one particular part of ourselves, that a true, lived pluralism can be found.

Some insight can be gained from bringing Beaman's and Maalouf's conception of identity into conversation with a Buddhist analysis. Beaman's and Maalouf's analysis of self is different from a Buddhist analysis. According to a Buddhist analysis, the very notion of self is problematic. It is our clinging to the very idea of a self—to an identity that is, in reality, a construct—that is at the root of our problems. But I believe the two can be connected in the following way. Both false senses of self—the reified self that is the object of the Buddhist critique, and the exclusive adherence to one allegiance of which Maalouf speaks—are inauthentic forms of self-awareness, reflecting a lack of insight into the true character of self as a complex, fluid, ever-emergent reality that is ultimately relational in nature. Both false senses of self involve a simplistic identification of the totality of one's being with some specific set of attributes. Both false senses of self are reinforced through habitual thought patterns. Both are based on fear—or negative desire, as a Buddhist would say—of self-annihilation. Finally, and most significantly, both lead to suffering, including violence.

Maalouf speaks of being asked, as someone who is both Arab and French, which of these two he really is "deep down inside."

> For a long time I found this oft-repeated question amusing, but it no longer makes me smile. It seems to reflect a view of humanity which, though it is widespread, is also in my opinion dangerous. It presupposes that "deep down inside" everyone there is just one affiliation that really matters, a kind of

"fundamental truth" about each individual, an "essence" determined once and for all at birth, never to change thereafter. As if the rest, all the rest–a person's whole journey through time as a free agent; the beliefs he acquires in the course of that journey; his own individual tastes, sensibilities, and affinities; in short his life itself–counted for nothing. And when, as happens so often nowadays, our contemporaries are exhorted to "assert their identities," they are meant to seek within themselves that same alleged fundamental allegiance, which is often religious, national, racial or ethnic, and having located it they are supposed to flaunt it proudly in the face of others. Anyone who claims a more complex identity is marginalized.[20]

According to Maalouf, violence really begins within ourselves, and with the suppression of our own inner complexity. From a classical Buddhist or Vedāntic perspective, this suppression is not the *ultimate* root of violence and suffering. The ultimate root of violence is instead ignorance of the true nature of self. However, when we are called upon, perhaps by political or other social or ideological forces, to suppress the complex totality of who we are and to fixate upon only one facet of our rich and full identity, we start down the path to violence. By obliterating ourselves—who we really are, in our full richness and novel individuality—we create the conditions that enable us, psychologically, to obliterate the other as well. If we can reduce ourselves to tokens of a singular identity—religious, ethnic, ideological, national, and so on–we can more easily reduce others in the same fashion.

What are the conditions that make violence possible? In an essay titled "War and Warriors: An Overview," Bruce Lincoln argues "that it is only when human actors come to regard others as 'things' that they become capable of employing force, particularly lethal force, against them."[21] If one is to engage in violence against another, one must blind oneself to the ways in which the other is like the self: the ways in which the other is also a rich, complex, and unique being, of ultimate value precisely for this reason.[22]

The virtue of inter-religious friendship is precisely that it militates against this process of de-humanization. Because you are my friend, I know many of the complex details of your life—not only your religious affiliation, but what makes you laugh, which of your family members drives you crazy with worry or irritation, what books you like to read, what movies you like to watch, what kind of music you like to listen to. And because you are my friend, we probably share many of these same interests. You are like me, even if we are religiously different. I may, indeed, share much with you that I do not share with some of my co-religionists, with whom I have a different set of bonds.

Can a focus upon inter-religious friendship indeed reduce the prospects for inter-religious violence? How can such friendships be encouraged and cultivated in a way that avoids artificiality and pretense? Are there ways that a society can create the conditions for such friendships without forcing the matter? One possibility, that has been pioneered by the Interfaith Youth Corps, is the development of service projects which consciously bring together people from diverse religious backgrounds, not to discuss their religious identities— an approach which all too often leads to mere tokenism—but to address issues of common concern. This cooperative process has been shown to be conducive to the cultivation of friendships, which cross religious boundaries, and which end up issuing in improved relations between communities.[23] Like the friendship of Krishna and Sudama, the friendships that issue from the kind of shared experiences that Interfaith Youth Corps facilitates are enduring and they transcend the religious identities which might otherwise separate people.

The wisdom of this approach is that it brings people together as whole people, and not, again, as tokens of their religious affiliation. It does not thereby force the issue of inter-religious harmony. Rather, it allows inter-religious issues to arise in an organic fashion, from out of the relationships and interactions of the whole persons involved.

At the same time, though, it should be pointed out that activities of this kind presuppose a certain measure of civil society: that the facilities exist for bringing people together in this way. In situations where civil society has broken down—such as the experiences in the nineteen nineties of the breakup of the former Yugoslavia, or the ethnic genocide of Rwanda—even friendships across the boundaries in the name of which violence occurred could not necessarily spare those involved from becoming victims. While individuals and organizations can do good work to bring about the kinds of relationships upon which deep equality can be built, governments also bear responsibility for maintaining the conditions that allow healthy human relations to flourish. And citizens bear a responsibility to hold their governments accountable, and to elect representatives who refrain from trafficking in religious and ethnic stereotypes. If the voices of leaders appear to give permission for citizens to indulge in stereotyping—in engaging in the violence of reducing complex persons to one single identity, and often a distorted caricature of that identity, at that—then one can expect violence in even more destructive senses to occur.

In my own career, as mentioned earlier in this chapter, I have sought to develop a model of religious pluralism at a theoretical, philosophical level. I do regard this work as worthwhile, for reasons articulated well by David Ray Griffin, whom I often cite in this regard:

> The human proclivity to evil . . . can be greatly exacerbated or greatly mitigated by a world order and its worldview. Modernity exacerbates it about as much as imaginable. We can therefore envision, without being naively utopian, a far better world order, with a far less dangerous trajectory, than the one we now have.[24]

Worldviews do matter. Ideas matter. It is also necessary, however, to find ways to translate one's ideals into action: to bring the ideal into the realm of concrete social and political interactions and human relations. How do concepts such as the relational self and the complementarity of the views articulated in the world's religions inform our actual, day-to-day existence?

The hope underlying this chapter is that the concepts of *mitratva*, of friendship that crosses all boundaries, and of deep equality, along with the living out of actual inter-religious friendships, with their cultivation of mutual appreciation and love across religious boundaries, can indeed lead to a world in which we all feel appreciated for who we are. In such a world, none of us will be treated as tokens of any one of the complex identities that make up each of our rich and unique realities.

NOTES

1. "Friendship as Devotion," *The Hindu*, June 30, 2016; updated October 18, 2016. (https://www.thehindu.com/features/friday-review/religion/Friendship-as-devotion/article14408782.ece, accessed April 7, 2022).

2. Swami Vivekananda, *Complete Works*, vol. 1 (Mayavati: Advaita Ashrama, 1979), 45.

3. Vivekananda, *Complete Works*, vol. 1, 222.

4. Vivekananda, *Complete Works*, vol. 1, 222.

5. Vivekananda, *Complete Works*, vol. 3, 95.

6. Vivekananda, *Complete Works*, vol. 3, 319.

7. Vivekananda, *Complete Works*, vol. 3, 444.

8. Lori Beaman, *Deep Equality in an Era of Religious Diversity* (Oxford: Oxford University Press, 2017), 1.

9. Vivekananda, *Complete Works*, vol. 2, 374.

10. Beaman, *Deep Equality,* 2.

11. Beaman, *Deep Equality,* 2.

12. Beaman, *Deep Equality,* 2.

13. Beaman, *Deep Equality,* 18.

14. Beaman, *Deep Equality,* 180.

15. Beaman, *Deep Equality,* 181.

16. Beaman, *Deep Equality,* 180.

17. Amin Maalouf, *In the Name of Identity: Violence and the Need to Belong*, trans. Barbara Bray, (New York: Arcade, 2000), 10.

18. Maalouf, *In the Name of Identity,* 10–11.

19. See Alfred North Whitehead, *Process and Reality* (New York: Macmillan, 1978).

20. Maalouf, *In the Name of Identity,* 2–3.

21. Bruce Lincoln, *Death, War, and Sacrifice: Studies in Ideology and Practice* (Chicago: University of Chicago Press, 1991), 144.

22. For a more in-depth exploration of the roots of violence in our human propensity toward tribalism and the relevance of Amin Maalouf's analysis to this topic, see my "Eliminating the Root of All Evil: Interdependence and the De-Reification of the Self," in Doug Allen, ed., *Comparative Philosophy in Times of Terror* (Lanham, MD: Lexington Books, 2006), 155–70, from which portions of this chapter are drawn.

23. Interfaith Youth Corps regularly gathers data which tests its methodologies.

24. Griffin, David Ray. "Introduction to SUNY Series in Constructive Postmodern Thought," xxi–xxvi, in Nicholas F. Gier, *Spiritual Titanism: Indian, Chinese, and Western Perspectives* (Albany: State University of New York Press), xxv–xxvi.

BIBLIOGRAPHY

Beaman, Lori. *Deep Equality in an Era of Religious Diversity* (Oxford: Oxford University Press, 2017).

Griffin, David Ray. "Introduction to SUNY Series in Constructive Postmodern Thought," xxi–xxvi, in Nicholas F. Gier, *Spiritual Titanism: Indian, Chinese, and Western Perspectives* (Albany: State University of New York Press), xxv–xxvi.

The Hindu. "Friendship as Devotion," *The Hindu*, June 30, 2016; updated October 18, 2016. (https://www.thehindu.com/features/friday-review/religion/Friendship-as-devotion/article14408782.ece, accessed April 7, 2022.

Lincoln, Bruce. *Death, War, and Sacrifice: Studies in Ideology and Practice* (Chicago: University of Chicago Press, 1991).

Long, Jeffery D. "Eliminating the Root of All Evil: Interdependence and the De-Reification of the Self," in Doug Allen, ed., *Comparative Philosophy in Times of Terror* (Lanham, MD: Lexington Books, 2006), 155–70.

Maalouf, Amin. *In the Name of Identity: Violence and the Need to Belong.* Translated by Barbara Bray. New York: Arcade, 2000.

Vivekananda, Swami. *Complete Works* (Mayavati: Advaita Ashrama, 1979).

Whitehead, Alfred North. *Process and Reality* (New York: Macmillan, 1978).

Chapter 3

Civic Friendship and Reciprocity

Ancient Biblical Exhortations, Contemporary Opportunities

Anne-Marie Ellithorpe

Of what relevance is friendship when it comes to civic practice? Does friendship have any relevance to how people and communities are to relate to one another? Answers to such questions may be found in the traditions that shape relationships and practices within communities, and the values inherent to those traditions. Here, I advocate for relationships within and between communities to be characterized by the values and practices of civic friendship, grounding this advocacy in traditions, values, and understandings communicated through ancient biblical texts.[1] Despite considerable differences between ancient agrarian communities and today's global economies and communities, similarities in power dynamics allow for an analogy between ancient and contemporary contexts.[2]

I begin by introducing key terminology and texts, namely the terminology of friendship, civic friendship, and reciprocity, along with Amos and Deuteronomy as sources for reflection on and advocacy for civic friendship. I then focus on reciprocity, interweaving an acknowledgment of diverse forms of reciprocity with an account of changes in Iron Age II Israel.[3] This historical and textual work lays a foundation for considering the relevance of civic friendship and various forms of reciprocity to contemporary communities and reflecting on practices that may contribute to living out civic friendship.

In relying on Amos, I am both following and going beyond earlier Biblical interpreters. Early commentators on the Hebrew Bible provide an example of interpreting texts for subsequent contexts. Rabbinic scholar Steven D. Fraade notes that early commentators on the Hebrew Bible were "double facing," looking toward both the text they were interpreting and the communities "for whom and with whom" they interpreted.[4] Admittedly, commentator attention to texts is uneven. Deuteronomy has had a significant impact on subsequent Jewish tradition and continues to play an important role in Jewish theology.[5] Yet it appears that the political and ethical aspects of Amos's message have consistently been downplayed. Its social critique has not featured as a prominent topic in rabbinic interpretations, patristic writings, or in premodern and early modern Christian interpretation.[6] It is only recently (relatively speaking) that the book of Amos has been a source of inspiration for various protest movements.[7] Writings from both Amos and Deuteronomy have the potential to be double-facing, informing contemporary understandings of civic friendship and promoting genuine reciprocity in the ways that people and communities relate to one another.

FRIENDSHIP, CIVIC FRIENDSHIP, AND CIVIC KINSHIP

Friendship is a relationship characterized by mutual affection and by reciprocity in willing and doing good for the other. In *Rhetoric*, written in the fourth century BCE, Aristotle describes *philia* (friendship) as characterized by reciprocity in desiring for another "what you believe to be good things, not for your own sake but for [the friend], and being inclined, so far as you can, to bring these things about."[8] The ancient Greek notion of *philia* is broader and richer than many contemporary perspectives on friendship. *Philia* includes special relations between those who are otherwise dissimilar, whether in "age, gender, class, religion, race or culture."[9] Reciprocity extends beyond personal friendship.[10] While reciprocity often refers to social norms of give-and-take, it may also refer to material transactions, or to both. In many contexts reciprocity implies balance, but with important exceptions relevant to the writings explored in this chapter.

Although many in modern Euro-Western contexts consider friendship to be merely a personal relationship, friendship has civic dimensions. Aristotle speaks of *politike philia*—political or civic friendship. Civic friendship extends willing and doing good to the broader community, where it may be expressed through a society's constitution(s), laws, institutions, and practices.[11] Political philosophers, including Danielle Allen and Sibyl Schwarzenbach, advocate for increased attentiveness to this form of friendship. One way that civic friendship may be outworked is through resistance to oppressive laws and practices.[12]

Contemporary writings regarding civic friendship, whether by political philosophers or theologians, typically begin with Aristotle's writings. Yet, as I have noted elsewhere, advocacy for societies characterized by willing good and doing good for the *other* is found in works authored significantly earlier by the ancient Hebrew prophets.[13] I write:

> Throughout centuries of significant socioeconomic change, various biblical prophets condemn practices that destroy community, including the injustices created by various forms of negative reciprocity. Implicitly then, these prophets critique a lack of civic friendship expressed through injustice—in the market-place, in the courts, and within patron-client relationships.[14]

Poetic oracles in the book of Amos, for example, critique oppression by the elite of eighth century BCE Samaria. These oracles depict marked social inequality indicative of an advanced agrarian society, disrupted by the process of urbanization, and the associated exploitation of peasants.

Advocacy for communities characterized by willing and doing good for the *other* is also evident in Deuteronomy. In this fifth book of the Torah, presented as an account of the renewal of covenant with God, but likely authored over several episodes of displacement, we find a view of what a theocracy could be like.[15] The Deuteronomic Code that forms its midsection has been described as "a socially oriented covenant charter bearing some semblance to a human rights charter."[16] Its social policies blend political, ideological, and theological thought. Deuteronomy promotes the inclusion of the marginalized triad (widows, orphans, strangers) in the life of the covenant community and advocates for genuine reciprocity.

FORMS OF RECIPROCITY IN ANCIENT ISRAEL

Reciprocity, as depicted by cultural anthropologist Marshall Sahlins, in his now classic *Stone Age Economics*, encompasses "a whole class of exchanges."[17] While reciprocity implies "action and reaction" between two parties, it does not necessarily imply balance, as in an "unconditional one-for-one exchange."[18] The spectrum of reciprocities include generalized reciprocity at one extreme, negative reciprocity at the other, and balanced forms of reciprocity at the midpoint.[19] Each of these forms of reciprocity were practiced in ancient Israel. While all three forms may have been practiced in a community on any one day, the following suggests specific contexts in which each was practiced.

Generalized Reciprocity, Kinship, and Survival

Generalized reciprocity, as described by Sahlins, takes place between "close kin, or people who one treats as if they were close kin."[20] In the context of everyday kinship, friendship, and neighborly relations, assistance is freely given. The obligation to reciprocate is relatively vague; to openly require return would be unsociable.[21] The giver is not deterred from giving by lack of return. Sustained by prevailing social relations, goods can move one way, towards those with less power or resources, for a significant period.[22] Generalized reciprocity can be found in stratified societies as well as in rural agrarian communities and may also include disinterested yet altruistic concern for the other party.

Rural agrarian peasants comprised a significant proportion of the population in Iron Age II Israel.[23] Peasants were reliant on generalized reciprocity through the labor of extended family.[24] Agrarian households were the basic unit of production and tended to be egalitarian.[25] Houses were clustered in twos or threes, with some sharing of walls, supporting intergenerational living whereby reciprocal relationships were nurtured over the course of a lifetime.[26]

A subsistence way of life was challenging. Climate or pestilence issues could provoke crop loss. Yet various forms of generalized reciprocity—within households, between households, and between villages—mitigated risk and contributed to survival.[27] This included the shared use of technology such as the iron plough, irrigation, terraces, processing facilities and storage facilities.[28] Such reciprocity enabled peasant households to survive and to be collaboratively effective, despite challenges posed by terrain, soil, and climate.[29]

Balanced Reciprocity, the Marketplace, and Patron-Client Relationships

Balanced reciprocity is yet another form of reciprocity sustaining agrarian communities. As identified by Sahlins, this form of reciprocity is characterized by "direct exchange"[30] and "governed by fairness."[31] Balanced reciprocity implies fair exchange and mutuality between parties and includes equitable business practices, gift exchange, friendship compacts, peace agreements, and "kinship, friendship, and neighborly relations."[32] In some cases, parity is not evident in any one moment of exchange but becomes evident over time. Failure to reciprocate within appropriate "time and equivalence leeways" disrupts social relationships.[33]

Early peasant markets in Iron Age II Israel utilized a system of barter, using weights to make payments in kind.[34] The balanced reciprocity inherent within friendship and kin-like relationships may be seen both metaphorically and practically as implicit in the Deuteronomic instruction to the covenant community to have accurate and honest weights and measures in their bags and in their houses (25:13–15 NJPS).[35]

You shall not have in your pouch alternate weights, larger and smaller. You shall not have in your house alternate measures, a large and a smaller. You must have completely honest weights and completely honest measures, if you are to endure long on the soil that the Lord your God is giving you.

As with generalized reciprocity, balanced reciprocity can be pursued in stratified societies as well as in rural agrarian communities. For example, balanced reciprocity can be an ethical principle within patron-client relationships necessitated by crises that have been exacerbated by crop specialization.[36] Some households successfully specialized in high value crops; others became indebted to patrons. As I write elsewhere:

> The ideal basis for the patron-client relationship is one of *balanced* reciprocity, through fair exchange, with goods and services exchanged between both parties. This can take place despite inequality in power or status. In what would *ideally* be a relationship of *mutual* benefit, goods flow steadily from villages to urban centers, in exchange for services and specialized commodities.[37]

However, sometime in the Iron Age, *balanced* reciprocity collapsed. Normal aspects of patron-client relationships became distorted, resulting in abusive practices.[38]

Negative Reciprocity and an Oracle against Dishonest Business Practices

Negative reciprocity names the breakdown of effective exchange, including exchanges characterized by the self-interest of those with greater power, as with the forced seizure of land or resources.[39] This form of reciprocity is critiqued within the oracle of Amos 8:4–6 (NRSV).

> Hear this, you that trample on the needy,
>   and bring to ruin the poor of the land,
> saying, "When will the new moon be over
>   so that we may sell grain;
> and the sabbath,
>   so that we may offer wheat for sale?
> We will make the ephah small and the shekel great,
>   and practice deceit with false balances,
> buying the poor for silver
>   and the needy for a pair of sandals,
>   and selling the sweepings of the wheat."

These verses condemn injustice created by negative reciprocity in the marketplace, deceit, and the dishonoring of others.[40] This oracle protests practices that are destructive of community.[41] It condemns dehumanizing business practices whereby "human beings become disposable goods for other human beings."[42] Such practices—likely on the part of unjust merchants—concern cost, quality, and time.

The development of regional specialization and trade enriched an emerging merchant class. Not all merchants became rich; many remained quite poor.[43] Merchants who accumulated wealth typically did so through developing skill in the use (and manipulation) of weights and measures. This oracle critiques the use of deceptive weights that result in the person purchasing paying too much and receiving too little, whether through dry measures (*ephah*) that are too small, counterweights (*shekel*) that are too heavy, or the use of fraudulent balances or scales (perhaps through the moving of the fulcrum).[44] The use of false weights and rigged scales in the marketplace increased the vulnerability of peasants.

Another unjust and dishonest business practice critiqued by this oracle is selling a product of inferior quality. "Selling the sweepings with the wheat" implies that "the chaff and trash left after winnowing would be remixed with clean grain, and presumably sold as clean grain."[45] Such practices, while always ethically inappropriate, would be particularly problematic during times of drought.

Lack of respect for restorative and celebratory time boundaries is yet another form of marketplace injustice. The Sabbath was—and is—a time for rest. The New Moon, on the first day of the lunar month, was a time for rest, festivities, and community building.[46] Amos implies that commerce was prohibited during these sacred times.[47] Yet merchants encroached on these occasions, rushing them in their eagerness "to trample on the needy" as they sold grain and wheat.[48]

Negative forms of reciprocity contribute to the *purchase* of the poor and needy for silver and a pair of sandals. The sandals may refer to bribery.[49] It is also possible that the exchange of sandals signifies the transfer of property rights from one party to another.[50] Regardless of the precise meaning of these phrases, peasants became victims of an emerging market economy as they borrowed to survive but eventually had to give up their land in order to pay their debts.[51] Ruined through deceptive commerce, with the help of *silver*, some became economically dependent and were effectively "bought" by their creditors.[52] Many peasants that were formally free holding were disenfranchised and "forced into wage labor" due to loss of household properties.[53]

Parasitic patterns, whereby one enlarged one's property and wealth at the expense of the poor, and through the perversion of justice, may be typical of advanced agrarian societies. It is not unusual for a small minority to enjoy significant luxury, while others are denied basic needs.[54] Nevertheless, engaging in unjust practices was an ethical failure of the elite and of more economically fortunate peasants who set aside ethical standards as they gained power and became patrons.[55]

Unethical business strategies have a destructive impact on communities. Thus, implicit within this Amos oracle and related texts is the value of marketplace behavior that cultivates community. As Gerhard Lenski notes, "it does not take much imagination to conceive of a more equitable method of distribution."[56] Exploitative relationships were challenged by the ideals of Deuteronomy and by the prophets. The failure of many to deal justly or humanely with others led to prophetic protests[57] and to advocacy for practices congruent with divine compassion, justice, and befriending.

Generalized Reciprocity, Imaging the Divine, and Kinship/Friendship Ethics

The earlier exploration of generalized reciprocity focused on its role in promoting survival for rural agrarian peasants engaged in a subsistence way of life; here I add to earlier insights by considering practices advocated for within Deuteronomy, in the context of what was likely a stratified society, and the ethics reflected therein. The instruction to befriend strangers in Deuteronomy 10:17–19 points towards important ways in which the community that Deuteronomy imagines is called to image the divine. Quoted here from the NJPS:

> For your God is God supreme and Lord supreme, the great, the mighty, and the awesome God, who shows no favor and takes no bribe, but upholds the cause of the fatherless and the widow, and befriends the stranger, providing food and clothing.—You too must befriend the stranger, for you were strangers in the land of Egypt.

These instructions do not settle for the status quo practices of a stratified society. Rather, as they advocate for practices that promote community, kinship, friendship, and justice, they also challenge the community to *Imitatio Dei*, that is, to image a God of justice, love, friendship.

Imaging the divine includes promoting justice and caring for the vulnerable. Imaging a God of justice begins with befriending and helping the marginalized and is outworked through all seeking the well-being of the community. Systems to promote fairness and rectify unfair situations within the community are also needed.[58]

Elsewhere in Deuteronomy the legal system, including the court, is specifically charged with this concern.[59] Judges are to image the impartial, non-bribable God of gods (10:17). The court has a role in protecting all but must specifically protect the marginalized and disadvantaged who would otherwise be without an advocate, including the socio-economically marginalized triad of stranger, widow, and fatherless (24:17).[60]

A kinship ethic, that recognizes all fellow human beings as siblings, is central to the social and theological vision of Deuteronomy.[61] "Deuteronomy fosters the inclusion of *gēr* as kindred."[62] The *gēr* has been variously translated as stranger, alien, or foreigner. Jewish biblical scholar Shani Tzoref considers the *gēr* to be a resident sojourner, "a person who lives within Israelite society but is marginalized due to their ethnic identity."[63] Mark Glanville interprets *gēr* in Deuteronomy more broadly, as designating "a vulnerable person who is from outside of the core family."[64] Regardless of the precise meaning of this term, the covenant community is to intentionally go beyond "the natural community of the extended family."[65] Ultimately *all* are kin, with responsibility to extend protection and care to one another.[66]

The Deuteronomic vision may also be expressed through an ethic of friendship. In this context, the translation of *'āhāb* ("love," with implications of affection expressed in action) as *befriend* is consistent with an ethic of friendship and provides its theological grounding.[67] Divine affection expressed through action is to be imaged by the covenant community: "You too must befriend the stranger, for you were strangers in the land of Egypt."[68]

FROM ANCIENT TO CONTEMPORARY CONTEXTS

Amos and Deuteronomy were originally composed and heard "within a social construct of collective identity."[69] There are clearly vast differences—socially, politically, and economically—between the agrarian society of ancient Israel that these biblical texts emerged from, and the contemporary hyper-individualistic Euro-Western contexts within which many of us live. Nonetheless, a friendship ethic is a needed corrective in our time.

Genuine friendship is characterized by "reciprocal awareness of the other, wishing the other well for their sake, and practical doing on behalf of the other."[70] This reciprocity is true of both personal and civic friendship. As described by political philosopher Sybil Schwarzenbach, civic friendship promotes the inclusion of these characteristics within the *structure* of society.[71] These characteristics would have been evident within the traditional reciprocity structures of agrarian village communities; biblical prophets and reformers encourage characteristics of genuine friendship within subsequent wider sociopolitical contexts. Both the marketplace and the court provide opportunities for the outworking of civic friendship.

Implicit within biblical texts promoting balanced and generalized reciprocity, and critiquing negative reciprocity, is the inherent dignity and value of every human being. Promoting personal dignity takes precedence over maximizing profits and is in alignment with the biblical call to the covenant community to image the divine in their relationships with those who are *other*.[72] As depicted in Deuteronomy, community life is to be shaped by imaging God, as all seek to proactively foster the flourishing of the broader community. Deuteronomy envisages a community that images God through promoting justice, socially, economically, and legally.[73]

Civic friendship is to be characterized by empathy for and the honoring of those who are *other*. Israel's own experience of being "displaced persons" is expected to "elicit an emotional response of empathy and kindness."[74] Tzoref notes that Deuteronomy directs the Israelites towards a constructive use of memory and narrative as they consider the needs of the *ger*, encouraging readers to "look back at their own suffering as a means to generate empathy, not because this is universal and natural, but precisely because it is a difficult and uncertain process, and requires cultivation."[75]

Lenski's *Power and Privilege*, with its focus on social stratification (most specifically, who gets what and why), traces the development of societies from hunting and gathering, to simple horticultural societies, advanced horticultural societies, agrarian societies, and finally industrial societies. The Amos and Deuteronomy texts appear to have been composed within the context of increasingly stratified agrarian contexts during the seventh and eighth centuries BCE. Lenski identified twentieth century Western societies as industrial societies.[76] Twenty-first century contexts are characterized by ongoing technological innovation and the pervasive spread of global capitalism, along with the neoliberal policies and practices that undergird it. Convinced that "trade enhances growth" and "growth reduces poverty," neoliberalism seeks an unfettered capitalist market that allows for the most "efficient" allocation of resources, nationally and globally.[77] Yet neoliberalism allows elites to prosper while the poor become more vulnerable.[78]

For many Euro-Westerners, neoliberalism permeates current socioeconomic contexts to the extent that its practices and policies are experienced as normal and resistance is muted.[79] Indigenous communities, however, experience neoliberal practices and policies as a form of colonization and seek to resist in multiple ways.[80] Māori professor Maria Bargh (of Te Arawa and Ngāti Awa descent) defines neoliberalism as "practices and policies which seek to extend the market mechanism into areas of the community previously organized and governed in other ways."[81] Resistance includes prioritizing relationships, remaining connected to place, continuing to take care of the collective, and challenging legal precedents based on global injustice.

Indigenous peoples have been impacted by a Euro-centered world economy that began to take shape in the late fifteenth and early sixteenth centuries, largely governed by "the competitive principles of capitalism."[82] Despite a 1537 decree by Pope Paul III opposing the enslavement of Indigenous

peoples, international law followed an earlier—unjust—papal bull in formu-
lating the so-called doctrine of discovery, a legal framework used to declare
lands held by Indigenous Peoples to be *terra nullius* (nobody's land) and to
justify European colonization.

Given significantly different socioeconomic contexts, and the legacy of
centuries of injustice, does advocacy for civic friendship—through the generalized and balanced forms of reciprocity encouraged by ancient Hebrew
writings—remain relevant? Do the insights gained from these reflections on
reciprocity and friendship inspired by Amos and Deuteronomy have implications for the contemporary practice of civic friendship? I argue that advocacy
for civic friendship and genuine forms of reciprocity continue to be relevant.
As in ancient contexts, on any one day all three forms of reciprocity earlier
articulated may be practiced.[83] The religious diversity of many contemporary
communities may not allow for the terminology of *imaging God* or of *theologically inspired civic friendship* (or *civic kinship*). Theocracies can clearly
be oppressive, and there may be few—if any—contemporary contexts in
which we could imagine a theocracy characterized by befriending and justice
to be viable. Nevertheless, the prophetic rebuke of Amos 8 and the reforming
critique of Deuteronomy 10 and associated texts continue to be applicable,
with their encouragement of positive forms of reciprocity, the pursuit of justice, empathy for and inclusion of the marginalized, and the valuing of all.[84]

Similarities in power dynamics provide a basis for an analogy between
ancient and contemporary contexts when it comes to issues of reciprocity and
relationality; "the dynamics of power continue to allow for negative reciprocity" and for the elite to prosper at the expense of the marginalized.[85] Rabbi
Abraham Joshua Heschel, in his 1969 *The Prophets*, notes that there is no
contemporary society to which Amos's critique is not relevant.[86] Martin Luther
King, Jr. spoke of Amos's words in Amos 5:24—"Let justice run down like
waters and righteousness like a mighty stream"—echoing across the centuries:[87]

Contemporary communities do not need to settle for societies, market-
places, and courts perpetuated by injustice. It is easy to be overwhelmed by
the extent of inequality, and to accept it as a given. After all, despite Lenski's
assertion that it does not take significant imagination to conceive of more
equitable methods of distribution,[88] Lenski asserts that "inequality among
societies has been a basic fact of human life" for thousands of years.[89] Yet
community traditions can dictate otherwise. Māori professor Margaret Mutu
(of Ngāti Kahu, Te Rarawa, Ngāti Whātua and Scottish descent) emphasizes
that Māori values do not allow Māori to *not* share: "Our culture will not allow
us to do that sort of thing, where just a few benefit and the rest are *pōhara*
[poor, impoverished]. You must share. Your primary aim is the well-being
of the people."[90] The Indigenous peoples of Turtle Island (North America)
hold similar values. Further, Abraham Ibn Ezra, a Jewish sage and important

"cultural broker" of the medieval period,[91] asserts that "only a just nation can endure, since justice is like a building, and injustice is like cracks that can cause a building to fall."[92]

LIVING OUT CIVIC FRIENDSHIP IN AND BETWEEN DIVERSE COMMUNITIES

Civic friendship has been described as "that form of friendship whose traits operate via a society's constitution, its public set of laws, its major institutions and social customs."[93] Customs, institutions, laws, and constitutional traditions—the diverse traditions and values that shape relationships and practices within and between communities—can all be shaped by the genuine reciprocity inherent to civic friendship.[94] Although communities may differ in their practices and traditions, the making and honoring of friendship treaties allow for connection, coexistence, and interdependence between diverse communities that share mutual aspirations.[95] To the extent that the honoring of such treaties is characterized by genuine reciprocity, each community is freed to learn from the other without threat of oppression.

While traditions carry the core values of a community, they do not necessarily remain static and unchanging. New stories can be told. Unjust laws and systems can be challenged, repealed, and replaced. Institutions that perpetuate injustice through distorted forms of reciprocity can be transformed, formed instead in ways that seek the good of all. Political philosopher Danielle Allen encourages her readers to recognize themselves as implicitly "founders of institutions," as they influence the shape of life in their communities.[96] It is appropriate for each one of us to consider the deepest values of the traditions that shape our communities and our institutions; ways in which personal, institutional, and perhaps even constitutional transformation may be needed; and our own sphere of influence in these areas.

The terminology of *civic friendship* may be complemented by that of *civic kinship*, the art of creating connections whereby kinship is recognized with non-kin. This is in alignment with the inclusive kinship ethic of Deuteronomy 10 as well as with Indigenous values. Indigenous traditions emphasize human kinship with all life, human and nonhuman. Kyle Powys Whyte, Potawatomi scholar and professor of environment and sustainability, describes kinship as referring to "relationships of mutual responsibility."[97] He identifies mutual care and responsibility as creating bonds that make not caring for each other unthinkable, and reciprocity as a key aspect of kinship.[98] Māori lawyer Māmari Stephens notes the transformative potential of a civic form of kinship (*whanaungatanga*, "the art of creating connection").[99] Speaking specifically to her own context of Aotearoa New Zealand, she asserts "we must move to understanding each other (and each other's practical needs) as *whanaunga*, relations, being deeply connected to one another, regardless of ethnic kinship."[100]

Living out civic friendship in currently colonized countries will contribute to all learning about the people of the lands on which they now live, deepening understandings of reciprocity from the perspective of Indigenous traditions, honoring treaties, taking responsibility for the actions of colonizing ancestors against Indigenous peoples through dismantling oppressive structures, and seeking to be rightly related.

Friendship may be costly and yet invaluable. Speaking specifically to the Māori struggle against British colonization, Margaret Mutu notes that: "At every stage on the journey, we have been supported by Europeans who have also seen through the myths [regarding issues such as discovery, land sales, and the ceding of sovereignty] and have fought beside us to tear them down."[101] While many—like Māori—have been vilified, ostracized, and marginalized for their support, such support contributed to the establishment of the Waitangi Tribunal (set up in 1975 to inquire into breaches of the 1840 treaty between Māori and the British Crown), which in turn "greatly strengthened" the Māori case in the United Nations.[102] United Nations human rights standards, once adopted by the government, will—Mutu asserts—contribute to the next generations' job becoming easier than the one her generation inherited.

There is no easy path to addressing contemporary forms of inequity and injustice. There are significant challenges—and quite possibly personal costs—to promoting civic friendship and genuine reciprocity. Nevertheless, we will all benefit from recognizing our common kinship with those who are marginalized and those who oppress, reflecting on reciprocity more carefully and paying attention to issues of reciprocity in terms of how we structure relationships. As we learn more about the various forms of power that contribute to oppression, we can challenge unjust power structures and promote various forms of transformation. As we consider how the prophetic rebuke of Amos and the reforming critique of Deuteronomy are relevant to our attitudes, lifestyle, and practices, we can—collaboratively—resist neoliberalism, recognize the dignity of all, and cultivate positive and active regard for each person within our communities.

NOTES

1. This chapter explores similar themes to my 2021 article in the Journal of Moral Theology. See Anne-Marie Ellithorpe, "Reciprocity Within Community: Ancient and Contemporary Challenges to and Opportunities for Civic Friendship," *Journal of Moral Theology* 10, no. 1 (2021). However, the article begins with a more explicit

focus on Amos 8:4–6, whereas this chapter begins with a more explicit focus on various forms of reciprocity. These themes are also evident in chapter four of my book *Towards Friendship-Shaped Communities: A Practical Theology of Friendship*. Oxford: Wiley Blackwell, 2022.

2. Similarities in power dynamics between ancient and contemporary contexts are also foundational to the analogy between radically different contexts made in Ellithorpe, "Reciprocity Within Community," 193.

3. Marshall Sahlins, *Stone Age Economics* (London: Routledge Classics, 2017), 175–77.

4. Steven D. Fraade, *From Tradition to Commentary: Torah and its Interpretation in the Midrash Sifre to Deuteronomy* (Albany: State University of New York Press, 1991), 14.

5. Jeffrey H. Tigay, *Deuteronomy: The Traditional Hebrew Text with the New JPS Translation* (Philadelphia: Jewish Publication Society, 1996), xxvi, xxviii.

6. Göran Eidevall, *Amos: A New Translation with Introduction and Commentary*, 29.

7. Eidevall, *Amos*, 30.

8. Aristotle, *Rhetoric*, trans. W. Rhys Roberts (New York: Dover Publications, 2012), 2.4, 1380b36–1381a2.

9. Sibyl A. Schwarzenbach, "Fraternity, Solidarity, and Civic Friendship," *AMITY* 3, no. 1 (2015): 9.

10. According to political philosopher Danielle Allen, reciprocity is friendship's "basic act." Danielle S. Allen, *Talking to Strangers: Anxieties of Citizenship since Brown v. Board of Education* (Chicago: The University of Chicago Press, 2004), 131.

11. See Schwarzenbach, "Fraternity, Solidarity, and Civic Friendship," 11.

12. Anne-Marie Ellithorpe, *Towards Friendship-Shaped Communities: A Practical Theology of Friendship* (Oxford: Wiley Blackwell, 2022), 56–60.

13. Ellithorpe, "Reciprocity Within Community," 178.

14. Ellithorpe, *Towards Friendship-Shaped Communities*, 81.

15. According to traditional rabbinic sources, Deuteronomy was written by Moses, late in his life. According to scholarly sources, Deuteronomy originated in the late pre-exilic period of the late seventh century BCE (around the time of Josiah's kingship). It may have been intensively revised in subsequent centuries or may alternatively be a post-exilic book employing traditions of the pre-exilic period. See also Tigay, *Deuteronomy*, xix–xviii.

16. Mark R. Glanville, *Adopting the Stranger as Kindred in Deuteronomy* (Atlanta: SBL Press, 2018), 49.

17. Sahlins, *Stone Age Economics*, 173.

18. Sahlins, *Stone Age Economics*, 169, 71.

19. Sahlins, *Stone Age Economics*, 175–78.

20. Sahlins, *Stone Age Economics*, vxii.

21. Sahlins, *Stone Age Economics*, 173.

22. Sahlins, *Stone Age Economics*, 176, 77.

23. See Carol Meyers, "Material Remains and Social Relations: Women's Culture in Agrarian Households of the Iron Age," in *Symbiosis, Symbolism, and the Power*

of the Past: Canaan, Ancient Israel, and their Neighbors from the Late Bronze Age through Roman Palaestina, ed. William G. Dever and Seymour Gitin (Winona Lake: Eisenbrauns, 2003), 426. See also Paula M. McNutt, *Reconstructing the Society of Ancient Israel* (Louisville: Westminster John Knox, 1999), 152, 68.

24. Such practices of generalized reciprocity continue to sustain rural agrarian peasants.

25. Meyers, "Material Remains and Social Relations," 429.

26. Carol Meyers, "The Family in Early Israel," in *Families in Ancient Israel*, ed. Leo G. Perdue et al. (Louisville: Westminster John Knox, 1997), 16. Clustered living allowed for distant kin without immediate family to be included within the "compound." Meyers, "The Family in Early Israel," 17.

27. Meyers, "The Family in Early Israel," 18.

28. David C. Hopkins, *The Highlands of Canaan: Agricultural Life in the Early Iron Age* (Decatur, GA: Almond Press, 1985), 261. For example, one processing installation typically provided for the processing of the entire village's crop. See Avraham Faust, "The Rural Community in Ancient Israel during Iron Age II," *Bulletin of the American Schools of Oriental Research* 317 (2000): 22.

29. Hopkins, *The Highlands of Canaan*, 243.

30. Sahlins, *Stone Age Economics*, 176.

31. Sahlins, *Stone Age Economics*, vxii.

32. Sahlins, *Stone Age Economics*, 175–77.

33. Sahlins, *Stone Age Economics*, 177.

34. William Domeris, *Touching the Heart of God: The Social Construction of Poverty Among Biblical Peasants* (New York: T&T Clark, 2007), 142.

35. Bible quotations are from *Tanakh: The Holy Scriptures: The New JPS Translation according to the Traditional Hebrew Text* (NJPS) or from the New Revised Standard Version (NRSV).

36. As the production of crops for the market limits the risk management inherent within the production of a variety of crops, the relative self-sufficiency of village communities is—over time—replaced with dependency on centralizing forces, and the exchange networks they administer. See Gerhard Lenski, *Power and Privilege: A Theory of Social Stratification* (Chapel Hill: The University of North Carolina Press, 1984), 201.

37. Ellithorpe, *Towards Friendship-Shaped Communities*, 82.

38. Eric R. Wolf, *Peasants* (Englewood Cliffs: Prentice-Hall, 1966), 16. Cited in Domeris, *Touching the Heart of God*, 91.

39. Sahlins, *Stone Age Economics*, 173, 75.

40. Jörg Jeremias, *The Book of Amos: A Commentary* (Louisville: Westminster John Knox, 1998), 147. In a similar oracle, the powerful grind "the heads of the poor into the dust" (2:7), possibly implying shaming, as the head is a symbol of honor. See Domeris, *Touching the Heart of God*, 115.

41. While Amos 8:4–6 appears to be one of the oracles delivered by Amos in the eighth century, it may be an adaption of Amos 2:6–8 by a subsequent seventh century editor. (The book of Amos appears to have been redacted and expanded a century after the delivery of the eighth century oracles.) See Robert B. Coote, *Amos among*

the Prophets: Composition and Theology (Philadelphia: Fortress, 1981), 93. Göran Eidevall considers this section to be a reinterpretation of the initial words of Amos. See Eidevall, *Amos*, 87.

42. Jeremias, *Amos*, 148.

43. Lenski, *Power and Privilege*, 252.

44. See also Hosea 12:7. Deceit may have involved the moving of the fulcrum or the modification of the stone sphere. A variety of weight measures used are depicted in Philip J. King and Lawrence E. Stager, *Life in Biblical Israel* (Louisville: Westminster John Knox, 2001), 195–98. Jeffrey Tigay notes that among those found, no two examples weigh exactly the same. He further asserts that while *some* may have been intentionally fraudulent, it is unlikely that *only* weights that were intentionally so have been discovered. Tigay, *Deuteronomy*, 235.

45. Ellithorpe, "Reciprocity Within Community," 185.

46. King and Stager, *Life in Biblical Israel*, 210, 353. See also Numbers 28:11–15.

47. King and Stager, *Life in Biblical Israel*, 353.

48. King and Stager, *Life in Biblical Israel*, 353. See also Domeris, *Touching the Heart of God*, 110.

49. Francis I. Andersen and David Noel Freedman, *Amos* (New York: Doubleday, 1989), 311–12. Bribery is referred to in Sirach 46:19. Sandals could also symbolize an insignificant debt for which people were sold into slavery, however Domeris notes that the idea of debt slavery is not explicit in the prophets. Domeris, *Touching the Heart of God*, 112.

50. Andersen and Freedman, *Amos*, 312. King and Stager, *Life in Biblical Israel*, 273. Ruth 4:7–8.

51. Richard D. Nelson, *Deuteronomy: A Commentary* (Louisville: Westminster John Knox, 2002), 190.

52. Jeremias, *Amos*, 148. See Deuteronomy 25:13–15.

53. Carol L. Meyers, *Discovering Eve: Ancient Israelite Women in Context* (New York: Oxford University Press, 1988), 195.

54. Lenski, *Power and Privilege*, 295.

55. Domeris, *Touching the Heart of God*, 91. Those who benefited from offering "protection" and patronage to peasants, in return for their loyalty and their surplus, through tax and rent, may rarely—if ever—have recognized their own practices as an ethical failure. Domeris, *Touching the Heart of God*, 86.

56. Lenski, *Power and Privilege*, 295.

57. Walter Houston, "Was there a Social Crisis in the Eighth Century?" in *In Search of Pre-Exilic Israel: Proceedings of the Oxford Old Testament Seminar*, ed. John Day (London: T&T Clark, 2004), 146.

58. Patrick D. Miller, *Deuteronomy* (Louisville: John Knox, 1990), 142.

59. Judges are to be elected and trusted by the people. They are to be discerning and wise. Judges are to judge righteously, pursue justice, and not distort justice (Dt 16:18–19). In showing no favor, and taking no bribes, God exemplifies qualities of the ideal judge. See also Dt 1:16–17 and Tigay, *Deuteronomy*, 108.

60. King and Stager, *Life in Biblical Israel*, 53.

61. Glanville, *Adopting the Stranger*, 119, 23.

62. Glanville, *Adopting the Stranger*, 265.

63. Shani Tzoref, "Knowing the Heart of the Stranger: Empathy, Remembrance, and Narrative in Jewish Reception of Exodus 22:21, Deuteronomy 10:19, and Parallels," *Interpretation* 72, no. 2 (2018): 121.

64. Glanville, *Adopting the Stranger*, 267.

65. Ellithorpe, "Reciprocity Within Community," 187.

66. Glanville, *Adopting the Stranger*, 122.

67. Tigay, *Deuteronomy*, 108.

68. This translation is used by Tigay, *Deuteronomy*, 108.

69. Glanville, *Adopting the Stranger*, 20.

70. Schwarzenbach, "Fraternity, Solidarity, and Civic Friendship," 11.

71. Schwarzenbach, "Fraternity, Solidarity, and Civic Friendship," 11.

72. See Deuteronomy 10:17–19, 24:17–18, 19–22. See also Leviticus 19:34.

73. Ellithorpe, "Reciprocity Within Community," 188.

74. Glanville, *Adopting the Stranger*, 220.

75. Tzoref, "Knowing the Heart of the Stranger," 126.

76. Lenski, *Power and Privilege*, 392–93. This is of course a generalization. Numerous Indigenous communities have resisted industrialization and sought to pursue more traditional ways of life that maintain a greater sense of connectedness to creation.

77. Jagdish N. Bhagwati, *In Defense of Globalization* (Oxford: Oxford University Press, 2004), 53.

78. Todd May, *Friendship in an Age of Economics: Resisting the Forces of Neoliberalism* (Lanham: Lexington, 2012), 11.

79. May, *Friendship in an Age of Economics*, 14–15, 11–12.

80. Maria Bargh, "Introduction," in *Resistance: An Indigenous Response to Neoliberalism*, ed. Maria Bargh (Wellington: Huia, 2007), 1, 2. Teanau Tuiono, "We are Everywhere," in *Resistance: An Indigenous Response to Neoliberalism*, ed. Maria Bargh (Wellington: Huia, 2007), 126.

81. Bargh, "Introduction," 1.

82. Lenski, *Power and Privilege*, xi–xii.

83. Some contemporary contexts are of course less dissimilar to ancient contexts than others; as Biblical scholar William Domeris notes, "peasants through time and place have a great deal in common." Domeris, *Touching the Heart of God*, 42. Regardless of context, there is value in strengthening genuine and balanced forms of reciprocity.

84. Ellithorpe, "Reciprocity Within Community," 179.

85. Ellithorpe, "Reciprocity Within Community," 179.

86. Abraham Joshua Heschel, *The Prophets*, vol. 1 (New York: Harper & Row, 1969), 3.

87. Cited in Eidevall, *Amos*, 30.

88. Lenski, *Power and Privilege*, 295.

89. Lenski, *Power and Privilege*, xii.

90. Whakaata Māori, "He Puni Wāhine: An Assembly of Women," in *Waitangi 2023*, aired February 6, 2023. https://www.maoriplus.co.nz/playback/item /6319893924112. Margaret Mutu's statement is at 2.28.46–2.29.10.

91. Tzvi Langermann, "Abraham Ibn Ezra," *The Stanford Encyclopedia of Philosophy* (2021), https://plato.stanford.edu/archives/fall2021/entries/ibn-ezra/.

92. Cited in Tigay, *Deuteronomy*, 235.

93. Sibyl A. Schwarzenbach, "Fraternity, Solidarity, and Civic Friendship," *AMITY* 3, no. 1 (2015): 11.

94. Law professor Robert Williams (Lumbee Tribe) identifies the body of values, customary practices, and traditions basic to a specific polity as (forming) a constitution. See Robert A. Williams Jr., *Linking Arms Together: American Indian Treaty Visions of Law and Peace, 1600–1800* (New York: Oxford University Press, 1997), 98–99. Williams describes this as the British use of the term constitution, in contrast with "the traditional American sense of one basic, written document of law." Similarly, law professor Carwyn Jones (of Ngāti Kahungunu and Te Aitanga-a-Māhaki descent) uses the term "constitutional tradition" to refer to "the collection of rules, principles, and practices that shape the way in which public power is exercised within a political community." Carwyn Jones, "Māori and State Visions of Law and Peace," in *Indigenous Peoples and the State: International Perspectives on the Treaty of Waitangi*, ed. Mark Hickford and Carwyn Jones (London: Routledge, 2018), 14.

95. See Jones, "Māori and State Visions," 14.

96. Danielle S. Allen, *Talking to Strangers: Anxieties of Citizenship since Brown v. Board of Education* (Chicago: The University of Chicago Press, 2004), xxi.

97. See Stan Rushworth, "Kinship," in *We Are the Middle of Forever: Indigenous Voices from Turtle Island on the Changing Earth*, ed. Dahr Jamail and Stan Rushworth (New York: New Press, 2022), 75.

98. Rushworth, "Kinship," 74.

99. Māmari Stephens, "'He Rangi tā Matawhāiti, he Rangi tā Matawhānui': Looking towards 2040," in *Indigenous Peoples and the State: International Perspectives on the Treaty of Waitangi*, ed. Mark Hickford and Carwyn Jones (London: Routledge, 2018), 193.

100. Stephens, "Matawhāiti," 193. Speaking specifically of Aotearoa New Zealand, Stephens acknowledges that kinship will inevitably retain importance.

101. Margaret Mutu, "'To Honour the Treaty, We Must First Settle Colonisation' (Moana Jackson 2015): The Long Road from Colonial Devastation to Balance, Peace and Harmony," *Journal of the Royal Society of New Zealand* 49, no. S1 (2019): 15.

102. Mutu, "Long Road," 15.

BIBLIOGRAPHY

Allen, Danielle S. *Talking to Strangers: Anxieties of Citizenship since Brown v. Board of Education.* Chicago: The University of Chicago Press, 2004.

Aristotle. *Rhetoric.* Translated by W. Rhys Roberts. New York: Dover Publications, 2012.

Andersen, Francis I., and David Noel Freedman. *Amos.* New York: Doubleday, 1989.

Bargh, Maria. "Introduction." In *Resistance: An Indigenous Response to Neoliberalism*, edited by Maria Bargh. Wellington: Huia, 2007.

Bhagwati, Jagdish N. *In Defense of Globalization.* Oxford: Oxford University Press, 2004.

Coote, Robert B. *Amos among the Prophets: Composition and Theology.* Philadelphia: Fortress, 1981.

Domeris, William. *Touching the Heart of God: The Social Construction of Poverty among Biblical Peasants.* New York: T&T Clark, 2007.

Eidevall, Göran. *Amos: A New Translation with Introduction and Commentary.* 2017.

Ellithorpe, Anne-Marie. "Reciprocity within Community: Ancient and Contemporary Challenges to and Opportunities for Civic Friendship." *Journal of Moral Theology* 10, no. 1 (2021): 176–96.

Ellithorpe, Anne-Marie. *Towards Friendship-Shaped Communities: A Practical Theology of Friendship.* Oxford: Wiley Blackwell, 2022.

Faust, Avraham. "The Rural Community in Ancient Israel During Iron Age II." *Bulletin of the American Schools of Oriental Research* 317 (2000): 17–39.

Glanville, Mark R. *Adopting the Stranger as Kindred in Deuteronomy.* Atlanta: SBL Press, 2018.

Heschel, Abraham Joshua. *The Prophets.* Vol. 1, New York: Harper & Row, 1969.

Hopkins, David C. *The Highlands of Canaan: Agricultural Life in the Early Iron Age.* Decatur, GA: Almond Press, 1985.

Houston, Walter. "Was There a Social Crisis in the Eighth Century?" Chap. 7 in *In Search of Pre-Exilic Israel: Proceedings of the Oxford Old Testament Seminar*, edited by John Day. London: T&T Clark, 2004.

Jeremias, Jörg. *The Book of Amos: A Commentary.* Louisville: Westminster John Knox, 1998.

Jones, Carwyn. "Māori and State Visions of Law and Peace." Chap. 1 in *Indigenous Peoples and the State: International Perspectives on the Treaty of Waitangi*, edited by Mark Hickford and Carwyn Jones. London: Routledge, 2018.

King, Philip J., and Lawrence E. Stager. *Life in Biblical Israel.* Louisville: Westminster John Knox, 2001.

Langermann, Tzvi. "Abraham Ibn Ezra." *The Stanford Encyclopedia of Philosophy* (2021). https://plato.stanford.edu/archives/fall2021/entries/ibn-ezra/.

Lenski, Gerhard. *Power and Privilege: A Theory of Social Stratification.* Chapel Hill: The University of North Carolina Press, 1984.

May, Todd. *Friendship in an Age of Economics: Resisting the Forces of Neoliberalism.* Lanham: Lexington, 2012.

McNutt, Paula M. *Reconstructing the Society of Ancient Israel.* Louisville: Westminster John Knox, 1999.

Meyers, Carol. *Discovering Eve: Ancient Israelite Women in Context.* New York: Oxford University Press, 1988.

Meyers, Carol. "The Family in Early Israel." Chap. 1 in *Families in Ancient Israel*, edited by Leo G. Perdue, Joseph Blenkinsopp, John J. Collins and Carol Meyers. Louisville: Westminster John Knox, 1997.

Meyers, Carol. "Material Remains and Social Relations: Women's Culture in Agrarian Households of the Iron Age." In *Symbiosis, Symbolism, and the Power of the Past: Canaan, Ancient Israel, and Their Neighbors from the Late Bronze Age through Roman Palaestina*, edited by William G. Dever and Seymour Gitin, 425–44. Winona Lake: Eisenbrauns, 2003.

Miller, Patrick D. *Deuteronomy.* Louisville: John Knox, 1990.

Mutu, Margaret. "'To Honour the Treaty, We Must First Settle Colonisation' (Moana Jackson 2015): The Long Road from Colonial Devastation to Balance, Peace and Harmony." *Journal of the Royal Society of New Zealand* 49, no. S1 (2019): 4–18.

Nelson, Richard D. *Deuteronomy: A Commentary.* Louisville: Westminster John Knox, 2002.

Rushworth, Stan. "Kinship." Chap. 6 in *We Are the Middle of Forever: Indigenous Voices from Turtle Island on the Changing Earth*, edited by Dahr Jamail and Stan Rushworth. New York: New Press, 2022.

Sahlins, Marshall. *Stone Age Economics.* London: Routledge Classics, 2017.

Schwarzenbach, Sibyl A. "Fraternity, Solidarity, and Civic Friendship." *AMITY* 3, no. 1 (2015): 3–18.

Stephens, Māmari. "'He Rangi Tā Matawhāiti, He Rangi Tā Matawhānui': Looking Towards 2040." Chap. 10 in *Indigenous Peoples and the State: International Perspectives on the Treaty of Waitangi*, edited by Mark Hickford and Carwyn Jones. London: Routledge, 2018.

Tigay, Jeffrey H. *The JPS Bible Commentary: Deuteronomy.* The Traditional Hebrew Text with the New JPS Translation. Philadelphia: Jewish Publication Society, 1996.

Tuiono, Teanau. "We Are Everywhere." Chap. 7 in *Resistance: An Indigenous Response to Neoliberalism*, edited by Maria Bargh. Wellington: Huia, 2007.

Tzoref, Shani. "Knowing the Heart of the Stranger: Empathy, Remembrance, and Narrative in Jewish Reception of Exodus 22:21, Deuteronomy 10:19, and Parallels." *Interpretation* 72, no. 2 (2018): 11931.

Whakaata Māori, "He Puni Wāhine: An Assembly of Women" in *Waitangi 2023.* Aired February 6, 2023. https://www.maoriplus.co.nz/playback/item/6319893924112.

Williams Jr., Robert A. *Linking Arms Together: American Indian Treaty Visions of Law and Peace, 1600–1800.* New York: Oxford University Press, 1997.

Wolf, Eric R. *Peasants.* Englewood Cliffs: Prentice-Hall, 1966.

Chapter 4

Becoming a Friend to the World

Śāntideva on "Bodhisattva Friendship"

John M. Thompson

"With a Little Help from my Friends," the second track of the Beatles' land-mark 1967 album *Sergeant Pepper's Lonely Hearts Club Band*, is loved by millions of people. Appropriately sung by Ringo Starr, the friendliest and most enduringly popular of the "Fab Four," this song attests to the central role that friends play in our well-being—we cannot live without them. This sentiment is so strong in U.S. culture that one of the most watched television shows ever is known simply as "Friends."

While there is no single universal notion of friendship, here I understand friendship as a voluntary relationship in which we choose to share our life with others, not just for our pleasure but for their own sake. Friendship, thus, involves communion, something that has a sacred dimension acknowledged across most all religions. Not surprisingly, this sacred dimension of friendship is central to the *Bodhicaryāvatāra* (Entry into the Activities of Enlightenment) by Śāntideva (ca. 695–743), a beloved religious "classic" outlining the path of the *bodhisattva* (awakening being), someone who seeks to awaken for the sake of all beings. Śāntideva's text is by no means an obscure treatise; it has been studied and commented upon by innumerable people and is integral to Mahāyāna tradition. I propose, however, that we read this text unconventionally, viewing it not as a way to get beyond the suffering of the world so much as an extended admonition on befriending the world, a notion I dub "*bodhisattva* friendship."

This chapter, then, is an exercise in reconceiving traditional aspects of the Buddha Dharma in ways that are relevant to the contemporary world. By re-examining a classic work of Mahāyāna Buddhism, we can see anew what it has to offer religious scholars and practitioners in the twenty-first century whose lives are increasingly informed by concerns shared by people of all faiths. After a brief look at views of friendship within Buddhism as a whole, I turn to Śāntideva's poetic treatise on the *bodhisattva* path, highlighting passages that speak directly or indirectly to the place of friendship in practices leading to Awakening. It will become apparent that pursuing and developing friendship is not only built into Buddhist spiritual life, but that such relationships invariably extend *beyond* the formal Buddhist community. To emphasize these points, I will also look at how two well-known contemporary Buddhist figures, the fourteenth Dalai Lama (Tenzin Gyatso) and the Vietnamese Zen teacher Thich Nhat Hanh, echo ideas in Śāntideva's verses and address them to a global audience. Finally, I will bring these ideas into conversation with notions of friendship in other religious faiths, namely Confucianism and Christianity. This last section, while brief, is important as a friendly invitation to other scholars to further exploration of friendship across cultural and religious boundaries.

AN INTERPRETATIVE POINT

From the outset, however, I need to address an interpretive issue relevant to *all* works exploring connections between religion and friendship. Features of any religious tradition (texts, doctrines, practices) arise in specific social, cultural, and historical settings. As such, they bear the marks (premises, unstated assumptions, etc.) of their originary contexts. Removing them from such contexts and then recontextualizing them in "new" historical and cultural situations invariably changes them. As David McMahan, a scholar of Modern Buddhism, aptly notes, "Ideas and practices that made sense in one cultural context atrophy like vestigial organs, and new ideas and practices are grafted on, sometimes uncomfortably, as the tradition is called upon to answer new questions, meet novel needs, and uphold—or join with those who oppose—the new culture's axiomatic assumptions."[1]

In terms of this chapter, my discussion of the *Bodhicaryāvatāra* as an extended Buddhist exhortation towards universal friendship amounts to a drastic de/recontextualizing of this text. It is unlikely that Śāntideva (or the scholar-monks commenting on his treatise over the centuries) ever grappled with notions of friendship in the same way that we in the globalized twenty-first century do. Indeed, all contributions to this volume entail such de/recontextualizing. This fact does not make our efforts illegitimate but will hopefully temper our claims with interpretive humility as we spin our words in our scholarly hermeneutic circles.[2]

FRIENDSHIP IN BUDDHISM

Buddhism highly values friendship, regarding it as crucial to spiritual life. In several early discourses, the Buddha praises friendship as central for both monastics and householders, declaring at one point that friendship is "the whole of holy life."[3] We also find evidence of Buddhist esteem of friendship in practices aimed at instilling "friendliness" (Pali, *metta;* Sanskrit, *maitri*), the foremost of the *brahmavihāras* (divine abodes), virtues that practitioners should cultivate as part of the path to Awakening.[4]

The importance of friendship within Buddhism is most obvious in the ideal of the *kalyāna-mitra* (good/admirable friend, sometimes glossed as spiritual friend), someone who encourages others to live according to Dharma (Skt. "Teachings"), as doing so is in the best interests of all beings. Typically, "good friends" should be motivated by compassion (*karunā*), be morally upright, have deep knowledge of the sacred canon, and extensive experience in meditation. In general, "good friends" in Buddhism should be one's spiritual superiors.

It may prove helpful to begin with some etymological analysis of these technical terms.[5] The Sanskrit term *kalyāna-mitra* (Pali, *kalyāna-mitta*) is a compound of two distinct words. The first, *kalyāna*, has a range of meanings, including "excellent," "beautiful," "lovely," and "auspicious." The second, *mitra*, means "friend," "associate," or "companion." *Mitra* is the name of the Vedic *deva* of harmony and is also cognate with related Sanskrit and Pali terms such as *maitrī* and *metta*. Thus, English translations of *kalyāna-mitratā* as "spiritual friendship" and *kalyāna-mitra* as "admirable/good friend" make sense. As Buddhist scholar Steven Collins observes, though, these terms not only have a complex history, they refer to concepts that are not specific to Buddhism nor, in fact, to Indian culture.[6]

Chinese and Japanese translations of these Sanskrit and Pali terms reveal other aspects of "good friendship" within Buddhism as well. The most common Sino-Japanese rendering of *kalyāna-mitra* is 善知識 (Ch. *shanzhishi*, Jpn., *zen chishiki*; lit. excellent/skillful knowledge acquaintance). Also translated as "good companion," the general sense here is someone who leads others to correct teaching or helps them along the way. Such a person strengthens one's faith and practice, often with the specific sense of being a "good teacher."[7]

Several points emerge from this brief etymological exploration. First, the notion of a "good friend" has aesthetic, ethical, and spiritual dimensions; a Buddhist "good friend" exemplifies both excellence and beauty, and the presence of such persons is a blessing for those around them. Second, the "goodness" of such an acquaintance is rooted in *knowledge* or rather, "know how."

Finally, a "good friend" in the technical sense is someone oriented towards others, aiming to assist them in following the Buddhist path. Implicitly, then, a Buddhist "good friend" would qualify as a *bodhisattva*, a follower of the Dharma who aids others as part of her own spiritual practice. It is little wonder, then, that such people are so revered, and it is in this light that we turn to Śāntideva's classic work.

ŚĀNTIDEVA ON THE *BODHISATTVA* PATH AND FRIENDSHIP

The ideal of the *bodhisattva* I touch upon above and its place within Buddhism calls for some explanation. Near the start of the Common Era, various changes were taking place within Buddhism that led to the rise of a reform movement that placed more emphasis on developing compassion and striving for full Buddhahood on behalf of oneself and all sentient beings. Although details are sketchy, this movement was likely rather marginal at first but grew over time, eventually becoming known as the Mahāyāna (Skt. "Great Vehicle"). New texts claiming to be "Buddha Word" (Skt. *buddhavacana*) such as the *Avataṃsaka* and *Vimilakīrti Nirdeśa sūtras* began to circulate, stressing the supremacy of the Buddha while also advocating the universal pursuit of Buddhahood. However, devotees of these texts constituted only a small minority and were not a united movement. Over several decades, followers of this new movement came to see themselves as a distinct group following a superior way to those who failed to appreciate their lofty goals. This Mahāyāna form of Buddhism gained traction as the Dharma spread north and east of the Indian cultural area, coming to dominate East Asia and much of the Himalayan region.[8]

The hallmark of Mahāyāna is the *bodhisattva,* someone who vows to become Buddha out of compassion for others, even postponing her own entry into *nirvana* to remain in *saṃsāra* until all beings Awaken.[9] We can find the notion of a *bodhisattva* in early Buddhism (e.g., the *Jataka Tales*, stories of Siddhartha's previous lives) but Mahāyāna expands upon it. Moved by the sufferings of those caught within *saṃsāra*, *bodhisattvas* draw on their store of *punya* (merit) to teach and comfort all beings. According to tradition, highly advanced *bodhisattvas* (often called *Mahasattvas,* Great Beings) may be reborn in heavenly realms from whence they can give aid to any who call upon them, much like saints in Christianity. At such advanced levels, *bodhisattvas* are virtually indistinguishable from Buddhas in that both *bodhisattvas* and Buddhas bestow grace upon faithful devotees.

One of the most beloved and memorized Buddhist texts, Śāntideva's *Bodhicaryāvatāra* takes its cues from depictions of *bodhisattvas* in Mahāyāna *sūtras* but expands upon them. Ironically, however, its origins are shrouded in mystery and its author Śāntideva (whose name literally means "god of peace") remains more a figure of legend than fact. According to traditional accounts, he was (like the historical Buddha) born into a royal family only to renounce the throne because the great *bodhisattva* Mañjuśrī appeared to him in a dream and proclaimed that the prince should commit himself to the monastic path. Soon after ordaining at Nālandā, one of the great centers of Buddhist learning, the poet-monk earned a reputation for laziness (supposedly spending his days eating, sleeping, and defecating rather than in study). However, when his fellow monks challenged him to recite some *sūtras* before the entire assembly in order to humiliate him, Śāntideva readily agreed, even asking if his brothers would like him to recite a well-known scripture or something new. The other monks requested something new, and to their amazement, their allegedly ignorant colleague began reciting from memory the beautiful verses of the *Bodhicaryāvatāra*. When he reached the thirty-fourth verse of the ninth chapter (the chapter on the "wisdom" that reveals the inherent "emptiness" of all things), Śāntideva rose up into the heavens and disappeared, while his disembodied voice finished the recitation.[10]

Setting aside such hagiographic tales, it is clear that Śāntideva has profoundly influenced Buddhist practice with his remarkable words—words that even after more than a millennium resonate for their profound humanity. Written primarily in the first person, the *Bodhicaryāvatāra* constitutes a condensed ten-chapter outline of the Mahāyāna spiritual path, beginning with the development of the aspiration for Awakening (Skt. *bodhicitta*) through nurturing and honing the practice of the "six perfections" (Skt. *pāramitās*), paying special attention to "patience" (Skt. *ksanti*). The tenth chapter ("Dedication") has become a popular Mahāyāna prayer. All told, this text aims to call people to the bodhisattva's vocation while giving instructions on infusing such spiritual aspiration into daily life.[11] It is also, I maintain, a powerful exhortation to befriend all beings.

One of the keys to understanding how the *Bodhicaryāvatāra* advocates for spiritual friendship lies in the attention the text gives to generating and stabilizing *bodhicitta*, the impetus that marks the beginning of the path and guides it through its ultimate fruition. Śāntideva entitles the first chapter of his work, "The Excellence of Bodhicitta," praising it as a source of "great beatitude" enabling the overcoming of sorrows and suffering.[12] A paradoxical and powerful idea, *bodhicitta* arises naturally when we recognize that suffering (*duhkha*) is inherent existence (*samsāra*) and affirm our desire to get beyond it. Yet at the same time, the aspiring *bodhisattva* also recognizes the suffering of others through developing and extending both friendliness and compassion, truly *feels* such common suffering, and resolves to shoulder the responsibility of relieving it. The initial stirrings of such intention are sudden, mysterious, yet very real; Śāntideva says, "As when a flash of lightning rends the night/And in its glare shows all the dark clouds hid," emphasizing their transient and fragile nature even as he proclaims that they are rooted in "the buddhas' power," the ultimate ground of our being.[13]

Intriguingly, as he goes on to laud *bodhicitta*, Śāntideva praises those who aspire to such a task as being far beyond even the most revered of beings, with their generosity and benevolence surpassing that of fathers, mothers, great teachers, even gods. Tellingly, Śāntideva's hyperbolic praise climaxes when he speaks of such aspirant *bodhisattvas* in terms of friendship, asking rhetorically, "What friend could be compared to them?"[14] This passage comes *after* he has praised *bodhisattvas* as surpassing parents, teachers, even gods, suggesting that the notion of friendship (or rather, *bodhisattva* friendship) may be the closest we can get to conceiving of the relation such "awakening beings" have towards us.

Śāntideva goes on in the next few chapters to confess his shortcomings in light of the daunting nature of such aspiration yet resolutely commits nonetheless, vowing in this moment "to take my birth in the Buddha's line" and "become the buddhas' child and heir."[15] Moreover, the text makes clear that this is not an idle fancy; Śāntideva details his deep awareness of the implications of taking on the *bodhisattva* way as a precious opportunity. It is at this point that he delves into actual *bodhisattva* practices and virtues, beginning with "Vigilance" (Pali, *sati*; Skt. *smrti*, mindfulness), a dedicated attentiveness aiming to tether the mind to the task at hand. This is a regimen of moral and mental discipline, adhering to monastic rules and regulations in one's outer behavior while guarding one's single-minded pursuit of awakening for the benefit of others. Crucial to this is following the examples of one's own mentors. Śāntideva explicitly invokes traditional Buddhist notions of "friendship" here, instructing the reader to never forsake their virtuous friend and teacher who understands the meaning of the Mahayana and practices the bodhisattva path.[16] As Śāntideva admonishes, one venturing on the path to Awakening must diligently follow those who have blazed the trail for us—the Buddhas and teachers whom he explicitly calls "virtuous friends" (*kalyāṇa-mitra*), the truest friends of all beings.

No section of the *Bodhicaryāvatāra* is as powerful and challenging as chapter six, the chapter dedicated to "Patience." This chapter amounts to a detailed admonition on developing forbearance as a way to counter the destructive powers of anger and aggression. Śāntideva anchors such control of the passions in a series of painstaking arguments against our deep-seated clinging to our egos. In fact, he argues rather ingeniously that our alleged "foes" provide us with the rare opportunity for developing spiritual virtues, thereby actually *helping* us along the *bodhisattva* path; our "enemies" are (perhaps unintentionally) among our most helpful "friends."[17] In turn, this realization prompts the poet to reflect on how the potential for Buddhahood in all beings can make us grateful for the ongoing guidance of all other Buddhas. Buddhas are steadfast friends and sources of endless benefits whose unfailing generosity can only be repaid by "making [all other] living beings happy."[18] Once again, Śāntideva speaks of spiritual striving and influence in terms of friendship.

The most striking section of the *Bodhicaryāvatāra* is chapter eight, which is dedicated to detailing various practices of *dhyana* (Meditation). This, the longest of all chapters, focuses especially on particularly powerful meditations often translated as "the equality of self and other," and "the exchange of self and other." Over the course of nearly 200 verses, Śāntideva explains that the *bodhisattva* path does not just entail developing sympathy for all beings (a laudable goal, of course) but moving beyond all barriers created by our egos. A *bodhisattva* must transcend the very distinction between "self" and "other" by coming to realize that the sufferings (and joys) of all beings are actually *our* sufferings and joys. This immediate mutual identification then becomes our primary motive to do what we can to relieve suffering and promote the happiness of everyone. We see directly that their sufferings and joys are ours, and ours are theirs—even down to the visceral sufferings and joys rooted in bodily existence. And once again, Śāntideva speaks of this realization in familiar terms, referring to "others" as "all my friends."[19] At this point in training, a *bodhisattva* has truly befriended all beings.

In the concluding chapter of the *Bodhicaryāvatāra*, the famous "Dedication" that many Buddhist devotees prayerfully recite for all beings, Śāntideva continues to remind his readers of the transformative wonder of "*bodhisattva* friendship." In dedicating the merit accrued through composing these verses, the poet wishes an end to the sufferings of all beings, most especially beings consigned to the hell realms. With vivid language Śāntideva conjures up the torments of those engulfed by the fiery lava-floods of Vaitarani, one of the eight hells of fire and flame, only to have the vast merit from his words (and the compassion of those trodding the *bodhisattva* path) quench the fires in a rain of blossoms and scented water. Filled with a bliss that assuages all their sufferings, the hell dwellers will gaze at the great *bodhisattva* Avalokiteśvara who appears to save and protect them all, as they will call to each other, saying, "Friends, throw away your fears and quickly gather here."[20] It seems that for Śāntideva, "*bodhisattva* friendship" can truly save *all* beings, even enabling those enmired in the worst of all sufferings to recognize each other as friends as well as those who seek to help in any way they can.

These passages give only a taste of Śāntideva's treatise, a call for intentionally engaging with the world instead of turning away and extending our hands in friendship to any and every being. Śāntideva's inspiring words advocate embracing the living and the dead, the saints and the sinners, the noble and the monstrous. Not surprisingly, the *Bodhicaryāvatāra* can come off as too vast and impractical, much like other spiritual texts. Certainly, its call to befriend the world may clash with our concerns for moral justice and a severe reckoning for wrong doers. Donald Lopez, one of the premier scholars of Buddhism and Tibetan culture, even calls the sage's *bodhisattva* vow to save all beings "a noble but insane sentiment."[21] Indeed, this compassionate embrace of *all* beings defies the ordinary prudence that the world typically counsels, with the text calling for a deep and transforming befriending that takes us beyond superficial "do gooderism" and strident moral indignation. In fact, the Padmakara Translation Group note in their introduction to the *Bodhicaryāvatāra*, "to cling to moral values in a spirit of self-righteousness and as a means of judging others is evidence of superficiality and ego-clinging and does not form part of the bodhisattva's mental horizon."[22]

The Influence of Śāntideva's *Bodhicaryāvatāra*: Tenzin Gyatso and Thich Nhat Hanh

The influence of Śāntideva's *Bodhicaryāvatāra*, including its lauding of "*bodhisattva* friendship," is extensive. For example, we catch echoes of such compassionate resolve clearly in the first of the "Four Great Bodhisattva Vows" recited in many Buddhist communities: "The many beings are numberless; I vow to save them."[23] While such words may initially strike a note of superiority (presuming a superior status as a "savior"), in fact one making this vow commits to standing with and helping ALL others no matter what. In other words, one resolves to be a genuine friend to anyone in all circumstances.

The current Dalai Lama, Tenzin Gyatso, is surely the most well-known Buddhist in the world. According to Tibetan teachings, he is also a contemporary manifestation of the *Mahasattva* Avalokiteśvara, the personification of the *bodhisattva* ideal. As the head of the Tibetan Government-in-Exile and the chief lama of the Gelugpa lineage, he draws upon his traditional monastic training and education in his own preaching, much of which has been shaped by his studies of Śāntideva's works. His Holiness has commented on the *Bodhicaryāvatāra* numerous times when addressing various audiences and one of his most notable publications, *For the Benefit of All Beings*, is the transcript of his own commentary on Śāntideva's classic treatise. In this particular book, His Holiness goes through each section of the *Bodhicaryāvatāra*, explaining the main points in simple terms but repeatedly stressing the importance of receiving the teachings with the "correct attitude," which he explicitly states as "the determined wish to attain the state of omniscience for the sake of all beings, who are infinite in number."[24] That is, he prods his listeners (readers) to commit themselves to the *bodhisattva* path. Tellingly, at the start of the very last chapter, the Dalai Lama addresses his *bodhisattva* audience as "spiritual friends," enjoining us all to further study and practice while reminding us that "Living for others is of immense importance for all of us, whatever our beliefs."[25] This is, I would say, encouragement towards "*bodhisattva* friendship."

The late Vietnamese master Thich Nhat Hanh, a prominent Buddhist almost as well known as the Dalai Lama, also preached upon the transformative power of compassion, and was a great advocate for following Śāntideva's guidelines. Buddhist scholar Dale Wright even calls Nhat Hanh a *bodhisattva* for his work, citing in particular the master's address "We are the Beaters; we are the Beaten" that was published as an op-ed article in the *Los Angeles Times* in response to the brutal beating of Rodney King at the hands of the police.[26] In popular addresses to Western audiences, Nhat Hanh often addresses people as "friends" as he encourages them to reach out to and support each other. In fact, he entitles one of his shortest and most direct pieces as "Investing in Friends," proclaiming this as a simple, practical way of creating global security rather than investing in money or arms:

> So, investing in a friend, making a friend into a real friend, building a community of friends, is a much better source of security . . . To create a good community, we first have to transform ourselves into a good element of the community. After that, we can go to another person and help him or her become an element of the community. We build our network of friends that way. We have to think of friends and community as investments, as our most important asset.[27]

Using contemporary metaphors that resonate with Śāntideva's own word, the Vietnamese master speaks of creating a network of friends as yet another way of conceiving the *bodhisattva* path.

Śāntideva's Text and "*Bodhisattva* Friendship"

Reading the *Bodhicaryāvatāra* as a discussion of "*bodhisattva* friendship" is fully in keeping with general Buddhist attitudes towards friendship. Most certainly it presents the *bodhisattva* path as a way of developing the virtue of *kalyāṇa-mitratā* and lays out in detail what striving to become a *kalyāṇa-mitra*, someone who encourages others to live according to Dharma, entails. Then, too, the Dharma has long encouraged practices aiming at developing *maitri* (friendliness). Such attitudes find their fullest expression in the person of *bodhisattva* Maitreya, the "Friendly One," the Buddha of the next world age who is available to us even now.

Not surprisingly, one of the most interesting aspects of the *Bodhicaryāvatāra* is how Śāntideva repeatedly invokes the loving presence of various *bodhisattvas* in his own striving (Samantabhadra, Avalokiteśvara, et al.), particularly in the aforementioned "Dedication" chapter. This chapter, essentially a prayer in which Śāntideva donates to all beings the merit from his composition (and by extension the merit from all who read his verses and put them into practice), is also a hymn of gratitude to the Buddhas and *bodhisattvas* for their continual support. In particular, he singles out Mañjuśrī (sometimes under the name Mañjughoṣa), the *bodhisattva* associated with *prajñā*, the "wisdom" that cuts through all dualities, and with whom he has an especially close relationship.[28] In these lines Śāntideva attests that it is "*bodhisattva* friendship" that has enabled his poetic work, and he thanks Mañjuśrī and all the "awakening beings," explicitly calling them his "virtuous friends" as he vows to stand with them in their compassionate work.

As this concluding chapter makes clear, Śāntideva is not just calling on these figures but pushing us to join their ranks; he is calling us to a shared endeavor with many others. This path is not really a matter of "faith" or "religion," so much as an intentional way of living positively with and for others. As contemporary scholar-practitioner Taigen Leighton puts it:

> The point is to take on bodhisattva commitment in our life here today. How we take care of this present life and the world that meets us does make a difference. Over the range of bodhisattva time our ongoing contribution to awakening conduct and awareness helps to actualize such an outlook for others. The ever-present reality of the radiant beauty of all things may also be universally recognized over time. This is the bodhisattva ideal.[29]

Although such words may lack the beauty of the words of the legendary Indian poet Santideva, they do help us see what the life of a *bodhisattva* should be. This is nothing less than a heart-felt embracing of "self" and "other" as inseparable, the "best of friends." In this light, then, the way of "*bodhisattva* friendship" becomes a mutual bettering and forms the basis for an informal "society of friends" potentially open to all beings. No doubt there are problems with such utopian aspirations but Śāntideva's text, a veritable paean to befriending the world, suggests new and highly creative ways of understanding human life.

I am *not* suggesting that we uncritically embrace the *Bodhicaryāvatāra*, reading it only through the eyes of faith. Nor am I claiming that these verses emerged directly from the lips of the Buddhas, even if it is clear that their examples inspired their author. Whatever else it may be, this text is obviously a document created by people and thus bearing all the traces of the time and place of its composition and the lives of generations who have studied it and passed it down to us. Yet such scholarly points do not preclude the idea that with the *Bodhicaryāvatāra* we are dealing with a true instance of "Buddha word." Buddhist tradition has long maintained that the Dharma *cannot* be limited to just what was (allegedly) spoken by the (historical) Buddha.[30] Setting such notions aside, however, this text provides us a unique opportunity to consider dimensions of spiritual friendship that offer important and timely insights to us in the twenty-first century.

CROSS-CULTURAL AND INTERFAITH COMPARISONS

This notion of "bodhisattva friendship" at the center of Śāntideva's masterpiece remains compelling even more than a millennium after its composition, but at the same it is also daunting. As such, it provides a sharp contrast to more limited and practical discussions of friendship by other thinkers, most notably by Aristotle. In the *Nichomachean Ethics* Aristotle praises friendship (*philia*) as a good and essential component of a fulfilling life, even claiming that a friend is a "second self." Yet he also states that friendship has necessary limits in actual life (1170b–1171a). Śāntideva, however, challenges us to go beyond Aristotelian conceptions and conceive of a deeper, more inspiring notion of what friendship might be.

In this vein, the notion of "*bodhisattva* friendship" in Śāntideva's work might actually provide a fruitful topic for interfaith work. For example, it would seem to resonate with the concept of "virtuous friendship" (*you*), one of the "five cardinal relations" (*wu lun* 五倫, lit. five duties) in Confucianism. According to Confucian tradition, one can only become truly human through our relations with other humans—relationships through which we exercise ethical virtues. The Confucian conception of a person as inherently relational goes back to the very beginnings of the religion, finding its most important articulation in the *Zhongyong* 中庸 ("Doctrine of the Mean"), in which Confucius himself lays out the ideal form of society in terms of "five cardinal relations":

> The universal Way of the world involves five relations, and practicing it involves three virtues. The five are the relations between ruler and minister, between parent and child, between husband and wife, between older and younger brother, and among friends. These five are the universal way of the world.[31]

Although most scholars stress the centrality of family in this Confucian relational view of humanity, it is highly significant that friendship, a *voluntary* relationship, is included. In fact, Ambrose King, a scholar of Chinese culture and modernization, goes so far as to claim that Confucian ethics is governed by an attitude of "self-centered voluntarism," and that the corner-stone of the entire system is *shu* 恕 (reciprocity), an empathetic ability to take on the role of others.[32] While it would be going too far to argue that this is "the same" as the notion of *"bodhisattva* friendship," the transformative nature of both ideas suggests promising areas for dialogue between these religions.

Moreover, we can find resonances to *"bodhisattva* friendship" in other faiths besides Confucianism. For the sake of brevity, I limit myself to one other example: Christianity. In a very personal essay Maria and Ruben Habito, Christian theologians who have long been involved in interreligious dialogue, speak of their own work as a spiritual journey with friends of various faiths. The Habitos take John 15:13, "Greater love has no one than this: to lay down one's life for one's friends" (NIV), as the guiding spirit that informs their faith. They go on to add, "The Spirit of Jesus Christ conveyed in the passage above, incidentally, coincides perfectly with the heart of the Bodhisattva, one who is no less willing to give oneself and one's entire life, and even die so that others may live, and have the fullness of well-being."[33] Once again, we find that notions of deep friendship lie at the heart of two world religions. This fact prompts several questions: to what extent might the love *(agapē)* enjoined and exemplified by Christ coincide with "bodhisattva friendship"? Is Śāntideva, like the Biblical writer Paul, calling us to give ourselves in love to others, perhaps in a sort of *kenosis,* or self-emptying, as Christ does (Philippians 2:7)? Such questions, of course, do not lend themselves to brief answers at the end of a chapter such as this one. My sense, though, is that the Habitos and Śāntideva might find much to discuss over a pot of freshly brewed Darjeeling.

CONCLUDING REFLECTIONS

I wrote the initial draft of this chapter during the fall of 2020, a year unlike any other in recent memory. A year of global pestilence that sickened or killed millions of people, raging wildfires that burned thousands of acres, floods that destroyed entire towns and displaced scores of people, and violent social unrest that laid bare deep-seated structural problems that humanity has created through our own short-sightedness. It was a year of apocalyptic dimensions that for many people was a literal hell on earth. Since then, the global situation has in many respects only deteriorated further. It is in such desperate times that we need friends more than ever. Even more importantly, though, we need to *be* friends with our fellow sentient beings, pledging in the words of Bruce Springsteen, "I will provide for you, and I'll stand by your side / You'll need a good companion now, for this part of the ride."[34]

Of course, we may rightly wonder if it is even possible to be friends under these circumstances. The coronavirus has already killed millions and continues to spread despite the availability of vaccines and other medical treatments, and while mask mandates and most travel restrictions are things of the past, many people still feel emotionally isolated and wary of engaging with others. Meanwhile social media continues to engender suspicion and hostility to anyone outside our immediate social circles (in person or online)—an attitude that certain political figures are only too happy to promote. In such circumstances, entering into (or even maintaining) true friendship that takes us beyond our immediate concerns for survival seems unimaginable. Yet it is precisely in such dire straits that we long to rise above worldly pettiness and entertain other possibilities.

Which brings us back to the *Bodhicaryāvatāra*, this beloved treatise whose words reaffirm the Buddha's reminder that friendship "is the whole of holy life." In fact, though, Śāntideva's words do more than just echo the World-Honored One's teachings, they draw out the deeper implications of what was always already there. This idea of "*bodhisattva* friendship" is radically transformative and positively exhilarating, particularly in a time of great suffering. In part, this seems to be because this idea enables us to marry our innate need for social support with our capacity to choose the direction of our life. "*Bodhisattva* friendship" challenges us to transcend our selfish concerns and embrace the entire world. For a *bodhisattva*, *everyone* really is (or can be) our friend. This sentiment, while initially ridiculous in its idealism, actually constitutes a sane response to our insane circumstances.

It is fitting to close these reflections on the words of one poet with those of another. In "A Servant to Servants," famous American poet Robert Frost gives voice to a long-suffering woman speaking to an unnamed man camping on the land she and her husband own. Touchingly understated, the poem reveals the woman's listless life as a perplexing cycle of doing "things over and over that just won't stay done." And yet weary as she is, she soldiers on, buoyed by her husband's grim motto that "the best way out is always through."[35] Tired but not bitter, her words suggest beauty and joy even in the midst of her toil—a faint but friendly *bodhisattva*-like hint that we can find nirvana within samsara. Such is Śāntideva's "*bodhisattva* friendship," a life that, while perhaps not for everyone, offers at least one way through.

NOTES

1. David L. McMahan, *The Making of Buddhist Modernism* (New York: Oxford University Press, 2008), 61–62.

2. As Heidegger observes. "What is decisive is not get out of the circle but to come into it in the right way." Martin Heidegger, *Being and Time*, trans. John Macquarrie and Edward Robinson, (San Francisco: Harper & Row, 1962), 195.

3. Thanissaro Bhikkhu, trans., "Upaddha Sutta: Half (of the Holy Life)" (SN 45.2), 1997, accessed October 15, 2019, http:/www.accesstoinsight.org/tiptaka/sn /sn45/sn45.002.than.html. This *sutta* is found in the *Samyutta-nikaya* ("Corrected Discourses"), a major section of the Pali Canon.

4. One famous discourse, the *Metta Sutta*, focuses entirely on the importance of "friendliness" and various techniques for instilling it. See Nanamoli Thera, trans., "Metta Sutta: Loving Kindness," (AN 4.125), 1998, accessed November 11, 2019, https://www.accesstoinsight.org/tipitaka/an/an04/an04.125.nymo.html

5. Here I follow John Grimes, *A Concise Dictionary of Indian Philosophy: Sanskrit Terms defined in English,* revised ed. (Albany: SUNY Press, 1996).

6. Steven Collins, "Kalyanamitta and Kalyanamittata," *Journal of the Pali Text Society*, vol. XI (1987): 51–72, accessed November 8, 2019, http://www.palitext.com /JPTS_scans/JPTS_1987_XI.pdf

7. "Good Friend," *Dictionary of Buddhism*, Nichiren Buddhism Library, accessed November 8, 2019, https://www.nichirenlibrary.org/en/dic/Content/G/56. A less common rendering of *kalyāṇa-mitra* is 善友 (Ch. *shanyou*).

8. For a summary of the scholarship, see Paul Williams, *Mahayana Buddhism: The Doctrinal Foundations*, 2nd ed. (New York: Routledge, 2009), 21–44.

9. For a classic scholarly discussion, see Har Dayal, *The Bodhisattva Doctrine in Buddhist Sanskrit Literature,* reprint, (Delhi: Motilal Banarsidass, 2004).

10. There are various versions of this tale, some replete with far more fanciful details. For a standard version, see Donald S. Lopez, "How to Be a Bodhisattva," 395–96, in Donald S. Lopez, Jr., ed., *Buddhism*, in *The Norton Anthology of World Religions*, (New York: W. W. Norton, 2015).

11. Donald S. Lopez, "How to Be a Bodhisattva," 395–96.

12. Shantideva, *The Way of the Bodhisattva: A Translation of the Bodhicharyavatara*, trans. by the Padmakara Translations Group (Boston & London: Shambhala, 1997), 34.

13. Shantideva, *The Way of the Bodhisattva,* 34.

14. Shantideva, *The Way of the Bodhisattva*, 37.

15. Shantideva, *The Way of the Bodhisattva*, 52.

16. Shantideva, *The Way of the Bodhisattva*, 76.

17. Shantideva, *The Way of the Bodhisattva*, 93–94.

18. Shantideva, *The Way of the Bodhisattva*, 95.

19. Shantideva, *The Way of the Bodhisattva*, 136.

20. Shantideva, *The Way of the Bodhisattva*, 164.

21. Lopez, "How to be a Bodhisattva," 396.

22. Shantideva, *The Way of the Bodhisattva,* 8.

23. Probably composed in China in the sixth century CE, these vows often conclude religious services at Mahāyāna centers. For an insightful explanation, see Robert Aitken, "The Bodhisattva Vows," *Tricycle: The Buddhist Review*, Summer 1992, accessed October 3, 2020, https://tricycle.org/magazine/bodhisattva-vows/

24. Tenzin Gyatso, *For the Benefit of All Beings: A Commentary on The Way of the Bodhisattva* (Boulder, CO: Shambhala, 2009), 8.

25. Gyatso, *For the Benefit of All Beings*, 124–125.

26. Dale S. Wright, "The Bodhisattva's Practice of Enlightenment," in *What is Buddhist Enlightenment?* (New York: Oxford University Press, 2016), 18–19.

27. Thich Nhat Hanh, *Peace is Every Step: The Path of Mindfulness in Everyday Life*, ed. Arnold Kotler (New York: Bantam Books, 1991), 87.

28. Shantideva, *The Way of the Bodhisattva*, 169–170.

29. Taigen Dan Leighton, *Faces of Compassion: Classic Bodhisattva Archetypes and Their Modern Expression*, revised ed. (Boston: Wisdom, 2012), 40–41.

30. Donald S. Lopez, Jr., *Elaborations on Emptiness: Uses of the Heart Sūtra* (Princeton: Princeton University Press, 1996), 28.

31. Irene Bloom, trans, "The Mean *(Zhongyong)*," in Wm. Theodore De Bary & Irene Bloom, eds., *Sources of Chinese Traditions: Volume One—From Earliest Times to 1600*, 2nd ed. (New York: Columbia University Press, 1999), 336–337.

32. Ambrose Y. C. King, "The Individual and Group in Confucianism: A Relational Perspective," in Donald Munro, ed., *Individualism and Holism: Studies in Confucian and Taoist Values* (Ann Arbor, MI: Center for Chinese Studies, University of Michigan, 1985), 57–70.

33. Maria Reiss Habito and Ruben L. F. Habito, "Friendship across Traditions: Buddhist Perspectives," in Alon Goshen-Gotstein, ed., *Friendship Across Religions: Theological Perspectives on Interreligious Friendship* (Eugene, OR: Rowman & Littlefield, 2015), 163.

34. "Land of Hope and Dreams," track 10 on Bruce Springsteen, *Wrecking Ball*, Columbia Records, 2012.

35. Robert Frost, "A Servant to Servants," accessed November 20, 2020, https://www.internal.org/Robert_Frost/A_Servant_to_Servants

BIBLIOGRAPHY

Aitken, Robert. "The Bodhisattva Vows," *Tricycle: The Buddhist Review*, Summer 1992, Accessed October 3, 202. https://tricycle.org/magazine/bodhisattva-vows/

Bloom, Irene, trans. "The Mean (Zhongyong)." In *Sources of Chinese Traditions: Volume One—From Earliest Times to 1600*, edited by Wm. Theodore De Bary and Irene Bloom. 2nd ed. New York: Columbia University Press, 1999.

Collins, Steven. "Kalyanamitta and Kalyanamittata," *Journal of the Pali Text Society*, vol. XI (1987): 51–72. Accessed November 8, 2021, http://www.palitext.com/JPTS_scans/JPTS_1987_XI.pdf

Dayal, Har. *The Bodhisattva Doctrine in Buddhist Sanskrit Literature*. Reprint, Delhi: Motilal Banarsidass, 2004.

Frost, Robert "A Servant to Servants." Accessed November 20, 2020. https://www.internal.org/Robert_Frost/A_Servant_to_Servants

Grimes, John. *A Concise Dictionary of Indian Philosophy: Sanskrit Terms Defined in English*. Revised edition. Albany: SUNY Press, 1996.

Gyatso, Tenzin. *For the Benefit of All Beings: A Commentary on The Way of the Bodhisattva*. Boulder, CO: Shambhala, 2009.

Habito, Maria Reiss, and Ruben L. F. Habito, "Friendship across Traditions: Buddhist Perspectives." In *Friendship Across Religions: Theological Perspectives on Interreligious Friendship*, edited by Alon Goshen-Gotstein. Eugene, OR: Rowman & Littlefield, 2015.

Heidegger, Martin. *Being and Time.* Translated by John Macquarrie and Edward Robinson. San Francisco: Harper & Row, 1962.

King, Ambrose Y. C. "The Individual and Group in Confucianism: A Relational Perspective." In *Individualism and Holism: Studies in Confucian and Taoist Values*, edited by Donald Munro. Ann Arbor, MI: Center for Chinese Studies, University of Michigan, 1985.

Leighton, Taigen Dan. *Faces of Compassion: Classic Bodhisattva Archetypes and Their Modern Expression.* Revised edition. Boston: Wisdom, 2012.

Lopez, Jr., Donald S. *Elaborations on Emptiness: Uses of the Heart Sūtra.* Princeton: Princeton University Press, 1996.

Lopez, Jr., Donald S. "How to Be a Bodhisattva," 395–96. In *Buddhism*, in *The Norton Anthology of World Religions,* edited by Donald S. Lopez, Jr. New York: W. W. Norton, 2015.

McMahan, David L. *The Making of Buddhist Modernism.* New York: Oxford University Press, 2008.

Nanamoli Thera, trans., "Metta Sutta: Loving Kindness," (AN 4.125), 1998. Accessed November 11, 201. https://www.accesstoinsight.org/tipitaka/an/an04/an04.125.nymo.html.

Nhat Hanh, Thich. *Peace is Every Step: The Path of Mindfulness in Everyday Life.* Edited by Arnold Kotler. New York: Bantam, 1991.

Nichiren Buddhism Library. "Good friend," *Dictionary of Buddhism.* Accessed November 8, 2019. https://www.nichirenlibrary.org/en/dic/Content/G/56.

Shantideva [Śāntideva]. *The Way of the Bodhisattva: A Translation of the Bodhicharyavatara.* Translated by Padmakara Translations Group. Boston: Shambhala, 1997.

Springsteen, Bruce. *Wrecking Ball.* 2012. Columbia Records.

Thanissaro Bhikkhu, trans. "Upaddha Sutta: Half (of the Holy Life)" (SN 45.2), 1997. Accessed October 15, 2019. http:/www.accesstoinsight.org/tiptaka/sn/sn45/sn45.002.than.html.

Williams, Paul. *Mahayana Buddhism: The Doctrinal Foundations.* 2nd ed. New York: Routledge, 2009.

Wright, Dale S. "The Bodhisattva's Practice of Enlightenment." In *What is Buddhist Enlightenment?* New York: Oxford University Press, 2016.

Chapter 5

Sacred Fellowship among Learners

A Kabbalistic Pedagogy for Our Times

Laura Duhan-Kaplan

The *Zohar,* a classic imaginative kabbalistic text, describes a community of friends who study esoteric theology together. One famous section of the *Zohar* reflects on the nature of that community. In times of spiritual drought, it says, members of the community adopt one another as family, build a world together, and model divine unity in diversity. It is an idealized vision, to be sure; but elements of it can come to life in a university classroom. In fall 2001 in the USA, in the weeks leading up to and following the 9/11 terrorist attack, I was teaching a philosophy course. That term, I was experimenting with several classroom strategies, including journaling, intentional listening, and a ritual activity. These strategies, I believed, would help us open as individuals to big existential questions. But they also helped our class bond as a group, travel to one another's social and personal worlds, and become a unity by honoring our diversity.

Below, I present a passage from the *Zohar* about the kind of friendship its community of comrades shares. Using appropriate hermeneutic tools, I draw out its many meanings. Next, I describe the social context of our philosophy class, with its diverse group of students learning together in a stressful time. I focus on our "WOW Journal" listening practice, and its impact on the group. Finally, I theorize about why the practice worked, drawing on Maria Lugones's understanding of "'world'-traveling," Lawrence Hoffman's concept of a "ritual moment," and Ray Aldred's discussion of "making relatives" through treaty. All these dynamics, I believe, are subtly present in the *Zohar*'s story.

THE *ZOHAR*

A famous passage in the *Zohar* expresses a theology of spiritual and intellectual friendship in a specifically Jewish idiom.[1] The *Zohar*, a classical work of kabbalah written in the twelfth century, is a kind of mystical novel set in the second century BCE.[2] It follows the adventures of the *hevraya*, or comrades, as they wander the land with their teacher, Rabbi Shimon bar Yochai.[3] Together, they explore deep metaphysical and existential issues. What underlies the reality we experience? Who was God before the world was created? How can we speak about the true nature of the divine? And, together, they scan the worlds of nature, sacred text, and ritual practice for clues.

Rabbi Shimon teaches in a homiletic style, full of story, allegory, and biblical allusion.[4] His style is consistent with some biblical texts, especially books of classical prophecy (c. 700–500 BCE). And it looks very similar to classical rabbinic *midrash*, early biblical interpretation (c. 200–600 CE). Thus, we can use some tools of *midrash*, biblical hermeneutics, to explore it—as long as we keep in mind ways that the *Zohar*'s style differs from more free-wheeling classical *midrash*. The *Zohar*'s main author, Moses de Leon, wrote a self-conscious allegory pointing to a particular theology. God is infinite energy, expressed through a finite set of spiritual qualities. Some of these qualities are gendered either masculine or feminine. When they are allegorically "married," (i.e., when they come into balance), positive divine energy fills the world.[5] To hint at this, many passages of *Zohar* use erotic male-female love as an allegory. Here, I do preserve the *Zohar*'s gender-binary language. But I also go beyond it, as is appropriate to the passage in question, which equates the intimacy of the *hevraya* with the intimacy of family.[6]

Comrades in Learning

The *Zohar* says:

> It has been taught [that] R. Yosi said: One time the world was in need of rain. So R. Yeisa, R. Hizkiya, and others from among the friends came before R. Shimon. They found him setting out to see R. Pinhas ben Yair. Because he saw them, he opened and said (Psalm 133:1), "A song of ascents. Behold how good and how pleasant it is when brothers dwell together! What is [the meaning of] when brothers dwell together? [It is like] what is said (Exodus 25:20): Their faces, each toward his brother. When they were one-to-one, gazing face-to-face, [it was like what] is written, Behold how good and how pleasant! But when the male turns his face away from the female, woe to the world!"[7]

Here, the *Zohar* weaves a dense homily. So, I will explicate it strand by strand. To do so, I will use a Kabbalistic four-fold interpretive framework, one the *Zohar* itself hints at.[8] The framework is called *PaRDes,* which means "orchard." It helps us study a text on four levels: (1) *Peshat,* or a relatively "simple," literal reading. (2) *Derash,* or "homily," an intertextual exploration of a core biblical value. (3) *Remez,* or "hint," an allegorical reading. (4) *Sod,* or "secret," an esoteric teaching about the nature of God. I will do my best to walk through those steps in a linear way, though they often layer in nonlinear ways.

The *peshat,* plain literal meaning, of this *Zohar* text tells a story about a group of male friends who delight in learning together. They travel together on a shared spiritual journey. Their teacher, Rabbi Shimon, also delights in their company. He celebrates it by spinning an exuberant homily. Our friendship, says Rabbi Shimon to his *hevraya,* is "good and pleasant." But, he cautions, do not let our friendship distract you from your marriage. Do not turn away from your wives; that is not good for you, or for anyone else.

Spiritual Friends Are Family

Rabbi Shimon's homily takes the form of a *derash,* an intertextual exploration of the spiritual value of friendship. Rabbi Shimon explicitly quotes only two different Biblical verses. But, because Rabbi Shimon presents a "chain" *midrash,* other Biblical stories and rabbinic homilies are at work in the background.[9] Rabbi Shimon opens his homily by quoting Psalm 133:1. But it helps if you know the full psalm:

> A song of ascents. Of David.
> How good and how pleasant it is
> Dwelling together like brothers.
> It is like fine oil on the head
> running down onto the beard,
> the beard of Aaron,
> that comes down over the collar of his robe;
> like the dew of Hermon
> that falls upon the mountains of Zion.
> There the LORD ordained blessing,
> everlasting life.[10]

Explicitly, the Psalm suggests that friends worshipping together in community are like close siblings. Implicitly, it evokes famous Biblical stories of friendship. Ruth and Naomi adopted one another as family. So, one could say, did David and Jonathan. If you keep those stories in mind, you understand Psalm 133 more deeply. Good friends are not just "like" family; they are family. Close friends adopt one another as siblings. When you create a family of choice, you take on sacred responsibilities. You are, in a sense, like the newly anointed high priest Aaron. At the same time, you open yourself to a wild, unpredictable relationship. Navigating a friendship is like climbing up to the snowfields of Mt. Hermon, 9232 feet above sea level. The ups and downs bring you closer to God's presence. Then, blessings rain down upon you.

Becoming part of the *hevraya*, Rabbi Shimon hints, is as sacred as getting married. But his homily does not say this explicitly. Again, Rabbi Shimon assumes you are familiar with a relevant rabbinic *midrash*. Explicitly, he begins by reaffirming Psalm 133 with a biblical verse describing the construction of the ark of the covenant. This ark will be housed inside the Holy of Holies, where the anointed high priest meets God. This sacred work of art will be decorated with golden cherubim. In Ancient Near Eastern iconography, these hybrid human-animal sculptures often guard the entrance to sacred places.[11]

> The cherubim will have wings spread above, making a screen over the cover, each facing his brother, their faces [also] turned towards the cover (Exod 25:20).[12]

If you read the text literally, the "brothers" are clearly a pair of identical sculptures. But we are reading homiletically along with Rabbi Shimon. So we know that our sacred friendships make us metaphorical high priests. But we must be careful: a high priest who encounters God directly does dangerous work. The priest needs to protect himself, and act with ritual precision.[13] Members of the *hevraya,* too, need to act with care. The metaphysical knowledge they seek can be overwhelming. And family, too, can be overwhelming! So, Rabbi Shimon issues a caution. One should not enter the *hevraya* lightly. On the contrary; the group's intimacy must be carefully tended. Friends must not turn away from one another.

Friends Build a World

Now, Rabbi Shimon slides into speaking about another kind of family of choice: a married couple. Rabbi Shimon says, "But when the male turns his face away from the female, woe to the world!" This change of focus calls the reader's attention to a classical rabbinic *midrash* that reimagines the cherubim not as siblings but as a married couple.

> Rav Ketina said: When the Jewish people would ascend for [one of the pilgrimage] Festivals, [the priests would] roll up the curtain for them and show them

the cherubs, which were clinging to one another, and say to them: See how you are beloved before God, like the love of a male and female.[14]

Rav Ketina is clearly on a flight of imagination as he describes this scene in the Jerusalem temple. He seems to be amplifying Rabbi Akiva's famous teaching about the erotic biblical love poem Song of Songs. Rabbi Akiva says, "all the writings are holy but the Song of Songs is the holy of holies."[15] So, Rav Ketina imagines the Song of Songs come to life in the holy of holies. And the priests invite the pilgrims in to learn two secrets. One, the cherubim move! Sometimes they embrace, like a couple making love. Two, the cherubim show that God loves the people as deeply as spouses (ideally) love each other. When spouses first meet, as the prophet Jeremiah says, they are romantic lovers.[16] Over time, they work through their differences, and become intimate friends.

Rav Ketina's word choice in the *midrash* is important. He does not liken the cherubim to a man and a woman, but to a "male and female." Thus, he evokes the original creation of human beings. Torah says,

> God created humankind in the divine image; creating it in the image of God; creating them male and female (Gen. 1:27).[17]

According to rabbinic *midrash,* this verse teaches us much about the first human being. The first human is androgynous, with two faces, one male and one female. Later, in the Garden of Eden, God divides this human in two. Then, God turns their faces towards one another.[18] They recognize each other, become the first family, and begin to build the human world. Every couple that unites into a family, the Talmud suggests, continues this mission. At every wedding, the Talmud recommends reciting it in a ritual statement:

> Blessed are You . . . Who made humanity in His image, in the image of the like-ness of His form, and out of His very self formed a building for eternity. Blessed are You, Lord, Creator of mankind.[19]

In Rav Ketina's *midrash,* spiritual friends also have the power to bring male and female together. They, too, come together in mutual recognition, and build the world in community. Clearly, Rabbi Shimon believes that the *hevraya* are building a world together, as well. And woe to the world when they turn away from one another!

Cosmic Dimensions of Friendship

Now, it is easy to identify an allegory (*remez*) in the *Zohar* text. Rabbi Shimon speaks into a time of drought. Allegorically, he speaks of a spiritual drought. The earth should be saturated with awareness of God's love. But it is not. So, someone needs to open a channel so that awareness can flow. Members of the *hevraya* can just do that. They open their hearts to one another, achieving intimacy as they study together. As they feel God's love, their minds open to God's true nature. They receive spiritual insight, and share it with all who can understand. But woe to the world if they cannot do this work!

Finally, we can begin to grasp the esoteric secret (*sod*), the allusion to God's true nature. The original human was created in the image of God. It was a unity in diversity, male and female in a single being. Once God split the human, its two halves became a couple. Thus, it was still a unity in diversity, male and female in a single community. The *Zohar* affirms that divine energy has both masculine and feminine facets. Sometimes these facets are in a natural unity, like the original human was. But sometimes they are alienated from one another, and need to come together, as the first human couple did. When God's masculine and feminine energies are integrated, we might say, the world is whole (*shalem*) and at peace (*shalom*).

What can bring God's scattered energies to together? Why, it is the action of human beings themselves! We can become a unity in diversity. Members of a couple can turn towards one another in love. Friends can adopt one another as family. A worshipping community can create a sacred interpersonal space. A *hevraya* can form and get to know God together. We humans have this power because we, like all of creation, are made of divine energy. When we love, divine love flows. But when our relationships fray, so does the spiritual energy of the world. And woe to us all if we let that happen!

TEACHING IN A TIME OF FRACTURE

I'd like to tell a story of a time a university class became a kind of secular *hevraya*. It's September 11, 2001, and I am teaching at the University of North Carolina at Charlotte. It's the fourth week of term, so students in my 11:00 a.m. Introduction to Philosophy class are well into discussing deep metaphysical and existential issues. In fact, they have their first formal course paper in hand. But everyone already knows that something crazy happened in New York, Pennsylvania, and Washington, DC. So, I tell them to discuss their papers in small groups, and I'll go find someone with a TV or radio. I come back to class and confirm what they have already pieced together. Multiple airplanes were hijacked. Two flew into the World Trade Center in New York and brought down the 110-story twin towers. An Iranian-American student says, "My mother is a flight attendant for American Airlines. Sometimes she's assigned to the eastern corridor routes. I hope we hear from her soon." A white Southern student says, "I'm here on an ROTC (Reserve Officer Training Corps) scholarship. I hope I don't get called up for military service." There's not much I can do, and not much the students can do, except listen to one another's fears.

Fortunately, supportive listening is already part of this class's group ethos. We are four weeks into our WOW Journal activity. This is my first use of the WOW Journal in a philosophy course. My mentor Rabbi Marcia Prager told me she sometimes asks twelve-year-old bar and bat mitzvah students to keep one. Spirituality, Prager believes, is a conscious practice of wonder.[20] Well, I believe, along with Plato, that philosophy is also a conscious practice of wonder, explored through dialogue.[21] So, I adapted Prager's WOW Journal into a group experience. Here is the description from the original Fall term 2001 syllabus:

> *Wow journal:* This journal is designed to encourage you to notice and write about things you find special or unusual in everyday life: events, activities, feelings, thoughts, movies, music, etc. that make you say, "Wow!" You will find that the topics we discuss in class make you notice at least some new and different things. Please write a minimum of 1 full page per week in the journal. Entries may be handwritten, as long as they are legible. Describe the "wow," try to put into words why the experience stands out, explain what it makes you think or wonder about. "Wow" journals will be collected twice during the semester for informal feedback, and once at the end of the semester for a grade. Also, during each class session in which there is no quiz, three people will be asked to read (or tell about something) from their "wow" journal, and other students will have the opportunity to respond.[22]

The most powerful part of this assignment turned out to be the sharing of journal entries. After our first class meeting, students signed up for their days to read. About twenty minutes before the end of each ninety-minute class, we would turn to the journals. We always approached them in the exact same way. One student would read, and I would call on three students to comment out loud. A second student would read, and three others would comment. A third student would read, and three would comment. Then, I would invite everyone in the class to write a personal comment for one of the readers. I would collect and sort the comments without looking at them, and deliver them immediately to the journal readers.

The process was the same, but the content was always different. Sometimes students read entries about happy experiences, like hearing a concert by the ocean at sunset. But, more often, students read entries about painful memories: witnessing a murder, or growing up as a refugee in a country at war. Sometimes students read entries about new challenges, like worrying how they, a foreign student, were becoming targets of hate. Classmates who commented aloud weren't experts in careful speech, but no one ever mis-stepped. And journal readers consistently told me, in private, that they received supportive comments from their classmates.[23] During that stressful term, everyone needed support. UNC Charlotte students were used to learning on a racially and ethnically diverse campus.[24] But this term was different. Many students on military scholarships did indeed withdraw from classes for deployment in Afghanistan and Iraq. Some angry American students did indeed attack foreign students. But our classroom was a bit of an oasis, where students formed new international friendships, laughing and learning together.

The WOW Journal activity surprised me. Initially, I had hoped to inspire individual students to shift their own ways of perceiving the world. I assumed each student would notice some wondrous things about the world. And, when they read from their journal, they would point out new things for fellow students to notice. I did not predict the intersubjective effect, that is, a shift in the class's perception of itself as a group. Nor did I predict the power of the activity to inspire friendship. In retrospect, however, I understand two factors were at work. One, the sharing gave students an opportunity to visit one another's life-worlds without prejudice. And, as propaganda and suspicion increased around them, they yearned for this special time. Two, the structure offered students a safe ritual container for their visits. Both of these factors became a foundation for creating friendships.

TRAVELING ACROSS LIFE-WORLDS

To understand more deeply what it meant for students to visit one another's life-worlds, I draw on phenomenology, the study of experience. The *lebenswelt,* or "life-world" became a popular idea through the work of philosopher Edmund Husserl (1859–1938). As Husserl sees it, we have a sense of a shared cultural world, a backdrop from which our academic research emerges.[25] We live into this intersubjective experience through a kind of empathy. For example, each of us experiences our own body as the center of our spatial field. Thus, we perceive things as near or far from us, to our right or our left. But we also know that other conscious beings experience the world from their own position.[26] And we understand that physical objects can be seen from multiple perspectives.[27] So, our sense of empathy helps us share our physical space. Normally, this empathy becomes part of our perception in what we might call an intuitive way. But we can take a closer look at how this integration works. To do so, we turn our focus away from the physical world and towards the structures of our consciousness. We "bracket off" our usual focus on the world itself and pay attention instead to the ways we are conscious of it. In this altered mode, we can begin to see how the life-world functions to structure our consciousness.

Philosopher Maria Lugones (1944–1920) deepens Husserl's analysis of the life-world, and adds an ethical dimension.[28] Lugones defines a "world" as a set of social and cultural relationships. Most people, she says, are part of multiple social circles, such as family, work, and school. Each circle has its own ethos. And, in each circle, we play a different role. Thus, in our lives, we travel between different worlds. If we are members of a nondominant subculture, the different worlds we visit may be dramatically different. And we may not always be at ease in those.

In different "worlds," we see from different perspectives. But that experience does not intuitively teach us empathy. Often, our default is "arrogant perception," seeing others *only* through the lens of our own "worlds." To achieve "loving perception," we must, as Husserl says, "bracket off" our usual focus. We must travel, without arrogance, to other people's worlds. We must be open to learning how others see themselves in various worlds. Why would we choose to do that? Ideally out of friendship, a reciprocity of care and understanding, or an obligation to right wrongs.[29]

I think about the students who shared their WOW journals in my class. They opened their worlds, and invited class members to travel in. Some took risks, not knowing if classmates would see them through arrogant or loving perception. A Black student chose to share about seeing a friend get shot. She wanted support from classmates as she recounted something that shocked her. But, with this story, she took a chance. Would some white students respond with arrogant perception? And see in her journal reading a confirmation of racist stereotypes of violent, disorderly Black Americans? Or would all students respond with loving perception, and see her as she saw herself, a grieving friend? The class chose to perceive with love. A Vietnamese student read a journal entry about his family's dangerous refugee journeys. He, too, took a chance. What would classmates think about this normally quiet student telling such a personal story? Would it be safe to step outside the cultural persona of a hardworking, stoic new immigrant to say, "Yes it was incredibly hard and my parents are deeply scarred"? Would classmates try to distance themselves from the pain using arrogant perception? Or would they listen with loving perception, seeing this burdened, dutiful, and resilient son as he saw himself? This time, too, they chose loving perception.

Role of Ritual

For many students, maybe for most, WOW journal sharing time was the best part of class. It was, as Lawrence Hoffman says, a "ritual moment." Group rituals, Hoffman says, help structure our emotional lives. Without them, life might be a meaningless succession of moments. To make meaning together, a group enacts a ritual script, a set of steps leading to a high point. Over time, the steps become invested with emotional memories, and thus become more meaningful. Hoffman offers an example of friends meeting regularly for lunch. One by one, they trickle in and greet one another. When everyone has arrived, drinks are poured. The friends raise their glasses and make a toast, dedicating the moment to celebrate, reflect on, or pray for what's happening in each other's lives. This, Hoffman says, is the ritual moment.[30]

When our class would meet, we would begin by greeting each other; I would lecture on the assigned reading. Then I would pose a question. Students would discuss it, sometimes in a free-wheeling way. Next, I would summarize the discussion. A pretty standard class structure so far! Then, I would announce the day's WOW journal readers, and remind the class of the process. The class would become silent, as if everyone quieted their own thoughts in order to listen to each other. The journal readers would read. Three well-spoken students would empathize aloud. Then all would sit and compose their personal notes for the readers. This final moment of empathic writing was the ritual moment. Students clearly looked forward to this opportunity to speak to one another from the heart—particularly in a time of social uncertainty and stress.

Becoming Relatives

Indigenous and Native American teachers say that ritual has a tremendous power to bring people together into relationships. As Ray Aldred writes, a treaty process is a ceremony that brings people into proper relatedness.[31] The spiritual teacher Black Elk describes treaty-making as one of seven sacred rites gifted to humanity by *Wakan-Tanka,* the Great Spirit. In a teaching recorded by Joseph Epes Brown, Black Elk tells the story of the Sioux and Ree people becoming one family through the wisdom of the Sioux sage, Matohoshila.[32] One day, Matohoshila, moved by a profound vision, found some corn and brought it back to his people. He learned that the patch of corn belonged to the Ree people, when they sent messengers asking for the corn's return. Matohoshila then understood that his vision pointed beyond corn to the making of new relatives. He proposed a ceremony, led by representatives of the two people. The ceremony began with two days of ritual in which Sioux and Ree leaders set up sacred spaces, exchanged gifts of sacred objects, and declared the intent of the gathering. On the third day, everyone gathered for a dramatic play, in which Ree warriors "captured" members of the Sioux nation. Chosen Ree helpers then dressed and painted the "captives" to look like fellow Ree, and introduced them to the crowd. Finally, everyone feasted together as one family.

Black Elk's story of this rite holds much wisdom for understanding my class's journey together. Without knowing it, we relied on principles taught by Matohoshila. Perhaps they came down to us, as many good American customs did, through Native American influences.[33] For that I am grateful. Our class did, in a sense, become relatives. In a world where these young adults were encouraged to misunderstand each other, they chose a different route. They did not literally wear one another's clothes, but they did metaphorically walk in one another's shoes. They did not literally enter each other's tents, but they did travel in thought and feeling to one another's worlds. During WOW journal sharing time, they were their own unique community. But we did not ever leap into this new relation. At each class meeting, we set up our spiritual space carefully. We followed a kind of protocol, defined by Aldred as "how we approach one another and hold and care for one another in a respectful manner."[34] Before each sharing, students waited patiently as I explained the instructions yet again. We all understood that the instructions were an important part of the ritual. They reminded us what our roles were, and helped us walk together towards the ritual moment of communication. This resonance with Indigenous thought places the *Zohar*'s homily in a larger context. Although the *Zohar* itself speaks in a particularly Jewish idiom, the *hevraya* it describes expresses a cross-cultural hope. This shared hope is just not an imaginative ideal; in fact, there are road maps to working towards it.

NOTES

1. Eitan Fishbane highlights this passage in his essay "God in the Face of the Other: Mystical Friendship in the Zohar," in *Friendship in Jewish History, Religion, and Culture,* ed. Lawrence Fine (University Park, PA: Pennsylvania State University Press, 2021), 38–54. Fishbane focuses his exploration on a community of mystics sharing esoteric experience. I move in a different direction with my own interpretation of the passage.

2. Daniel C. Matt, *Zohar: The Pritzker Edition,* vol. 1. (Stanford: Stanford University Press, 2004), xvii. Rabbi Shimon is a key teacher cited in early rabbinic literature. Rabbi Moses de Leon, a key author of the *Zohar,* attributed his own mystical homilies to Rabbi Shimon to give them greater credibility. See Gershom Scholem, *Major Trends in Jewish Mysticism* (New York: Schocken Books, 1974), 156–204.

3. Ariel Evan Mayse, "Gardens of the Spirit: Land, Text, and Ecological Hermeneutics in Jewish Mystical Sources," *Dibbur Literary Journal* 11 (Spring 2022), 62.

4. Laura Duhan-Kaplan, "Tradition and Innovation: Metaphor in Philosophy and Philosophy of Religion," *Philosophic Exchange* (2002–2003): 49–59.

5. *Tikkunei Zohar* 70:122b, 57:91b at *Zohar,* Sefaria, https://www.sefaria.org/ Zohar. See also Isaiah Tishby, *The Wisdom of the Zohar* (London: Littman Library of Civilization, 1991), 368–370.

6. For contemporary challenges to the *Zohar*'s gender binary, see for example, Arthur Green, *Ehyeh: A Kabbalah for Tomorrow* (Woodstock, VT: Jewish Lights, 2003), 55–58; Chava Weissler, "Meanings of Shekhinah in the 'Jewish Renewal' Movement," *Nashim: A Journal of Jewish Women's Studies & Gender Issues* 10 (2006), 53–83.

7. *Zohar* 3:59b. Eitan Fishbane does not cite the translator; I assume this is his translation.

8. *Zohar* 3:152a. Eitan Fishbane does not himself use this framework. For more about it, see Michael Fishbane, "Ethics and Sacred Attunement," *The Journal of Religion* 93:4 (October 2013), 421–33.

9. Jill Hammer, "Midrash," in *The JPS Guide to the Jewish Bible* (Philadelphia: Jewish Publication Society, 2008), Kindle edition, loc. 3269–3283.

10. New Jewish Publication Society (NJPS) translation, adapted.

11. Exodus does not describe the cherubim's form, but cross-cultural research into Ancient Near Eastern religious iconography suggests this description. See, for example, Carl S. Ehrlich, "Ezekiel's Vision of God and the Chariot," TheTorah.com, https://www.thetorah.com/article/ezekiels-vision-of-god-and-the-chariot.

12. Translation mine.

13. See, for example, Exod 28:35; 28:43; Lev 16:13.

14. Babylonian Talmud, Yoma 54a. Steinsaltz translation. Cited in Zev Farber, "The Cherubim: Their Role on the Ark in the Holy of Holies," TheTorah.com, https://www.thetorah.com/article/the-cherubim-their-role-on-the-ark-in-the-holy-of-holies.

15. Mishnah Yadayim 3:5, trans. Joshua Kulp, Sefaria, https://www.sefaria.org/ Mishnah_Yadayim. Some interpret Rabbi Akiva's statement to mean he views the Song as an allegory of God's love for Israel. See, for example, Rachel Adler, *Engendering Judaism: An Inclusive Theology and Ethics* (Boston: Beacon Press, 1998), 134.

16. Jer 2:2.

17. NJPS.

18. Bereishit [Genesis] Rabbah, 8:1. See also Rashi on Gen 1:27.

19. Babylonian Talmud, Ketubot 8a. Steinsaltz translation. Please note, this description of marriage expresses an archetypal and spiritual ideal, and does not imply that every marriage is perfect. In practice, rabbinic law recognizes divorce.

20. Marcia Prager, *The Path of Blessing* (Woodstock, Vermont: Jewish Lights Publishing, 2003) Kindle edition, loc. 248–282.

21. Plato, *Theaetetus* in *Selected Dialogues of Plato: The Benjamin Jowett Translation.* (New York: Modern Library, 2001), 155c–d.

22. Laura Duhan-Kaplan, Course syllabus, "PHIL 2101–009, Introduction to Philosophy," University of North Carolina at Charlotte, fall term 2001.

23. Report on the structure and results of the group process adapted from Laura Duhan-Kaplan, "Autobiographical Writing in the Philosophy Classroom," *Teaching Philosophy* 29:1 (March 2006).

24. UNC Charlotte Demographics & Diversity Report, College Factual, 2021, https://www.collegefactual.com/colleges/university-of-north-carolina-at-charlotte/student-life/diversity/. Student body composition was similar in 2001.

25. Edmund Husserl, *The Crisis of the European Sciences* (Evanston IL: Northwestern University Press, 1970), 108–109.

26. Christian Beyer, "Edmund Husserl," *The Stanford Encyclopedia of Philosophy.* Winter 2020 Edition, ed. Edward N. Zalta, https://plato.stanford.edu/archives/win2020/entries/husserl/.

27. Edmund Husserl, *Ideas Pertaining to a Pure Phenomenology and a Phenomenological Philosophy* (Dordrecht: Kluwer), 1990; Laura Duhan-Kaplan, "Edmund Husserl" in *The Great Thinkers A to Z*, ed. Julian Baggini (London: Continuum Press, 2003), 122–124.

28. Maria Lugones, "Playfulness, 'World'-Traveling, and Loving Perception," *Hypatia* 2:2 (1987): 3–19. For an application of the experience of "world"-traveling to inter-religious learning, see Francis X. Clooney, *Comparative Theology: Deep Learning Across Religious Borders* (Malden, MA: Wiley Blackwell, 2010).

29. Maria C. Lugones and Elizabeth V. Spelman, "Have We Got a Theory for You! Feminist Theory, Cultural Imperialism and the Demand for 'The Woman's Voice,'" *Women's Studies International Forum* 6:6 (1983), 573–581.

30. Lawrence A. Hoffman, *The Art of Public Prayer: Not For Clergy Only,* 2nd ed. (Woodstock, VT: Skylight Paths, 1999), Kindle edition, loc. 198–573.

31. Raymond C. Aldred, "Invitation to Reconciliation" in Raymond C. Aldred and Laura Duhan-Kaplan (eds.), *Spirit of Reconciliation* (Toronto, ON: Canadian Race Relations Foundation), 2020, 9–10.

32. Joseph Epes Brown. "Hunkapi: The Making of Relatives," in *The Sacred Pipe: Black Elk's Account of the Rites of the Oglala Sioux* (Norman, OK: University of Oklahoma Press, 2012), 101–115.

33. Paula Gunn Allen, *The Sacred Hoop: Recovering the Feminine in American Indian Traditions* (Boston: Beacon Press, 1992), 215–221.

34. Raymond C. Aldred, "Embracing Indigenous Values for Theological Education" in *Before Theological Study: A Thoughtful, Engaged, and Generous Approach,* eds. Richard Topping, Harry O. Maier, and Ashley Moyse (Eugene, OR: Wipf & Stock, 2021), 162–169.

BIBLIOGRAPHY

Adler, Rachel. *Engendering Judaism: An Inclusive Theology and Ethics*. Boston: Beacon Press, 1998.

Aldred, Raymond C. "Embracing Indigenous Values for Theological Education" in *Before Theological Study: A Thoughtful, Engaged, and Generous Approach,* edited by Richard Topping, Harry O. Maier, and Ashley Moyse. Eugene, OR: Wipf & Stock, 2021, 162–169.

Aldred, Raymond C., "Invitation to Reconciliation." In Raymond C. Aldred and Laura Duhan-Kaplan, eds. *Spirit of Reconciliation.* Toronto, ON: Canadian Race Relations Foundation, 2020, 9–11.

Allen, Paula Gunn. *The Sacred Hoop: Recovering the Feminine in American Indian Traditions.* Boston: Beacon Press, 1992.

Babylonian Talmud, William Davidson edition, with translation by Adin Steinsaltz. Sefaria, https://www.sefaria.org/texts/Talmud.

Bereishit [Genesis] Rabbah, Sefaria. https://www.sefaria.org/Bereishit_Rabbah.

Beyer, Christian, "Edmund Husserl," *The Stanford Encyclopedia of Philosophy.* Winter 2020 Edition, Edward N. Zalta, ed. https://plato.stanford.edu/archives/win2020/entries/husserl/.

Brown, Joseph Epes. "Hunkapi: The Making of Relatives" in *The Sacred Pipe: Black Elk's Account of the Rites of the Oglala Sioux.* Norman, OK: University of Oklahoma Press, 2012, 101–115.

Clooney, Francis X. *Comparative Theology: Deep Learning Across Religious Borders.* Malden, MA: Wiley Blackwell, 2010.

Duhan-Kaplan, Laura, Course syllabus, "PHIL 2101-009, Introduction to Philosophy." University of North Carolina at Charlotte, fall term 2001.

Duhan-Kaplan, Laura, "Autobiographical Writing in the Philosophy Classroom." *Teaching Philosophy* 29:1 (March 2006).

Duhan-Kaplan, Laura. "Tradition and Innovation: Metaphor in Philosophy and Philosophy of Religion." *Philosophic Exchange* (2002–2003): 49–59.

Duhan Kaplan, Laura. "Edmund Husserl." *The Great Thinkers A to Z*, edited by Julian Baggini. London: Continuum Press, 2003, 122–124.

Ehrlich, Carl S. "Ezekiel's Vision of God and the Chariot," TheTorah.com, https://www.thetorah.com/article/ezekiels-vision-of-god-and-the-chariot.

Farber, Zev. "The Cherubim: Their Role on the Ark in the Holy of Holies," TheTorah.com, https://www.thetorah.com/article/the-cherubim-their-role-on-the-ark-in-the-holy-of-holies.

Fishbane, Eitan P. "God in the Face of the Other: Mystical Friendship in the Zohar," in *Friendship in Jewish History, Religion, and Culture,* edited by Lawrence Fine. University Park, PA: Pennsylvania State University Press, 2021, 38–54.

Fishbane, Michael. "Ethics and Sacred Attunement," *The Journal of Religion* 93:4 (October 2013), 421–33.

Green, Arthur. *Ehyeh: A Kabbalah for Tomorrow.* Woodstock, VT: Jewish Lights, 2003.

Hammer, Jill. "Midrash," in *The JPS Guide to the Jewish Bible.* Philadelphia: Jewish Publication Society, 2008. Kindle edition, loc. 3112–3428.

Hoffman, Lawrence A. *The Art of Public Prayer: Not For Clergy Only,* 2nd ed. Woodstock, VT: Skylight Paths, 1999. Kindle edition.

Husserl, Edmund. *The Crisis of the European Sciences.* Evanston: Northwestern University Press, 1970.

Husserl, Edmund. *Ideas Pertaining to a Pure Phenomenology and a Phenomenological Philosophy.* Dordrecht: Kluwer, 1990.

Lugones, Maria. "Playfulness, 'World'-Traveling, and Loving Perception," *Hypatia* 2:2 (1987): 3–19.

Lugones, Maria C. and Elizabeth V. Spelman, "Have We Got a Theory for You! Feminist Theory, Cultural Imperialism and the Demand for 'The Woman's Voice.'" *Women's Studies International Forum* 6:6 (1983), 573–581.

Matt, Daniel C., trans. *Zohar: The Pritzker Edition,* vol. 1. Stanford: Stanford University Press, 2004, xvii.

Mayse, Ariel Evan. "Gardens of the Spirit: Land, Text, and Ecological Hermeneutics in Jewish Mystical Sources." *Dibbur Literary Journal* 11 (Spring 2022), 59–88.

Kulp, Joshua. "Mishnah Yadayim." In *Mishnah Yomit.* Sefaria, https://www.sefaria.org/Mishnah_Yadayim.1?ven=Mishnah_Yomit_by_Dr._Joshua_Kulp&lang=bi.

Plato. *Selected Dialogues of Plato: The Benjamin Jowett Translation.* New York: Modern Library, 2001.

Prager, Marcia. *The Path of Blessing.* Woodstock, VT: Jewish Lights Publishing, 2003. Kindle edition.

Rashi on Genesis. Sefaria. https://www.sefaria.org/Rashi_on_Genesis?tab=contentshttps://www.sefaria.org/Rashi_on_Genesis?tab=contents.

Scholem, Gershom. *Major Trends in Jewish Mysticism.* New York: Schocken Books, 1974.

Tishby, Isaiah. *The Wisdom of the Zohar.* London: Littman Library of Civilization, 1991.

UNC Charlotte Demographics & Diversity Report, College Factual, 2021. https://www.collegefactual.com/colleges/university-of-north-carolina-at-charlotte/student-life/diversity/.

Weissler, Chava. "Meanings of Shekhinah in the 'Jewish Renewal' Movement." *Nashim: A Journal of Jewish Women's Studies & Gender Issues* 10 (2006): 53–83.

Zohar. Sefaria. https://www.sefaria.org/Zohar.

Chapter 6

God, Prophecy, and Friendship in Islam

A Theological Perspective

Hussam S. Timani

Who is included in *walaya,* the friendship of God? This chapter attempts to establish a theology of friendship with God from the sources of Islamic traditions. It discusses friendship with God in different Islamic traditions, bringing together three quite different concepts of friendship with the divine within Islam. First, friendship as a spiritual energy that pre-existed the creation of the world. This type of friendship is prevalent in Shiʻi traditions and is exclusive to the family of Muhammad and the Shiʻi imams. Second, friendship as a spiritually elevated relationship with God is found in mystical Islam and can be discovered only by those who are able to recognize it. These first two approaches are based on the concept of *walaya* in the Shiʻi and Sufi traditions. For the Shiʻas and Sufis, the Imams and the Saints serve as the friends of Gods for God's friendship extends to them in a hierarchical order but does not proceed beyond them. However, friendship with God can also be experienced in the first pillar of Islam, the *shahada* (testimony). The divine friendship that God has established with Muhammad through the prophecy is not exclusive to Muhammad but extends to the Prophet's heirs and successors and eventually to all the believers.

This chapter advocates for a third understanding of the friendship of God, that is, friendship as performing ethical actions in the Muslim community. This latter type of friendship is experienced through the *shahada.* It is extended to all Muslims by way of Muhammad and to all religions by way of Muslims. All believers are able to experience God's friendship by their linkage to Muhammad through their confession of the *shahada.* God's divine friendship extends from the abodes of Shi'ism and Sufism to all adherents of the religion; God's friendship with all is the foundation of Islamic faith. This essay discusses friendship from multiple Islamic perspectives and then demonstrates how various approaches to friendship culminate in the prophecy of Muhammad through the *shahada* (testifying that there is no god but God and that Muhammad is the Messenger and Servant of God).

The *walaya* is a doctrine that is mainly prevalent in both Shi'i and Sufi traditions. The Shi'as believe that the Imams[1] are the friends of God and the Sufis contend that Sufi saints have earned that title, too. The Shi'i approach understands friendship as a spiritual energy that pre-existed the creation of the world. This friendship is available exclusively to the family of Muhammad and the Shi'i imams. The mystical Sufi approach sees friendship as a spiritually elevated relationship with God. This friendship can be discovered only by those who are able to recognize it. Traditional and Salafi[2] Muslims, however, have shunned both views as blasphemous and insisted that God has no relationship with this world except through prophetic experiences, which ended with the prophecy of Muhammad. In this chapter, I propose a third perspective: friendship as performing ethical actions in the Muslim community that is experienced through the *shahada*.

I argue that the doctrine of the friendship of God can be realized not only in Shi'ism and Sufism, but also in all of the Islamic faith. God's friendship *is* at the heart of Islam, for our friendship with God is experienced in the *shahada*, the first pillar of Islam. To this end, I explore the definition of *walaya* (the friendship of God) in Shi'i and Sufi sources and then argue that while the *walaya* is regarded as exclusively Shi'i and Sufi, it is at the heart of the Islamic faith through the *shahada*. Furthermore, this chapter demonstrates that while Shi'ism and Sufism limit God's friendship to imams and saints, respectively, the *shahada* breaks those limitations and extends God's loving relationship to all, Muslims and non-Muslims alike.

The goal of this essay is to demonstrate that God's friendship is available to creation first in a vertical order from God to Muhammad and then in a horizontal order from Muhammad to the rest of humanity, for the *shahada* makes God's friendship available to all people by way of Muhammad. I begin by exploring the concept of *walaya* in Shi'i and Sufi sources and then move to discuss the *shahada* as a path to God's friendship with the believers. The objective for discussing the concept of friendship in Shi'ism and Sufism is (1) to show the centrality of friendship in the Islamic tradition, (2) to demonstrate the ontological nature of the concept of friendship in Islam, and (3) to offer insights on how friendship is a shared experience across Islamic traditions. I conclude by arguing that God's loving relationship can also be experienced by every Muslim in the *shahada*, making the first pillar in Islam a necessary link between God's friendship and the people.

More than a simple act of faith, the Islamic doctrine of the *shahada* serves as a model for friendship and a loving relationship. Loving friendship between God and creation, as expressed in the *shahada*, can be used to shape relations between the Muslims and the Other. The loving friendship between God and Muhammad in the *Shahada* can help adherents of Islam and other religions come together in friendship and realize that their basic Islamic belief is an act of faith that is ontologically based on God's loving relationship with all of us. Mutuality and friendship are at the heart of the *shahada,* as friendship "guides and initiates mankind into the mystical or inner truth of religion."[3]

WALAYA: THE FRIENDSHIP OF GOD

Walaya is an important concept in both Shi'ism and Sufism that emerged as an alternative to prophecy.[4] It was developed in Shi'i and Sufi traditions in the eighth and ninth centuries, respectively,[5] as a substitute for prophecy. Friends of God emerged as substitutes (*abdal* or *budala'*) to the prophets, being mediators between God and humanity. According to the Qur'an, prophecies ended with Islam thus making Muhammad "the seal of the prophets" (Q. 33:40),[6] the last prophet sent by God to humankind. This Qur'anic view challenges the notion that humans are always in need for "charismatic religious figures who can function as mediators between [humanity] and God."[7] The concept of *walaya*, therefore, was a solution to this problem as it continued the role of prophecy (the mediation between God and humanity) through "friends of God" who are "much like the prophets themselves" but "not considered to be prophets in the true sense of the word."[8] The *walaya*, according to both Shi'ism and Sufism, existed prior to the creation of the world.

The abstract term *walaya* (friendship) occurs twice in the Qur'an (Q. 8:72 and Q. 18:44) and the words *wali* (sing. friend) and *awliya'* (pl. friends) are mentioned eighty-six times in the text. While such friends are identified as the prophets and the believers, as well as the enemies of the prophets and the unbelievers who are friends amongst themselves, a number of verses designate God as friend (*wali*) (Q. 2:107, 2:257, 3:68, 5:55, 7:196, 12:101, and 45:19).

The Friendship of God in Shi'ism

Shi'i sources tell us that the friends of God were created from a light before the creation of the material world. According to these sources, Muhammad and the friends of God were conceived in their "mystical dimension" as being a light that God created before the creation of the world and that light became "the cause and instrument of all the rest of creation."[9] The sources also present Muhammad as a light formed by God and "then passed to Adam, via his chosen descendants and the prophets known from sacred human history, to Muhammad."[10] The following Shi'i tradition is attributed to the first Imam, 'Ali:

> God is one; He was alone in His singleness and so He spoke one word and it became a light and He created from light Muhammad and He created me and my descendants . . . then He spoke another word and it became a Spirit and he caused it to settle upon that light and He caused it to settle on our bodies. And so we are the Spirit of God and His word.[11]

Consequently, the friends of Gods are distinct from ordinary human beings and have a special relationship with the Divine.

In Shi'i traditions, the *shahada* "implicitly contains a triple profession of faith: the unicity of God, Prophet Muhammad's mission, the *walaya* of 'Ali and the imams in his lineage."[12] This Shi'i inclusion of 'Ali makes the latter the second friend of God after Muhammad, and from 'Ali, the friendship with God extends only to 'Ali's family and descendants, the Imams. The position of 'Ali after Muhammad in the Shi'i version of the *shahada* corresponds to the creation account in Shi'i traditions where Muhammad was the first to be created from light followed by 'Ali's creation. The sources also tell us that without 'Ali and the imams, "there would be no religion at all."[13] God does not accept any of the religious duties without the *walaya* of 'Ali and the imams.[14] It is important to note here that since there is no *walaya* without the imam, this *walaya* was cut off and ceased from rolling down the hierarchy with the mysterious disappearance of the twelfth imam in the tenth century, therefore denying the believers and the rest of the humanity the *walaya*. Moreover, according to Shi'i *hadiths*, only a small group of creation pledged allegiance and received God's *walaya*.[15] This special group consists of the "Closest (*al-muqarrabun*) among angels, the Messengers (*al-mursalun*) among prophets, and the tested ones (*al-mumtahanun*) among believers."[16] Furthermore, in Shi'ism, the *walaya* denotes devotion to 'Ali and the imams from the house of Muhammad and also applies the position of 'Ali "as the single, explicitly designated heir and successor to Muhammad in whom all responsibility for the guidance of the Muslims was subsequently vested."[17] This account above provides more examples that the *walaya* is strictly hierarchical (vertical) and ontologically not available to anyone beyond the "elite of creation."[18] This Shi'i concept of a hierarchical *walaya* is also shared by the Sufis who claim that, "all Muslims can potentially belong to the *awliya'* hierarchy."[19]

The Friendship of God in Sufism

In the Sufi tradition, the primordial being of the Prophet Muhammad is described as a light or the light of Muhammad (*nur muhammad*). The concept of *nur muhammad* is found in the writings of Sufi masters such as al-Hakim al-Tirmidhi (d. 869), Sahl al-Tustari (d. 896), Mansur al-Hallaj (d. 922), and Muhyiddin ibn 'Arabi (d. 1240).[20] According to Ibn 'Arabi, the greatest Sufi master, or *al-shayhk al-akbar*, the motif of *nur mahammad* is reflected in the concept of *al-haqiqa al-muhamadiyya* ("the true essence of Muhammad"), which "was, in effect, the first being to emerge out of the Divine light" and "from *al-haqiqa al-muhammadiyya* and by means of it, all other beings were created."[21] For Ibn 'Arabi, the imitation of Muhammad (following the Prophet's examples) is an act of "love and intimacy, another word for *walaya*."[22]

Although Islamic mysticism recognizes that all believers are "participants in a general *walaya*,"[23] Ibn 'Arabi created a special category of friendship with God and restricted it to a group of people who are recognized as: a knower (*'arif*); one embarked upon spiritual realization (*muhaqqiq*); one blamed or blameworthy (*malami*); an heir (*warith*); a mystic (*sufi*); a servant/slave (*'abd*); and a man (*rajul*).[24] Moreover, Ibn 'Arabi designates certain people who have received the highest degree of sainthood/friendship with God (*walaya*). "They are the hidden ones, the pure ones, the ones in this world who are sure and sound, concealed among men . . . they are the solitary ones (*al-afrad*)."[25]

In *al-Futuhat al-Makkiyya*, Ibn 'Arabi refers to the "Perfect Man" or "Complete Man" who is both a representation of the divine and the origin of all human spirits[26] and who is also identified with the spirit of Muhammad, "or the eternal Muhammadan Reality, which became incarnated in the persons of the prophets" before the coming of Muhammad.[27] Only the Complete Man, according to Ibn 'Arabi, reflects God's image and through him God sees and knows Himself and the people see the clearest manifestation of God. The Sufi thinker 'Abd al-Karim al-Jili (d. 1408) writes, "The Perfect Man is the *Qutb* (axis) on which the spheres of existence revolve from first to last . . . His own original name is Mohammed."[28] For this reason, the Complete Man, or the spirit of Muhammad, forms the highest boundary or point of mediation (*al-barzakh al-a'la*) between God and this world.[29] Through the Complete Man (Muhammad) who is the Supreme Barzakh and the perfect link between God and humanity, the people are able to form a relationship with God that they are never able to do on their own. The notion that a relationship with God is possible through Muhammad only is expressed by Ibn 'Arabi in his *al-Futuhat*.[30] According to Ibn 'Arabi, the rank of Muhammad in the knowledge of God is above all ranks. He is the mirror where God discloses Himself to the believers in that mirror. The manifestation of God in "the mirror of Muhammad is the most perfect, most balanced, and most beautiful manifestation."[31] For Ibn 'Arabi, Muhammad alone has the constitution to form a link between God and the people, for without Muhammad, "human beings are veiled by their persons"[32] from making a loving relationship with the Creator. Muhammad's role, in Ibn 'Arabi's point of view, as mediator for the Muslims and the only "accessor to the presence of God are logical corollaries of his unique cosmic status as the Supreme Barzakh."[33]

Al-Jili writes that Muhammad is the *barzakh* linking God and creation and that Muhammad's special creation from the Divine and Adam's creation in the likeness of Muhammad allow every human being to partake of God's friendship.[34] Muhammad's role as the only intercessor for the Muslims is supported by the Qur'an in verse 21:107: "We sent [Muhammad] only as a mercy for the peoples." God's mercy on all things is mediated through Muhammad, and it is through the Muhammadan Reality alone that human beings are able not only to receive God's love but also to form a loving relationship with Him. This loving relationship between God and human beings is the highest state of perfection, according to al-Jili, and "were it not for Muhammad, [God] would not have created the spheres"[35] to form this friendship. Therefore, Muhammad was the originally intended object to receive God's friendship and love and his community is loved only because its members follow him, as the Qur'an states: "If you love God, follow [Muhammad]; God will love you" (Q. 3:31).

Al-Jili nicely demonstrates how Muhammad serves as a link between God and other humans. He writes: "One of the characteristics of the Prophet is that whenever any saint sees him in one of the divine manifestations wearing one of the robes of perfection, he [the Prophet] grants that robe to the one who has this vision, and it then belongs to him." The prophetic robe then passes from Muhammad to other saints and this goes on indefinitely.[36] This example supports the thesis of this essay that the *shahada* is an act of friendship that brings the people closer to God, for the closer a person is to the Prophet, the more perfect and complete is this relationship with God. Al-Jili writes, "The more the saint increases his knowledge of the Prophet, the more perfect he is than others, and the more established in the divine presence, and the more profoundly he enters into the knowledge of God."[37]

The Shi'i and Sufi *walaya* hierarchy is obvious again in the *shahada,* for Muhammad is part of the *shahada* after God (no god but God and Muhammad is His Messenger and Servant) making him the first friend of God. This hierarchy is apparent in Islam where the dominant belief emphasizes the righteousness and purity of Muhammad's family, his companions or *al-salaf al-salih* (the pious ancestors), the later Muslims—those closest to Muhammad's time—as the perfect interpreters of the *shari'a* (Islamic law), and the believers at large. Therefore, Muhammad's presence in the *shahada*, as the discussion below demonstrates, is instrumental for making God's friendship a universal reality starting with Muhammad, at the top of the hierarchy, to the stars in the celestial sphere and then down to all creatures in the terrestrial world.

The Friendship of God in the *Shahada*

In the Islamic tradition, friendship is a major theme. The Qur'an and *Hadith* (the sayings of Muhammad) set some guidelines on the selection of right friends, both Muslim and non-Muslim. Friendship is important not only in the relationship between the people but also between select individuals and God. For instance, in the Qur'an 4:125, God took Abraham for a friend (*khalil*). Tenth-century polymath Aḥmad Abū 'Alī ibn Muḥammad Miskawayh (d. 1030) writes:

> [God] is loved only by the person of virtuous well-being (*sa'īd*) and goodness who knows true virtuous well-being and the real good (*al-sa'ādah wa-l-khayr*). And he who shows such love of God . . . will be loved by God and will become worthy of His friendship—that friendship to some men by the Law wherein Abraham is called "the friend (*khalil*) of God" and Muhammad "the Beloved (*ḥabīb*) of God."[38]

According to Islamic studies scholar Roy Parviz Mottahedeh, "One would expect that in a strongly monotheistic system . . . God would be too remote to be a friend. Yet both the Bible and the Qur'ān call Abraham the friend of God. Such friendship between God and man is a persistent theme in the Islamic tradition."[39] In fact, says Mottahedeh, "it is in man's relation with God that friendship reaches its apotheosis."[40]

Faith and friendship are strongly linked together, both in this world and the next. For example, the Prophet Muhammad is reported to have said, "You shall not enter Paradise until you believe; and you shall not believe until you love one another."[41] Friendship, then, is key to the fulfillment of *iman* (faith). Loving friendship, according to the above *hadith*, is the key to the gates of Paradise as it enhances the chances of intercession and, consequently, salvation. The medieval theologian Nasir al-Din al-Tusi (d. 1274) tells us that, "The virtue of love and friendship is the greatest of virtues."[42] For al-Tusi, friendship is the love and hunger for perfection and for the Divine.

To enter Heaven, a righteous Muslim must act according to faith rather than simply believing internally. Faith in Islam is about action, and doing things together as friends is more meaningful, and it would result in a stronger faith. Toshihiko Izutsu tells us that faith (*iman*) must be judged by actions rather than internal beliefs.[43] Since the first pillar in Islam, the *shahada*, represents a relationship between God and other persons, the *shahada* then is an act of faith rather than an internal belief. This act of faith becomes an act of friendship. Moreover, the *shahada*, the most important pillar in Islam, is the acknowledgment of the loving relationship between God and other persons, and true faith is to act on this relationship. In both Sunni and Shi'i traditions, God is a being that represents a loving relationship. Thus, as the first pillar of Islam is an act of faith—an act of friendship—God expects us to act in this faith—this friendship—accordingly.

The *shahada* serves as the clearest and most definite elaboration of both monotheism (to testify there is no god but God) and Muhammad's prophecy and messengership (Muhammad is the Messenger of God). The *shahada* expresses the Islamic belief in "one God . . . this belief is the foundation stone of Islam. It governs the religious faith, designs the social patterns and gives life to the oral codes."[44] Believing in the *shahada* in the heart and speaking it on the tongue is the acknowledgment and affirmation of a special relationship between God and Muhammad. The testimony that there is no god but God (*la ilaha illa lah*) is enough to make a person a monotheist, but the acknowledgment that Muhammad is the Messenger of God (*Muhammad rasul Allah*) is the affirmation and belief that Muhammad and God are linked together in a special relationship. To acknowledge this relationship is to make the believer a Muslim (i.e., a member in the Muslim community). The names of God and Muhammad are joined together and are the pinnacle of the Muslim creed. According to Lamin Sanneh, the name of God and Muhammad's name "stand at the pinnacle of devotion and obligation. It is impossible to respond to the call of God without hearing in that the strains of his human instrument. It is not for nothing that the early Muslims were first identified as the *ummatu Muhammadiyah*, 'the Muhammadan community.'"[45]

God's relationship with Muhammad began long before Muhammad became a prophet, and Muhammad's capacity to be a great friend emerged long before the sending down of the Qur'an. According to Sam Agnoli, "Muhammad needed to be a friend *first*, and a prophet second . . . and this is the basis for God's choosing of Muhammad as the final prophet of Islam."[46] Muhammad needed to be a great friend as a prerequisite to becoming a prophet. God and Muhammad had to come together in friendship *first* so the prophet would be able to serve his Creator.

The *shahada*'s statement, "Muhammad is the Messenger of God," reveals a relationship between God and Muhammad that transcends the conventional, earthly God-prophet encounter. Muhammad's special relationship with God can be illustrated in the Prophet's direct encounter with God during Muhammad's night journey to heaven (*al-isra' wa al-mi'raj*). The night journey, according to the Qur'an, takes Muhammad from Mecca to Jerusalem and from Jerusalem to a direct encounter with God (Q. 17:1; 53:1–10). The Qur'an tells us that Muhammad drew near God two bows' length (*qab qawsayn*), or even nearer (*aw adna*) (Q. 53:9). This Qur'anic narrative demonstrates the levels of intimacy between Muhammad and God. Now, while Muhammad in the presence of God, the Prophet sees not with his eyes but rather with his heart (*fu'ad*): "The heart did not lie in what it saw" (Q. 53:13–18). According to the *hadith* tradition, even the angel Gabriel had to withdraw from Muhammad, covering his eyes with his hands, fearing that his sight would be destroyed by the intensity of divine love.[47] Angel Gabriel said that "he himself could not go a finger's length further, but that Muhammad must cross the river and travel on."[48] Muhammad alone enters the divine presence and ascends to a level of intimacy with God that angels were so reluctant to do.

Through friendship, Muhammad made a covenant with God. He became God's mediator and His beloved. Muhammad is referred to as the "beloved of God."[49] God's very name for Muhammad is *al-Habeeb*, or "the beloved."[50] When pressured to stop preaching the word of God, Muhammad replied that he will be ashamed in front of God if he stops relaying His words. Muhammad's relationship with God was so profound that he was willing to sacrifice his life relaying His message. Confessing the *shahada* by every Muslim, therefore, is the constant renewal of this loving relationship with God that Muhammad accepted and passed on to the Muslims; it is a constant reminder of God's friendship with Muhammad. Therefore, the *shahada* is the covenant with God that reminds people of their natural duties: justice and righteousness. These duties are "fulfillable through friendship,"[51] as Muhammad demonstrated in his prophetic experience.

CONCLUSION

This chapter has argued that the *walaya* (God's friendship with the world) is at the heart of the Islamic beliefs. This divine friendship can be found not only among certain believers or groups as Shi'ism and Sufism claim, but it is also given to the people through the *shahada*. This essay has argued for a wider concept of friendship within the Islamic traditions that transcends the mystical realm. It has also demonstrated that through the *shahada*, our friendship with God is real and possible. The *shahada* is more than a simple act of faith; it defines our relationship with the Divine. Through it, God has established a loving relationship with Muhammad, the believers, and all of humanity.

NOTES

1. In Shi'i theology, there are twelve Imams whose line of blood is traced to the family of the Prophet Muhammad. The first Imam was Muhammad's son-in-law and cousin 'Ali b. Abi Talib (d. 661), followed by his two sons, Hasan (d. 669) and Husayn (d. 680). The last and twelfth Imam was al-Mahdi al-Muntazar, who mysteriously disappeared in the tenth century. The line of the Imamate was therefore cut off or ended with his disappearance. These Imams, according to the Shi'i tradition, are the sole successors of the Prophet Muhammad. The Shi'as consider the Imams infallible and the closest to God, hence, the friends of God (*awliya' Allah*). For more on the Imamate, see Moojan Momen, *An Introduction to Shi'i Islam: The History and Doctrines of Twelver Shi'ism* (New Haven: Yale University Press, 1985).

2. Salafism is a modern traditionalist movement that adheres to the literal interpretation of the Qur'an. Salafis believe that true Islam was the one practiced by the Prophet Muhammad and the early Muslim community; hence, all Muslims should literally imitate the pious ancestors (*al-salaf al-Salih*).

3. Momen, *An Introduction to Shi'i Islam*, 157.

4. Michael Ebstein, *Mysticism and Philosophy in al-Andalus* (Leiden: Brill, 2013), 123.

5. Ebstein, *Mysticism and Philosophy*, 124.

6. Jane McAuliffe, ed., *The Qur'an* (New York: W. W. Norton, 2017) is used for Qur'anic translation.

7. Ebstein, *Mysticism and Philosophy*, 123.

8. Ebstein, *Mysticism and Philosophy*, 123.

9. Momen, *An Introduction to Shi'i Islam*, 148.

10. Momen, *An Introduction to Shi'i Islam*, 143–144.

11. Momen, *An Introduction*, 148.

12. Mohammad Ali Amir-Moezzi, *The Spirituality of Shi'i Islam: Beliefs and Practices* (London and New York: I.B. Tauris, 2011), 243.

13. Amir-Moezzi, *The Spirituality of Shi'i Islam*, 243.

14. Amir-Moezzi, *The Spirituality of Shi'i Islam*, 243.

15. Amir-Moezzi, *The Spirituality of Shi'i Islam*, 257.

16. Amir-Moezzi, *The Spirituality of Shi'i Islam*, 257–258.

17. Wahyuddin Halim, "The Complex Relationship Between Sufism and Shi'ism as Reflected in the Concept of *Walayah*," *Kanz Philosophia* 5, 1 (June 2015): 81.

18. Amir-Moezzi, *The Spirituality*, 257.

19. Ebstein, *Mysticism and Philosophy*, 128.

20. Ebstein, *Mysticism and Philosophy*, 145.

21. Ebstein, *Mysticism and Philosophy*, 144–145.

22. Todd Lawson, "Friendship, Illumination and the Water of Life," *Journal of the Muhyiddin Ibn 'Arabi Society*, vol. 59 (2016): 17.

23. Lawson, "Friendship, Illumination and the Water of Life," 31.

24. According to Sufi scholar Todd Lawson, *rajul* does not refer to gender; rather, it means "valiant" or "steadfast" or "accomplished" and may be applied to women such as female mystic woman Rabi'a al-Adawiyya (d. 801) whom fellow Sufis in

early Islam refer to as a "real man," someone who perseveres on the path of spiritual accomplishment. See, for example, Lawson, "Friendship, Illumination and the Water of Life," 31. See also Annemarie Schimmel, *Mystical Dimensions of Islam* (Chapel Hill: University of North Carolina Press, 1975), 426.

25. Lawson, "Friendship," 44; See also Claude Addas, *Ibn 'Arabi, ou La quete du soufre rouge* (Paris: Gallimard, 1989), 71.

26. Ibn 'Arabi, *al-Futuhat al-Makkiyya* (Beirut: Dar Sadir, 1966), 1:134–35, 144–45.

27. Valerie J. Hoffman, "Annihilation in the Messenger of God: The Development of a Sufi Practice," *International Journal of Middle East Studies* 31, 3 (August 1999): 352.

28. Rebecca Masterton, "A Comparative Exploration of the Spiritual Authority of the *Awliya'* in the Shi'i and Sufi Traditions," *The American Journal of Islamic Social Sciences* 32, 1 (2015): 56.

29. Hoffman, "Annihilation in the Messenger of God," 352.

30. Ibn 'Arabi, *al-Futuhat al-Makkiyya*, 3:251.

31. Quoted in Hoffman, "Annihilation in the Messenger of God," 353.

32. Hoffman, "Annihilation in the Messenger of God," 353.

33. Hoffman, "Annihilation in the Messenger of God," 354.

34. Hoffman, "Annihilation in the Messenger of God," 355.

35. Hoffman, "Annihilation in the Messenger of God," 357.

36. Hoffman, "Annihilation in the Messenger of God," 358.

37. Hoffman, "Annihilation in the Messenger of God," 358.

38. Quoted in Roy Parviz Mottahedeh, "Friendship in Islamic Ethical Philosophy," in *Essays in Islamic Philology, History, and Philosophy*, eds. Alireza Korangy, Wheeler M. Thackston, Roy P. Mottahedeh, and William Granara (Berlin: De Gruyter, 2016), 232.

39. Mottahedeh, "Friendship in Islamic Ethical Philosophy," 232.

40. Mottahedeh, "Friendship in Islamic Ethical Philosophy," 232.

41. Muhammad Fu'ad 'Abd al-Baqi, ed., *Sunan Ibn Maja*, vol. 1 (n.c.: Dar Ihya' al-Kutub al-'Arabiyya, n.d.), 1217–18.

42. G.M. Wickens, trans., The Nasirean Ethics (London: George Allen & Unwin, 1974), 252.

43. Toshihiko Izutsu, *Ethico-Religious Concepts in the Qur'an* (Montreal: McGill-Queens University Press, 2014), 203.

44. Rahman Doi, *The Cardinal Principles of Islam* (Lagos: Islamic Publication Bureau, 1972), 38.

45. Lamin Sanneh, "Muhammad, Prophet of Islam, and Jesus Christ, Image of God: A Personal Testimony," *International Bulletin of Missionary Research*, vol. 8, no. 4 (October 1, 1984): 170.

46. Sam Agnoli, "On Friendship as the Essential Teachings of the Qur'an," https://oberlin164.rssing.com/chan-44497996/latest.php.

47. Arthur Jeffrey, ed., *Islam: Muhammad and His Religion* (New York: Bobbs-Merrill, 1958), 43.

48. Eliot Weinberger, "Muhammad," *Conjunctions*, no. 46 (2006): 246.

49. Michael Sells, *Approaching the Qur'an: The Early Revelations* (Ashland, OR: White Cloud Press, 2007), 209.
50. Fazlur Rahman, *Major Themes of the Qur'an* (Minneapolis, MN: Bibliotheca Islamica, 1999), 103.
51. Agnoli, "On Friendship."

BIBLIOGRAPHY

'Abd al-Baqi, Muhammad Fu'ad. *Sunan Ibn Maja*, vol. 1. N.c.: Dar Ihya' al-Kutub al-'Arabiyya, n.d.

Addas, Claude. *Ibn 'Arabi, ou La quete du soufre rouge*. Paris: Gallimard, 1989.

Agnoli, Sam. "On Friendship as the Essential Teachings of the Qur'an." https://oberlin164.rssing.com/chan-44497996/latest.php.

Amir-Moezzi, Mohammad Ali. *The Spirituality of Shi'i Islam: Beliefs and Practices*. London: I. B. Tauris, 2011.

Doi, Rahman. *The Cardinal Principles of Islam*. Lagos: Islamic Publication Bureau, 1972.

Ebstein, Michael. *Mysticism and Philosophy in al-Andalus*. Leiden: Brill, 2014.

Halim, Wahyuddin. "The Complex Relationship Between Sufism and Shi'ism as Reflected in the Concept of *Walayah*." *Kanz Philosophia* 5, 1 (June 2015): 73–87.

Hoffman, Valerie J. "Annihilation in the Messenger of God: The Development of a Sufi Practice." *International Journal of Middle East Studies* 31, 3 (August 1999): 351–369.

Ibn 'Arabi. *al-Futuhat al-Makkiyya*. Beirut: Dar Sadir, 1966.

Izutsu, Toshihiko. *Ethico-Religious Concepts in the Qur'an*. Montreal: McGill-Queens University Press, 2014.

Jeffery, Arthur, ed. *Islam: Muhammad and His Religion*. New York: Bobbs-Merrill, 1958.

Lawson, Todd. "Friendship, Illumination and the Water of Life." *Journal of the Muhyiddin Ibn 'Arabi Society*, vol. 59 (2016): 17–56.

Masterton, Rebecca. "A Comparative Exploration of the Spiritual Authority of the *Awliya'* in the Shi'i and Sufi Traditions." *The American Journal of Islamic Social Sciences* 32, 1 (2015): 49–74.

McAuliffe, Jane. *The Qur'an*. New York: W. W. Norton, 2017.

Momen, Moojan. *An Introduction to Shi'i Islam: The History and Doctrines of Twelver Shi'ism*. New Haven: Yale University Press, 1985.

Mottahedeh, Roy Parvis. "Friendship in Islamic Ethical Philosophy." In *Essays in Islamic Philology, History, and Philosophy*, edited by Alireza Korangy, Wheeler M. Thackston, Roy P. Mottahedeh, and William Granara. Berlin: De Gruyter, 2016.

Rahman, Fazlur. *Major Themes of the Qur'an*. Minneapolis: Bibliotheca Islamica, 1999.

Sanneh, Lamin. "Muhammad, Prophet of Islam, and Jesus Christ, Image of God: A Personal Testimony." *International Bulletin of Missionary Research*, vol. 8, no. 4 (October 1, 1984): 169–174.

Schimmel, Annemarie. *Mystical Dimensions of Islam*. Chapel Hill: University of North Carolina Press, 1975.

Sells, Michael. *Approaching the Qur'an*: The Early Revelations. Ashland, OR: White Cloud Press, 2007.

Weinberger, Eliot. "Muhammad," *Conjunctions*, no. 46 (2006): 231–246.

Wickens, G. M., trans. *The Nasirean Ethics*. London: George Allen & Unwin, 1974.

Chapter 7

Ineffable Accompaniment

Towards a Theology of Friendship and the Human Animal

Dorothy Dean

Reflecting on friendship through religious and theological lenses can illuminate previously hidden dimensions of both religion and friendship itself. In this chapter, I suggest that nonhuman animal capacities for friendship, as well as friendships between humans and animals, have a spiritual tone, and argue that affect theory provides scholars with the vocabulary to speak about the spirituality of human-animal friendships. (I use "human" and "animal" as shorthand throughout, but what I mean in each case is "human animal" and "nonhuman animal," respectively. I use "human" and "animal" to facilitate smoother reading, not to reify the divide between humans and nonhumans.) To make this case, I take an interdisciplinary approach, as animals have been refracted in different ways through the lenses of numerous scholarly fields. Through an exploration of work by scholars in critical animal studies, affect theory, theology, and religious studies, I propose a spirituality of friendship that rethinks human-animal and animal-animal relationships, and opens new avenues onto theorizing concepts of divinity. After introducing affect theory in the study of religion, I analyze human and animal friendships as affects. I then explore the spiritual significance of human-animal encounters through the pastoral theological model of wordless accompaniment. Based on this friendship beyond words, I go on to sketch the possibility of an apophatic theology inspired by animal friendship. Ultimately, I conclude by showing how this work adds to the growing scholarship challenging human exceptionalism and contributes to the idea of the spiritual human animal.

AFFECT THEORY AND THE STUDY OF RELIGION

Rationality, symbolic language, and verbalized intellection have generally been presumed to be prerequisites for both religion and friendship.[1]
Therefore, when engaging the subject of nonhuman animals, it is necessary
to find a way of accessing meaning that does not require words or reason.
The recent turn to affect in theology and religious studies provides the means
to do this.

Broadly speaking, affect theory analyzes power relations, cultural phenomena, and other realms of human life with an emphasis on the feelings,
emotions, and sensations experienced by bodies, in contrast to the traditional
academic approach of privileging verbal discourse. In *Religious Affects:
Animality, Evolution, and Power*, scholar of religion Donovan Schaefer
argues that religiosity is a bodily phenomenon shared by human and nonhuman animals. By applying an affect-based approach to studying religion in
humans and animals, Schaefer is able to focus on the ways bodies respond to
each other and the world, and the role of embodied states of being in networks
of religiosity. Affect theory connects bodies to each other on a material level
by highlighting "the wormlike processes flowing through bodies, rather than
the intact agents resolutely moving through their worlds."[2] To examine the
affects of religious experience is to study the processes that move and connect
bodies. Friendship, in this context, is a force that pulls two beings together
and moves them beyond their usual patterns.

Because language loses its privileged status when classically human traits
are viewed through the lens of affect theory, many aspects of religion (especially as it has been understood through a Protestant lens) require reevalu-
ation. Language is not the pinnacle of evolution, but "a wormlike process"
that emerges, animalistically, from certain apes.[3] Far from being the primary
locus of religion, language becomes for Schaefer simply one in a range of
expressions of and contributors to human affect. "Affect theory sees the passion for belief that is unique to the human bodily experience of religion as
one facet of the broader matrix of animal religions . . . Discourse is just one
of many intransigent shapes grafted onto the worldwide creature of animal
religion."[4] Humans, when moved by affects of religiosity, often experience
"this incredible need to believe" (to borrow a phrase from psychoanalyst
Julia Kristeva), yet it is not *belief* that is constitutive of religious feeling; it
is the religious *affect* that propels the verbally inclined human species into
cognizing their feelings as beliefs, creeds, theologies, and doctrines. In this
understanding, "religion is a place that bodies go, a flame to which bodies
are drawn like moths."[5] That same affect, moving through another species,

might elicit a variety of different behaviors, in accordance with each species' or individual's particular idiom.

Teya Pribac, an interdisciplinary animal studies scholar, makes a case for the noncognitive aspects of religion and bodily spirituality. Because the spiritual is seen as "above and beyond the cognitive" and is presumed to be "metaphysical," scholars have neglected to expand our knowledge of spirituality in "the body and the more ancient regions that humans share with other animals."[6] Pribac argues that the transcendent experiences of spirituality and religion are more self-extension than self-transcendence—they are an extension of the "affective self" through expanded relationality with others. "Attending to the present moment aids in uncovering a multitude of relationality that may otherwise remain undetected. It is in this space of implicit relationality that self-extension materializes."[7]

Religion and Animal Affects

Affect theory illuminates truths about our commonalities with nonhuman others that have been occluded in Christian reasoning. Philosopher of religion Stephen R. L. Clark observed that it is practically an article of faith in Western Christianity that "nonhuman animals can have no sense of justice, let alone religion, and are moved only by 'natural' lusts and affections."[8] This is not a universal attitude, however. Clark points out that it was self-evident for many peoples around the world that animals were engaged in their own kind of worship or had a place in the larger valuation of the world—that animals were moral agents of some kind, as stories in Ancient Greek writings about animals (and animal religiosity), as well as various Jewish, Muslim, and Buddhist stories attest.[9] These people might not have found the notion of animal friendships to be controversial at all.

Since humans are animals, religion must be an animal trait. According to Schaefer, religion itself emerges from the intertwining affects that push, pull, and move through bodies, and is viewed by affect theory as primarily relevant to bodies and is "a massing of affects, a core response of bodies in the world prior to ideas, words, thoughts."[10] Religion, viewed this way, de-constitutes individual subjectivity and prioritizes the myriad movements of affect. Thus, a definition of religion founded in affect connects human beings, even in those moments that we consider to be the most human, to the rest of the animal kingdom, because this understanding of religion means it is not contingent on assent to propositional statements. An affect-based interpretation of friendship also suggests that our own friend-making, friendly relationships, and the religious dimensions of those relationships also exist on a continuum with other animals.

FRIENDSHIP THROUGH THE
LENS OF AFFECT THEORY

It is possible to experience powerful emotions within friendships that resemble religious experiences—a transporting leave-of-self in the ecstatic connection with the other, when one connects with the friend unselfconsciously.[11] Friendship can involve connecting on a prelinguistic level where one does not *cognize* the relationship but instead *lives* it. It is thus a bodily experience that can be described in many of the same ways as affect theorists describe bodily religion. Movement away from material reality into a spiritual realm may actually be a return to the prelinguistic mode of being in the body—a movement that exceeds and precedes verbalization, returning us to something that predates *Homo sapiens* as a species.[12]

Animal Friendships

Affect theory provides a framework for understanding the extant scientific evidence for friendship in nonhuman animals. There are grounds for attributing the existence of empathy and attachment to many species, and some researchers (drawing on the work of affective neuroscientist and psychobiologist Jaak Panksepp[13]) have suggested that human emotions bear marked similarities to other animals' emotions. Humans and most other vertebrates share structures in the brain (also known as the limbic system) that are central to the ability to feel emotions. "It is now widely accepted that the human limbic system has a prominent role in both emotion and memory."[14] Moreover, neuroscientists have argued that the idea that "the limbic system is an early development of the vertebrate brain gives support to the antiquity of the emotions and to the idea that they exist not only in reptiles, but also in their predecessors."[15] While being able to feel is not the same thing as feeling friendship in particular, it is one crucial trait without which friendship would be impossible.

Panksepp identified certain "primary emotional systems" that all mammals have. In addition to the emotional systems in most vertebrates that drive seeking food, fighting, fleeing, and mating,

> mammals with their more social orientation acquired the motivational system for nurturing their offspring (CARE[16]); the powerful separation distress system for maintaining social contact and social bonding (PANIC/Sadness); and the complex system stimulating especially young animals to regularly engage in physical activities like wrestling, running, and chasing each other (PLAY/ Social Joy).[17]

These three additional emotional systems all come into play in the formation and maintenance of friendships in humans: care for the other, desire to stay close to the other, enjoyment in interacting with the other. In other words, while the language-processing areas of human brains are distinct from many other animals, the parts of our brains connected to the regulation of affects and emotions necessary for friendship—including and especially empathy— are often remarkably similar. From a scientific perspective, it is therefore reasonable to assume that friendship is not a fundamentally human phenomenon but a fundamentally *animal* relational capacity. Moreover, Panksepp's categories are affects—evolutionary forces that move, drive, and shape creatures, processes flowing amidst animal bodies. As is the case with religion, understanding friendship through an affect-based approach can help to see nonhuman animals as capable of considerably more depth of feeling and can also help humans see the animality of our modes of relating.

THE SPIRITUAL SIGNIFICANCE OF HUMAN-ANIMAL ENCOUNTERS

Friendship as Accompaniment

Human-animal and animal-animal encounters may be analyzed through the model of pastoral care. Concretely, the model of friendship that emerges from a theological study of animal-human and animal-animal friendships is one that will be familiar to those in pastoral ministry: it is based on the idea of "accompaniment." In the case of human-animal friendships, there is a mutual accompaniment that ebbs or flows in one direction or another depending on the circumstances. Importantly, it is not the animal accompanying the human, with the human as the main actor at all times; the human may also accompany the animal and provide a supportive presence.

Nonverbal physicality is an essential element of pastoral care—and is also a primary mode by which animals relate to us and each other. Pastoral and practical theologians provide helpful resources for addressing this phenomenon. Pastoral theologians Barbara McClure and Peter Capretto have both written about the importance of *being with* in a pastoral setting. McClure observes that "it is through *accompanying others*, or *being with* them in intentional ways, that modern caregivers help create opportunities for reflection, for deeper awareness of self and of others."[18] Although her intended audience is pastors and those who train them, her advice about accompaniment can apply to all those who abide together without words mediating the distance between them. McClure highlights the significance of one's physical presence—being with and attending to the suffering person without words.

Meanwhile, Capretto explicitly acknowledges the importance of silent, embodied presence in the pastoral relationship during times of grief. "As a concession to the unicity of the other's experience of the loss in immeasurable ways, silence establishes respect for the strangeness of the new world in which the griever finds herself, yet stands resolutely in the theological task of nonabandonment despite the inability of the caregiver to understand."[19] In silence, one cares for the other. This care and compassion transcend, through silent presence, the otherwise insurmountable differences between the two parties. Silence respects the fact that there is a boundary between the subjects that cannot be crossed, while at the same time providing comfort that *can* traverse that divide. Naturally, the relationship between pastor and parishioner is not strictly analogous to the friendship that pertains between equals. However, the existence of this discourse on the subject does show that there is an extant theological framework for considering caring relationships that exist beyond words. I would also argue that friendships do contain informal moments of pastoral care.[20] Our animal companions may do this for us as well; and, perhaps, we do this for them. (Humans are not the common denominator in this phenomenon; consolation is likely present amongst social animals interacting with other members of their own species, as well; it does not excessively strain credibility to imagine an elephant providing similar, silent solidarity to her grieving companion after the death of the latter's calf, for example.) When we are present with each other not only in loss, but in life, as individuals offer the comfort of their presence to one another, words are not required—indeed, they may only impede that communion between two individuals.

The pastoral model of silent accompaniment may provide a way to understand what transpires in the wordless relationship between human and animal, or between one animal and another: it is a friendship that is based on mutually affirming presence. Even though our inner states may be alien to each other, humans and animals can be with each other in a way that affects each of them profoundly. The silence of bodily presence mediates the unknowable reality of the other. Without words, friendship becomes a matter of presence and the emotions elicited by that presence: joy, comfort, and solidarity.

The value of a silent friendship can be seen clearly in relationships between humans and dogs.[21] Psychologist Joel Gavriele-Gold explores how, from a therapeutic perspective "the human-canine bond offers a unique, nonverbal communication."[22] The communication and relationship that exist in a friendship between human and dog is a thing unto itself that has unique and specific value, and does not function solely as a stand-in for "real" human friendships, Gavriele-Gold contends.[23] The embodied presence of the dog is *enhanced* by its silence and is a relationship that stands on its own merits. Dogs "say no words that hurt, offer no advice and ask no questions, keep their silence, yet they bear witness . . . Interacting with our dogs offers us . . . a way to reconnect with our feelings and ourselves."[24] Put another way, the dog speaks no representative language, and yet she is able to exist as a complete individual. By her presence, she reminds her human companion of the importance of being-with, and the nonfungibility of specific, embodied presence.

Although canine companions are immediately relatable to most people, dogs, as domesticated, social mammals, make it easy for people to ignore the divide between human and animal experiences, and thus overlook the theological importance of relating across an abyss of difference. By contrast, a radically different animal makes plain the potential for experiencing something of the divine through keeping affectionate company with the utter strangeness of the other. The 2020 Netflix documentary, *My Octopus Teacher*, is one example. Unlike Panksepp's mammals, octopi do not care for their young or socialize with each other, so it seems reasonable to assume that the documentary's titular octopus was simply interacting with Craig Foster as an intriguing and benign part of its environment. In spite of that, the affects of friendship that Foster felt within *himself*—the emotions of bonding, loyalty, pleasure, and concern—were all real.

This may be revelatory of theological possibilities within human friendships with animals, regardless of whether or not those friendships are reciprocated. In Foster's case, there was another level of friendship: a level of that being-with that does not descend from maternal relationships in mammals and birds, but a kind of presence with nature, metonymized in this case in the presence of the octopus. The nature of friendship would thus exceed interpersonal relationships and would also encompass a multitude of ways of being in and with bodies in the world. Author Christopher Karr has suggested that there is a Job-like quality to Foster's friendship with the octopus, in the sense that Foster encounters the presence of God in this relationship with the octopus and her habitat.[25]

AN APOPHATIC THEOLOGY OF ANIMAL FRIENDSHIP

Academic theology has imagined a God who is characterized and received almost exclusively through verbal discourse and cognitive comprehension. I agree with Stephen Clark that this is an error.[26] That is not to say that verbally cognized revelation and the works of the great mystics and theologians are unimportant—just that they are *insufficient*. Apophatic animal friendship makes it possible to imagine divinity as something more limbic than cerebral, less like human thoughts and more like the capacity for love that we arguably share with many other creatures. Human intellect is many things, a gift simultaneously wonderful and terrible, and no doubt it does provide us with a unique perspective on the divine. However, that fact does not preclude the possibility that intellection of God is something that emerged later in the evolutionary process and, hence, does not reflect the core of creaturely reception of divinity. That would in turn imply that humans reflect the divine image not only in our cogitation but also in our feeling and relating.

There is great potential in the Christian apophatic theological traditions to address this wordless friendship and its theological connotations. Apophatic theology uses mutually contradictory concepts to deliver the mind to a point that escapes language. For example, as philosopher and theologian Denys Turner has observed, Pseudo-Dionysius (an early Christian monk and thinker writing around the turn of the sixth century) negates all the names for God in a systematic fashion, progressing "up the scale of language until at the end of the work the last word is that all words are left behind in the silence of the apophatic."[27] The result is that the reader "step[s] off the very boundary of language itself, beyond every assertion and every denial, into the 'negation of the negation' and the 'brilliant darkness' of God."[28] Language, then, is a barrier to deeper understanding. It takes us only so far, and then must be abandoned. Because we humans are creatures accustomed to understanding our world through verbal signals, it takes considerable effort to renounce our concepts.

It may be possible to think of nonhuman animals, with different means of interpreting their respective worlds, as already existing in a realm without verbalizable concepts. Perhaps that space beyond the boundary of language is inhabited by those relational creatures who do not possess a symbolic vocabulary. Without words to get in the way, they begin at the last rung of the apophatic ladder, and always already dwell within that brilliant darkness of the divine. Friendship with an animal—as mutual silent accompaniment—may therefore provide another point of access to understanding God for humans. In inhabiting the wordless relationality of friendship with an animal, or contemplating their friendship with each other, we may touch, for a moment, a manifestation of the love of God.[29]

FRIENDSHIP AS A CHALLENGE TO
HUMAN EXCEPTIONALISM

Sentimental Anthropomorphism?

Do nonhuman animals behave in a way that could be called "friendly," and, if so, is it intellectually responsible to term that behavior "friendship"? To the casual observer, something like friendship appears to be visible in a variety of animal species and between different species of animals, humans amongst them, and yet it continues to be controversial to suggest that friendship is something that can be found throughout the animal kingdom. On the one hand, a scholar might be accused of being too "sentimental" if she were to imagine that savage beasts, red in tooth and claw, could actually experience something like friendship. On the other hand, anyone proposing complex emotional states in animals risks being charged with anthropomorphism.

Some of the resistance to the question of whether animals have friendships is related to sex-based inequalities and biases found in certain human societies. Until recently, researchers ignored friendly and peaceful behaviors amongst animals, especially females of a species, similarly to the way sociologists and historians often ignored women's experiences and perspectives. Anne I. Dagg, feminist and zoologist, argues that both wild and domestic animal friendships are often missed because researchers focus on fighting and power struggles over peaceful activities.[30] The category of friendship was denied even to our own species, as there was a bias toward assuming that "aggression was central to human evolution."[31] Even when ostensibly friendly behaviors can be observed, there are those who object to the idea that animals have friendships because saying so seems to be an instance of anthropomorphism—assuming that nonhuman animals have inner lives like our own.[32] Certainly, to uncritically label animal behaviors using human categories is problematic. There comes a point, however, when a dogmatic resistance to anthropo*morphism* just becomes anthropo*centrism*: the idea that only humans have been gifted with the ability to feel, love, and enjoy, and that we must assume that all other creatures know nothing of these states of being. It also presupposes a human-animal divide: *nothing of my own inner experience could have descended from or be related to the animal kingdom.* At a certain point, the risks of distortion due to anthropocentrism exceed those due to anthropomorphism. I agree with feminist and critical animal theorist Kari Weil that there are uses for strategic empathy and anthropomorphism that can acknowledge the multifaceted nature of relating and of our own individual subjectivity:

> We might then want to call an ethical relating to animals (whether in theory or in art) "critical anthropomorphism" in the sense that we open ourselves to touch and be touched by others as fellow subjects and may imagine their pain, pleasure, and need in anthropomorphic terms but must stop short of believing that we can know their experience. In addition, critical anthropomorphism must begin with the acknowledgment that the irreducible difference that animals may represent for us is one that is also *within* us and within the term human.[33]

There will always be a mysterious divide between self and other, whether that other is animal or human. This gap must not be allowed to preclude the possibility of empathy. Moreover, the point is not to project human reality onto all other living things, but to see the commonalities shared between multiple, disparate species. I consider the finding of such commonalities to be less a case of anthropomorphizing animal behavior and more a "zoo-morphizing" of human experiences. Seeing ourselves in others and others in ourselves, while maintaining an awareness of our epistemic limitations, may indeed be the most ethical way forward.

Although, as discussed above, there is evidence to suggest that animals have friendships with one another, it is ultimately irrelevant whether or not we can prove that an animal "thinks" that the two of you are "friends." Those are words created by our distinctively verbal species to understand and label this embodied relationship. We do not need to wait for the science to be unmistakable to theologize human-animal friendships. Even if we only have the *perception* of the animal as our friend, the simple act of presuming that friendship is found throughout the animal kingdom could enrich our lives and benefit the lives of the animals with whom we interact.[34] Sharing the category of friendship opens up a much more capacious theological anthropology that makes room for human animality.

The Human Animal

From an ecotheological perspective, discussing friendship in a way that is inclusive of animals is part of the ongoing project to disrupt the ecologically deleterious human/animal binary. If friendship is an object of religious reflection, and religion is an animal affect, then theologies of friendship may reveal something about nonhuman experiences of divinity. The theological implications of friendship further destabilize the human-nonhuman binary and helps to bolster a robust sense of "human nonexceptionalism."[35]

Finding human religiosity in a well of animal affects makes it possible to see many of our other "higher" behaviors, like forming friends, as something shared with animals.[36] It also blurs the lines between those things that are labeled "animal" and those that are "religious." Teya Pribac has similarly critiqued the contingency of human identity on distancing the self from non-human animals.

> The Western human's ontological fabric is to a significant extent defined by the human/nonhuman animal binary . . . In order to secure this extremely vulnerable mode of being, separatists have over time built a domino castle of "exclusively human" attributes, only to see it progressively collapse as knowledge and understanding of humans and other animals rapidly increases. Spirituality is one such attribute, jealously guarded by those whose humanity may feel under threat if it

turns out that the sacrificial lamb has equal, or greater, spiritual depth compared to her killer.[37]

Human self-understanding is challenged when animals, whom Christian theology has predominantly viewed as spiritually inert or, at best, as vehicles for expressions of human spirituality (as sacrificial offerings), must be reconsidered as possessing their own kind of spirituality. Allowing that nonhuman animals may have what we consider a full complement of emotions and experiences, not to mention ways of being in the world that are beyond our ability to understand due to the specificity of their positions in "lifeworlds"[38] unique to their species, challenges our lonely human exceptionalism and makes it possible to theorize a spirituality of friendship for both the human and the animal in a human-animal encounter.

Religious responses to friendship viewed through affect theory combine both religion and friendship to highlight the spirituality of the human animal. If, as Donovan Schaefer has argued, religion is meant to be the thing that makes us human by "severing our animality," then animal friendships may be crucial for reintegrating the spiritual into the animal.[39] Theologizing the affective, embodied spirituality of friendship with our animal others reconnects us with our animality, and opens new pathways to thinking the human animal.

NOTES

1. See, for example, almost all contemporary Christian theology since René Descartes, in which humans are defined as being created in the image of God because of our capacity to reason—a feat predicated on the capacity for making verbal arguments.

2. Donovan O. Schaefer, *Religious Affects: Animality, Evolution, and Power* (Durham: Duke University Press, 2015), 211.

3. Schaefer, 208.

4. Schaefer, *Religious Affects*, 209.

5. Schaefer, *Religious Affects*, 216.

6. Teya Brooks Pribac, "Spiritual Animal: A Journey into the Unspeakable," *Journal for the Study of Religion, Nature and Culture* 11, no. 3 (2017): 356, https://doi .org/10.1558/jsrnc.31519.

7. Pribac, "Spiritual Animal," 353–54.

8. Stephen R. L. Clark, "Ask Now the Beasts and They Shall Teach Thee," in *Animals as Religious Subjects: Transdisciplinary Perspectives*, ed. Celia Deane-Drummond, David L. Clough and Rebecca Artinian-Kaiser (London: Bloomsbury, 2013), 16.

9. Indeed, as Laura Duhan-Kaplan has observed, there are threads in the Jewish tradition that honor the spiritual uniqueness of all creatures. Kaplan highlights *Perek Shira*, "an anonymous medieval Jewish work of eco-spirituality. . . . [in which] each

animal, plant, and geographic feature sings a different bible verse," reflecting Psalm 148, which features animals (among other aspects of creation) praising God. Laura Duhan-Kaplan, *Mouth of the Donkey: Re-imagining Biblical Animals* (Eugene, OR: Cascade, 2021), 12.

10. Schaefer, *Religious Affects*, 211.

11. I am indebted to Margaret Gower's insights on the concept of "ecstatic friendship," which she presented in her conference paper at the 2021 American Academy of Religion Annual Meeting.

12. I am grateful for Hussam Timani's insight that, in Islam, friendship is believed to have existed prior to the creation of humans.

13. See, for example, Kenneth L. Davis and Christian Montag, "Selected Principles of Pankseppian Affective Neuroscience," *Frontiers in Neuroscience* 12 (2019), https://doi.org/10.3389/fnins.2018.01025.

14. Joseph L. Price, "Limbic System," in *Encyclopedia of the Human Brain*, ed. V. S. Ramachandran. Academic Press, 2002.

15. R. V. Rial et al., "The Evolution of Consciousness in Animals," in *Consciousness Transitions*, ed. Hans Liljenström and Peter Århem (Amsterdam: Elsevier Science B.V., 2007), 45–76, https://doi.org/10.1016/B978-044452977-0/50004-8.

16. Panksepp wrote these words in all caps to distinguish them from their common usage.

17. Kenneth L. Davis and Christian Montag, "Selected Principles of Pankseppian Affective Neuroscience," *Frontiers in Neuroscience* 12 (2019), https://doi.org/10.3389/fnins.2018.01025.

18. Barbara McClure, "Pastoral Care," in *The Wiley Blackwell Companion to Practical Theology*, ed. Bonnie J. Miller-McLemore (Wiley, 2011), 272.

19. Peter Capretto, "Empathy and Silence in Pastoral Care for Traumatic Grief and Loss," *Journal of Religion and Health* 54, no. 1 (2015): 340.

20. Incidentally, animals already factor into the language of pastoral theology. "Pastoral" of course is the conventional shepherd/flock metaphor for the minister's relationship to the congregation.

21. Naturally, dogs are not representative of the majority of animals, which do not choose to live amongst humans. However, because most people have some level of experience with canine companions, what follows is perhaps the most relatable possible example.

22. Joel R. Gavriele-Gold, "The Human-Canine Bond: New Learnings and a Changing Rationality from a Psychoanalytic Perspective," *Psychoanalytic Review; New York* 98, no. 1 (February 2011): 104, http://dx.doi.org.ezproxy.lib.uh.edu/10.1521/prev.2011.98.1.91.

23. Gavriele-Gold, "The Human-Canine Bond," 104–5.

24. Gavriele-Gold, "The Human-Canine Bond," 105.

25. Karr, Christopher, "Why 'My Octopus Teacher' Is the Best Film of 2020," Highbrow Magazine, October 1, 2020, https://www.highbrowmagazine.com/10896-why-my-octopus-teacher-best-film.

26. There is a mystical vein through Christianity (Meister Eckhart comes to mind) that radically deemphasizes words and insists on truth through silence.

27. Denys Turner, "Apophaticism, Idolatry and the Claims of Reason," in *Silence and the Word: Negative Theology and Incarnation,* ed. Oliver Davies and Denys Turner, (Cambridge: Cambridge University Press, 2008), 19.

28. Turner, 20, citing Pseudo-Dionysius' *Divine Names* (817D), and *Mystical Theology* (997B), respectively.

29. It is not incidental that I said "touch" rather than "glimpse." As many have noted, theological language is saturated with visual metaphors that themselves relay upon verbal abstraction. It is in contemplation of prelinguistic bodily states that a theology of animal friendship finds resources for talking about God.

30. Dagg, Anne Innis. *Animal Friendships.* New York: Cambridge University Press, 2011, 2.

31. In general, "the activities of females, who are virtually always more friendly than males no matter what the species, were largely ignored." More recent studies have found that primates spend "Between 85 to 96 percent of their activity time in affiliative behavior—grooming, playing, huddling, cooperative infant care, food sharing . . . [etc.]," (Dagg, *Animal Friendships*, 5–6). That is not to say that all animals make friends. Some form such tight-knit societies that scientists cannot discern any outstanding, special friendships; others are naturally solitary. That said, there are plenty of nonhuman animals who relate to each other in ways that can best be described as friendship.

32. Most of us have heard a dog owner describing their pet as "feeling guilty," when the dog is simply exhibiting classic submission behavior in front of an agitated pack member. But what if guilt is internalized submission behavior?

33. K. Weil, "A Report on the Animal Turn," *Differences* (Bloomington, IN) 21, no. 2 (2010): 16, https://doi.org/10.1215/10407391-2010-001.

34. The other important thing to consider is the human affect of friendly feeling that can exist regardless of whether or not the object of that feeling reciprocates it in a measurable or similar way. Our capacity for friendship is a way of being in and with bodies in the world—maybe of trees, maybe of octopi. Octopi don't care for their young, they don't socialize, so it seems reasonable to assume that the octopus was simply interacting with Foster as a curious and benign part of its environment. But the friendship that Foster felt—the emotions of bonding, loyalty, pleasure, and concern—these were all real. Perhaps there was another level of friendship—a level of that being-with that doesn't descend from maternal relationships in mammals and birds, but is a kind of presence with nature. But this will need to be explored in a future paper.

35. For more about the need to construct human nonexceptionalism, see Dean, Dorothy. "'At Home on the Earth': Toward a Theology of Human NonExceptionalism." *Journal for the Study of Religion, Nature & Culture* 14, no. 4 (2020).

36. Teya Pribac makes a case for the noncognitive aspects of religion and bodily spirituality. Because the spiritual is seen as "above and beyond the cognitive" and is presumed to be "metaphysical," scholars have neglected to expand our knowledge of spirituality in "the body and the more ancient regions that humans share with other animals." (Pribac, "Spiritual Animal," 356.)

37. Pribac, "Spiritual Animal," 356.

38. "Lifeworlds" or *Umwelten*, formulated by early twentieth-century biologist Jakob von Uexküll, refer to the subjective sense of the "world" that members of a given species inhabit, which is produced by the specific interactions of an organism with its environment. See Jakob von Uexküll, *A Foray into the Worlds of Animals and Humans: With a Theory of Meaning* (Minneapolis: University of Minnesota Press, 2010). It is the world as the animal encounters it, based on that animal's ecological niche and evolutionary adaptations. A particular animal's lifeworld is something about which humans can speculate, but can never adequately know. For example, what it is like to *be* a dolphin—aquatic, equipped with sonar—and what the world and its boundaries *feel like* to a dolphin are vastly different from what humans experience.

39. Schaefer, *Religious Affects*, 204.

BIBLIOGRAPHY

Capretto, Peter. "Empathy and Silence in Pastoral Care for Traumatic Grief and Loss," *Journal of Religion and Health* 54, no. 1 (2015) 339–357.

Clark, Stephen R. L. "Ask Now the Beasts and They Shall Teach Thee." In *Animals as Religious Subjects: Transdisciplinary Perspectives*, edited by Celia Deane-Drummond, David L. Clough and Rebecca Artinian-Kaiser, 15–34. London: Bloomsbury, 2013.

Dagg, Anne Innis. *Animal Friendships*. New York: Cambridge University Press, 2011. https://doi.org/10.1017/CBO9780511794155.

Davis, Kenneth L., and Christian Montag. "Selected Principles of Pankseppian Affective Neuroscience." *Frontiers in Neuroscience* 12 (2019). https://doi.org/10.3389/fnins.2018.01025.

Dean, Dorothy. "'At Home on the Earth': Toward a Theology of Human Non-Exceptionalism." *Journal for the Study of Religion, Nature & Culture* 14, no. 4 (2020).

Duhan-Kaplan, Laura. *Mouth of the Donkey: Re-imagining Biblical Animals*. Eugene, OR: Cascade, 2021.

Gavriele-Gold, Joel R. "The Human-Canine Bond: New Learnings and a Changing Rationality from a Psychoanalytic Perspective." *Psychoanalytic Review; New York* 98, no. 1 (February 2011) 91–105. http://dx.doi.org.ezproxy.lib.uh.edu/10.1521/prev.2011.98.1.91.

Karr, Christopher. "Why 'My Octopus Teacher' Is the Best Film of 2020." Highbrow Magazine, October 1, 2020. https://www.highbrowmagazine.com/10896-why-my-octopus-teacher-best-film.

McClure, Barbara. "Pastoral Care," in *The Wiley Blackwell Companion to Practical Theology*, ed. Bonnie J. Miller-McLemore (Wiley, 2011), 272.

Oliver, Kelly. *Animal Lessons: How They Teach Us to Be Human*. Columbia University Press, 2009.

Pribac, Teya Brooks. "Spiritual Animal: A Journey into the Unspeakable." *Journal for the Study of Religion, Nature and Culture* 11, no. 3 (2017) 340–60. https://doi.org/10.1558/jsrnc.31519.

Price, Joseph L. "Limbic System." *Encyclopedia of the Human Brain*, edited by V. S. Ramachandran. Academic Press, 2002.

Rial, R.V., et al. "The Evolution of Consciousness in Animals." *Consciousness Transitions*, edited by Hans Liljenström and Peter Århem (Amsterdam: Elsevier Science B.V., 2007), 45–76, https://doi.org/10.1016/B978-044452977-0/50004–8.

Ruether Rosemary Radford. *Sexism and God-Talk: Toward a Feminist Theology.* Boston: Beacon Press, 1983.

Schaefer, Donovan O. *Religious Affects: Animality, Evolution, and Power.* Durham: Duke University Press, 2015.

Turner, Denys. "Apophaticism, Idolatry and the Claims of Reason." In *Silence and the Word: Negative Theology and Incarnation*, edited by Oliver Davies and Denys Turner. Cambridge: Cambridge University Press, 2008.

Uexküll, Jakob von. *A Foray into the Worlds of Animals and Humans: With a Theory of Meaning.* Minneapolis: University of Minnesota Press, 2010.

Weil, Kari. "A Report on the Animal Turn," *Differences* 21, no. 2 (2010) 1–23. https://doi.org/10.1215/10407391-2010-001.

Chapter 8

"I Have Called You Friends"

Friendship in the New Testament and Early Christianity

Liz Carmichael

Christian theology and ethics are grounded in the New Testament (NT), so the NT is fundamental to all thinking and research on friendship in the Christian tradition, throughout history. In the world today, the churches are called to be a sign of friendship, and the dynamic of God's open friendship, revealed in Jesus, continues to drive Christian compassion, humanitarian outreach, and peacemaking. This chapter introduces the theme of friendship in the NT and the early Christian centuries. Beginning with a key passage in the Gospel according to John, it sketches the rich background of thinking about friendship among classical writers and in the Hebrew scriptures, the Old Testament, and explores how Jesus builds on these to break new ground. In Christ, God's friendship-love reaches out to all people, even sinners, in an open offer of friendship that transcends the usual human limits of friendship. In this kind of love, commitment to God—in Christ—replaces classical virtue as the ground of firm mutual friendship between human beings and between humans and God. The chapter then traces how these new themes modify classical thinking in the work of major early Christian theologians.

FRIENDSHIP IS AT THE HEART OF THE NEW TESTAMENT

Friendship is central to the gospel message. In the Gospel according to John, Jesus speaks at length to his closest disciples during their last supper together.

They are in Jerusalem on the night of his arrest. In John this is the night before Passover. During his talk Jesus makes a key statement about friendship.

His teaching begins with a symbolic action. Before the meal, assuming the role of a servant, he takes a towel and bowl of water and, to their surprise, washes his disciples' dusty feet. Then he explains: "If I, your Lord and Teacher, have washed your feet, you also ought to wash one another's feet" (John 13:14).[1] Shortly afterwards, when Judas, who intended to betray Jesus, has left the room, Jesus says: "I give you a new commandment, that you love one another. Just as I have loved you, you also should love one another. By this everyone will know that you are my disciples, if you have love for one another" (13:34–5). A little later he returns to this new commandment:

> This is my commandment, that you love one another as I have loved you. No one has greater love than this, to lay down one's life for one's friends. You are my friends, if you do what I command you. I do not call you servants any longer, because the servant does not know what the master is doing, but I have called you friends, because I have made known to you everything that I have heard from my Father. You did not choose me but I chose you. And I appointed you to go and bear fruit. . . . (15:12–16a)

Jesus promises his disciples the gift of the Holy Spirit, and prays "not only on behalf of these, but also on behalf of those who will believe in me through their word, that they may all be one" (John 17:20–21). So God, incarnate in Christ Jesus, draws humans into intimate friendship with himself and one another. The Oxford scholar John Burnaby called these verses in John the "Holy of Holies of the New Testament."[2]

The Classical Background: The *"Topos"* of Friendship

The use of the language of friendship in the New Testament reflects the rich tradition of thought on this subject that had built up, primarily in Greek philosophical literature, over previous centuries. Friendship, *philia* in Greek, *amicitia* in Latin, formed a *topos*, literally a place or landscape of ideas and discussion, that was widely known and was familiar to New Testament and early Christian writers.[3] This cluster of ideas reflected, and in turn helped shape, the popular consciousness. Thus it was generally accepted that the ultimate sign of true friendship was willingness to die for one's friend. Cicero remarks in *De amicitia* ("On Friendship") written in 44 BC, how a theatre audience would burst into applause when characters showed themselves willing to die for one another, thus showing proof of their virtuous friendship.[4] The Greek word *philia* could denote the harmony of the cosmos, or of a well-governed state, or of personal friendship. "Friendship" could also refer to political alliances and mutual loyalty between clients and patrons. We see this use, too, in the New Testament.[5]

Aristotle, in a key text on friendship in his *Nicomachean Ethics*, said that *philia* is ultimately grounded in our sharing (communion, *koinōnia*) in human nature. Therefore, he remarks, a free man can befriend a slave as a human being, but not as a slave, for in that capacity they are merely a tool.[6] Aristotle analyses friendships according to three desirable goals: usefulness (as in business partnerships); pleasure (often the aim in youthful friendships), and goodness or virtue.[7] Only virtue-friendship between persons of good character is true, perfect, and lasting friendship. Cicero elaborates: "friendship (*amicitia*) is nothing else than accord in all things, human and divine, conjoined with mutual goodwill (*benevolentia*) and affection (*caritas*)."[8]

In classical literature, a few legendary pairs of men served as paradigmatic friends: Achilles and Patroclus, Orestes and Pylades, Damon and Phintias.[9] Friends were usually assumed to be male although Aristotle allows that a wife may be virtuous in her own way,[10] and he cites selfless maternal love as the perfect example of altruistic loving with affection and well-doing.[11]

For classical writers, it became axiomatic that a friend is "another self"; that true friends entrust each other with their inmost thoughts and secrets; and friends become as it were one soul in two bodies. Friends might share a combined household. The philosopher-mathematician Pythagoras, whose followers reportedly pooled their possessions and entered a communal lifestyle, was much quoted as saying that friends share everything in common. Classical writers discussed how to choose friends, debating whether persons who are like, or unlike, attract or repel one another; whether friends become like one another; and whether or not it was possible, given human limitations, to have many friends.

Friendship with the divine was occasionally mentioned. The preclassical writers Hesiod and Empedocles looked back to a golden age when love and virtue reigned and humans were friends with the gods. In Xenophon's account, Socrates acclaims the gods as friends of the noble and good.[12] Plato's Socrates says those who conceive a true virtue are destined for friendship with the gods.[13] In Herculaneum in the first century BC the Epicurean teacher Philodemus, who hailed from Gadara above the Sea of Galilee, allowed that when the wise strive joyfully in prayer to draw close to the divine and to be transformed by it, it was possible to call "wise men the friends of the gods, and the gods friends of the wise."[14]

Virtuous friendship was, it seems, inherently altruistic. Already in Plato we encounter the idea that to love a person entails desiring their happiness.[15] For Socrates's young Athenian friend Lysis, happiness lay in becoming a good and useful citizen, so that is what his friends wish for him. Aristotle makes it explicit that we love a friend "for his own sake" (*NE* 1155b31). On the question of how self-love relates to love of others, he says that right self-love is the pursuit of virtue, and is free of selfishness, hence to love a friend as one's self means desiring that they too will grow in virtue (*NE* 1166a32).

Classical friendship has limits. Friends should be chosen carefully. One should not associate with wicked persons: it is bad for one's reputation, and one is in danger of becoming like them. Instead, stay with those who strive to become virtuous. One should respond to a friend's request, but only if the request is honorable. If they wander from the right path we should disengage and end the friendship.

Scriptural Background in the Old Testament and Apocrypha

References to friendship in the Old Testament (OT), the Hebrew Bible, also help lay a foundation for NT writers. For example, both Abraham and Moses are called friends of God. Isaiah speaks of "Abraham, my friend" (Isaiah 41:8); Chronicles of "your friend Abraham" (2 Chronicles 20:7). Exodus says, "Thus the Lord used to speak to Moses face to face, as one speaks to a friend" (Exodus 33:11). The OT offers paradigmatic pairs of friends in David and Jonathan and, as more recent commentators point out, Ruth and Naomi.

Proverbs in the OT, and two Apocryphal books, the Wisdom of Ben Sirach (Ecclesiasticus) and the Wisdom of Solomon, transmit sayings on friendship typical of the "wisdom" tradition that flourished in scribal circles around the eastern Mediterranean. Proverbs offers two much-quoted sayings: "A friend loves at all times" (Proverbs 17.17) and: "The wounds of a friend are better than the kisses of an enemy" (27:6). Ben Sirach (Ecclesiasticus) boasts a collection of sayings, ranging from encouragement: "Pleasant speech multiplies friends . . . " (Sirach 6:5); "Faithful friends are a life-saving medicine . . . " (6:16), to warning: "In great and small matters do no harm, and do not become an enemy instead of a friend" (5:15–6:1); "When you gain friends, gain them through testing, and do not trust them hastily, for there are friends who are such when it suits them, but they will not stand by you in time of trouble. And there are friends who turn into enemies . . . " (6:7–9).

Friendship with God appears as a divine gift in the "Wisdom of Solomon," probably written in the half-century before Christ:

> I called on God, and the spirit of wisdom came to me, . . . I do not hide her wealth, for it is an unfailing treasure for mortals; those who get it obtain friendship with God, commended for the gifts that come from instruction. . . . in every generation she passes into holy souls, and makes them friends of God, and prophets. (Wisdom 7:7, 14, 27)

In scripture it is grace, the divine gifts of wisdom and love, and not simply the moulding of virtues by human effort, that forms the character of the friend. And, according to Song of Songs 2:4 in the Latin Vulgate, love should be rightly "ordered": "he ordered love in me (*ordinavit in me caritatem*)."

FRIENDSHIP IN THE NEW TESTAMENT

The verses from John's Gospel quoted above use classical friendship motifs, but add striking new developments. In John, Jesus says, "No one has greater love than this, to lay down one's life for one's friends" (John 15:13). In classical thought, willingness to give one's life was the ultimate sign of friendship, but it was assumed that the friend for whom one died was virtuous, and worthy of such sacrifice. Here, however, Jesus was about to die for sinners. This was astonishing, as Paul makes clear:

> For while we were still weak, at the right time Christ died for the ungodly. Indeed, rarely will anyone die for a righteous person—though perhaps for a good person someone might actually dare to die. But God proves his love for us in that while we were still sinners Christ died for us. (Romans 5:6–8)

Humanly speaking it is countercultural to act as a friend to a person who has forfeited, or rejected, our friendship; but God's friendship in Christ transcends such limitations. Christ acts as our friend while we are still his enemies, precisely in order to reconcile us to himself, transforming us into friends. We have only to respond to the love he offers, and to grow in that open, healing friendship.

The Greek noun for "love" used throughout the New Testament is *agapē*, a word that never appeared in classical literature but had evolved more recently, replacing an older form, *agapēsis*. *Agapē* and *philia* were related to two verbs "to love," *agapan* and *philein*, which were close synonyms in the NT era.[16] *Philia* could mean "love" but it primarily indicated the *state* of harmonious relationship. *Agapē* first appeared in writing in the Septuagint, the Greek translation of the OT; then it became the sole noun for "love" in the NT, where it happens it always denotes virtuous love, the kind of love a good friend gives.[17] In Latin *agapē* became *caritas* or *dilectio*, and in older English "charity." In modern NT translations it is again simply "love," but always understood as love grounded in goodness, given by God and offered to all.

Jesus' next words are "You are my friends, if you do what I command you" (John 15:12). They are often read in a conditional sense: "you are my friends, *if* you do as I command you." Instead, Ambrose suggests a consequential reading. We, like Abraham, first become God's friends by obeying him. Thereafter we obey out of love, as a friend, not out of fear as a servant.[18]

Jesus continues, "I have called you friends, because I have made known to you everything that I have heard from my father" (John 15: 15). Here Jesus is like a true friend, as described in classical literature: having chosen one another with care, friends entrust one another with their innermost thoughts and secrets. Jesus now affirms that he has indeed chosen this group who are to continue his work as evangelists, teachers, and leaders: "You did not choose me but I chose you. And I appointed you to go and bear fruit, fruit that will last . . . " (John 15:12–16a).

At times, Jesus' opponents insulted him by saying he was "a friend of tax-collectors and sinners," and asking why he ate with such people (Matthew 11:19, Luke 7:34). Tax collectors collaborated with unpopular authorities, and were despised as corrupt. Ironically, the insult expressed the truth. Jesus *was* a friend to sinners. Jesus responds that he was not sent to the healthy, but to those who needed a physician (Mark 2:17, Matthew 9:12, Luke 5:31). Matthew (Levi) himself had been a tax collector (Matthew 9:9, 10.3; Mark 2:14–17, Luke 5:27), as was Zacchaeus who after climbing a tree in Jericho to see Jesus pass by, found himself entertaining Jesus at a feast in his home, announcing he will give half of his goods to the poor and promising restitution to any he has wronged (Luke 19:1–10).

The writer of Luke's Gospel and its sequel, the Acts of the Apostles, is traditionally identified with "Luke, the beloved physician" (Colossians 4:14) a friend of Paul who shared some of Paul's journeys including his final voyage to Rome. Luke dedicates both his Gospel and Acts to "Theophilos." While Theophilos may well have been an actual person, the name, which was a common one, means "friend," "lover," or "beloved" "of God," so it has also been read generically. Ambrose comments: "the gospel was written for Theophilos, that is to him who loves God. If you love God, it is written to you."[19]

Luke is particularly attuned to human stories and to friendship. His Gospel contains 18 of the 29 NT occurrences of the word "friend." In his Gospel, as in John, Jesus addresses his disciples as "my friends" (Luke 12:4) but he also warns of persecutions to come, when Christians must expect to be "delivered up even by parents and brothers, kinsmen and friends . . . " (21:16).

In Luke it is a Roman army officer, a centurion, who sends a request to Jesus to come and heal his sick slave. Hearing that Jesus is on his way, the centurion sends his friends to ask him simply to give the command, and his slave would be healed (Luke 7:6). Jesus commends the faith of this Gentile, and the slave is well.

Luke recounts many of Jesus' parables. A whole string of friends feature in a parable about persistence in prayer. Suppose that we have a friend, whose friend arrives late one night, unexpectedly, from a journey. Having no food at home, our friend knocks on the door of another friend, his neighbor, asking to borrow three loaves. At first the neighbor protests: it is too late, the family is asleep; and yet: "I tell you, even though he will not get up and give him anything because he is his friend, at least because of his persistence he will get up and give him whatever he needs" (Luke 11:8).

To teach humility and warn against presumptuousness, Jesus advises that on arrival at a banquet we should take the lowest seat, "so that when your host comes, he may say to you, 'Friend, move up higher'" (Luke 14.10). In a different mode Jesus urges those who host banquets not to invite their friends and relatives who can return the invitation, but to entertain "the poor, the lame, the blind, and you will be blessed, because they cannot repay you, for you will be repaid at the resurrection of the just" (Luke 14.13–14).

Then Jesus tells the curious, semicomic story about the "dishonest steward" who, when he realizes he is about to be sacked, devises a way to ensure he will have friends in the future. He calls in his master's debtors, one by one, and alters the records so that they now owe much less. Consequently, they will be ready to "welcome" him "into their homes." His master, Jesus drily recounts, is impressed by the steward's wiliness: "for the children of this age are more shrewd in dealing with their own generation than are the children of light" (Luke 16:8). Jesus goes on, "And I tell you, make friends for yourselves by means of dishonest wealth [*literally:* unrighteous mammon] so that when it is gone, they may welcome you into the eternal homes" (16:9). Ambrose comments that "they" are the inhabitants of heaven, including angels, who will welcome those who give this world's wealth to the poor.[20]

Luke has much to say about joy, rejoicing, and making merry with friends. He records three parables about finding a precious thing that was lost, all to illustrate how the return of a lost soul brings joy to heaven. A woman finds a lost coin, a shepherd finds a lost sheep, and each calls their friends together to celebrate. The third parable is that of the "prodigal son" who takes his inheritance, leaves home and spends it on riotous living. He returns home penniless and repentant. His father, overjoyed, kills the fatted calf and throws a great party. His elder brother refuses to take part, complaining that his father had never given him so much as a young goat for a merry-making with his friends. His father tries to cajole him: "you are always with me, and all that is mine is yours," but the finding of his brother who was lost, who seemed dead but is alive, absolutely necessitates a celebration (15:31–32).

The Gospels depict Jesus as engaging almost continually with his human friends and audiences, except for moments of withdrawal for prayer. He enjoys the hospitality of Martha, Mary, and their brother Lazarus at their village home in Bethany. He depends on friends who travel with him and support his work, a number of whom, as Luke records, are women:

> ... he went on through cities and villages, proclaiming and bringing the good news of the kingdom of God. The twelve were with him, as well as some women who had been cured of evil spirits and infirmities: Mary, called Magdalene, from whom seven demons had gone out, and Joanna, the wife of Herod's steward Chuza, and Susanna, and many others, who provided for them out of their resources. (Luke 8:1–3)

John names Mary Magdalene as one of the women who stood beside the cross, with Jesus's mother Mary and Mary the wife of Clopas. Among the men, John "the disciple whom Jesus loved" alone records himself as being close to the cross. The same group of women took spices to Jesus' tomb on the morning of his resurrection, and John's account of Jesus' resurrection appearance to Mary Magdalene testifies to their close friendship.

THE EARLY CHRISTIAN COMMUNITY, BONDED IN FRIENDSHIP

Luke's interest in friendship continues in his sequel, the Acts of the Apostles. The classical *topos* is echoed in his description of the Christian community in Jerusalem: they are bound together in devotion "to the apostles' teaching and fellowship (*koinōnia*), to the breaking of bread and the prayers" (Acts 2:42). They practice a radical sharing of possessions like that ascribed to the Pythagoreans (and which, according to Josephus, was also practiced within the Essenes, another contemporary Jewish group). Luke writes:

> All who believed were together and had all things in common; they would sell their possessions and goods and distribute the proceeds to all, as any had need. Day by day, as they spent much time together in the temple, they broke bread at home [*or* from house to house] and ate their food with glad and generous hearts, praising God and having the goodwill of all the people. (Acts 2:44–7)

Christian monasticism took its cue from this description and especially from Luke's second summary: "Now the whole group of those who believed were of one heart and soul, and no one claimed private ownership of any possessions, but everything they owned was held in common" (Acts 4:32).

The second half of Acts describes Paul's missionary adventures. Friends and co-workers feature constantly, sharing his journeys and supporting him during long stays in different cities. Acts mentions "friends" who assist him in Ephesus and Sidon (Acts 19:31, 27:3). Paul himself prefers familial language, speaking of fellow Christians as brothers (and sisters, when specifically mentioning women). Mutual friendship between Paul and the Christians at Philippi shines through his letter to them. He easily makes new friends, such as Aquila and Priscilla, the Jewish couple from Rome with whom he stayed in Corinth, who shared his own profession as tent-makers. They joined him in his missionary work (Acts 18:2–3, 18, 26). Paul ends his Letter to the Romans with special greetings to a long list of people, including Priscilla and Aquila and other "co-workers"; and he commends to the community at Rome one of his most striking friends and benefactors, Phoebe, a deacon in the church at Cenchreae, the eastern sea-port of Corinth, where the church meets in her house. Phoebe, it seems, is carrying Paul's letter to Rome, possibly on a business trip (Romans 16:1–2).

The Letter of James shifts the focus from friendships between human beings, and refers to Abraham's friendship with God (James 2:23). James warns against enmity with God: "Adulterers! Do you not know that friendship with the world is enmity with God? Therefore whoever wishes to be a friend of the world becomes an enemy of God" (James 4:4). Several early Christian writers, but not the NT, refer to Moses's friendship with God. Only a few years earlier, the Jewish scholar Philo of Alexandria (ca. 20 BC–ca. AD 50) moved the philosophical ground of friendship to common commitment to the worship of the one true Creator God, so that all who worship God, both Israelites and proselytes, are friends and relatives to one another.[21] Christians were making the same move, seeing true friendship as grounded in common commitment to Christ.

EARLY CHRISTIAN WRITERS

Among the earliest Christian writers, Justin Martyr (ca. 100–165) and Clement of Alexandria (ca. 150–215) show themselves familiar with the terms "friend of Christ" and "friend of God." Origen (ca. 185–ca. 254) commenting on Psalm 23, contrasts how Christ, as shepherd, once led his sheep to pasture, but now as friend he calls his friends to the eternal table. The fear of God makes us his servants; the knowledge of God's mysteries makes us his friends. The Egyptian Pachomius (ca. 290–346), founder of the first organized monastery, emphasized equal love between all the monks, and forbade particular friendships among the younger ones, revealing a tension between universal and particular friendship that ran on down the centuries in monastic circles.

The early Christian period culminates in the late fourth century when Christianity became the official religion of the Roman Empire. Theologians brought their classical training to bear on scripture, in a flowering of

Christian scholarship. The leading scholars in the Greek-speaking east were the "Cappadocian Fathers" and in the Latin-speaking west Ambrose and Augustine. The monastic movement was burgeoning at the same time, and began to provide Christian scholarship with its chief home.

Cappadocians

The Cappadocians mention friendship, without exploring it as a topic in itself. Gregory of Nyssa (ca. 330–95) presented the life of Moses, a biblical "friend of God," as an allegory of the spiritual life, urging his readers to long to be "known by God" and "become his friend."[22] In his commentary on the Song of Songs he combines the verse, "I am wounded by love" (Song 2:5), with Proverbs 27:6, saying that Christ is our true friend, wounded by love yet loving those who wound him, so that his wounds "are better than the kisses of an enemy."[23] Gregory of Nazianzus (ca. 330–390) quotes the prodigal son's father: "'all that is mine is yours,'" commenting that friends share everything because they are united in love and in the fellowship (*koinōnia*) of the Spirit.[24] For Basil of Caesarea (ca. 330–379), father of eastern Orthodox monasticism, monastic life is one of growth in *koinōnia*, in love for God and for all members equally, with all the ardent depth of *philia* (*Shorter* Rules 242).

Ambrose

The first Christian text on friendship comes from Ambrose (ca. 339–397), Bishop of Milan, then the imperial capital of the western Roman Empire, from 374 to 397. Writing in Latin, Ambrose placed an extended exhortation to friendship, for his priests and other ministers, at the close of his instructions "On the Duties of the Clergy" (*De officiis ministrorum*).[25] The "Duties" draws on scripture and two works of Cicero: "On duties" (*De officiis*) written for his son, and "On friendship" (*De amicitia*).

Ambrose addresses his clergy as his beloved "sons" whom he has chosen and tested—the language of choosing friends (*De off.* 1.24). Following Cicero he explores duty in terms of the four classical virtues, which, in another place, he names the "cardinal virtues." These are prudence (practical wisdom), fortitude (courage, determination), temperance (balance, moderation) and justice (righteousness, which includes goodwill, generosity, and mercy, making justice the seat of love, *caritas*). Ambrose illustrates his points from scripture, chiefly the OT, weaving in the advice on friendship from scripture's wisdom tradition:

> Goodwill (*benevolentia*) makes wounds inflicted by a friend more beneficial than kisses given freely by an enemy. Goodwill makes those who were many

to become one, for though friends may be many they do become one, with one spirit and one mind. We see, too, that even rebukes are agreeable when they are delivered in the context of friendship, for while they carry the power to sting, they do not carry real pain. We are stung by the critical words, but we are pleased by the thoughtfulness or goodwill which lie behind them. (1.173)

Cicero advised his son that it is more expedient and honorable for a leader to seek the love (*caritas*) of the people rather than their fear; and such a leader will not lack friends. Conversely, Ambrose suggests, a leader who exemplifies faithful friendship will attract general goodwill:

No wonder the wise man says: "Lose money for a brother and a friend" (Sir. 29:10). And in another passage: "I will not blush to greet a friend, and I will not hide myself from his face" (Sir. 22:25), since in a friend there is "the medicine of life and of immortality," (Sir. 6.16) as the words of Ecclesiasticus testify; and no one should be in any doubt that it is in love that our strongest defence lies, for the apostle says: "it bears all things, believes all things, hopes all things, endures all things; love never fails" (1 Cor. 13:7–8). (II.37)

It is through a discussion of integrity and conflicting loyalties, that Ambrose launches into his final exhortation on friendship. He starts with a fundamental rule: "Friendship is only commendable . . . when it preserves what is honourable" (III.125). For Ambrose, faith is honorable; therefore he says, "It is never right to break faith for the sake of friendship. No one can be a true friend to man if he has been unfaithful to God" (III.133). But nothing is more beautiful than a friendship that is marked by truth and frankness, able to accommodate friendly correction. "Open your heart to your friend so that he will be faithful to you, and so that you will know joy in your own life from him. For: 'a faithful friend is the medicine of life,' the grace of immortality" (Sir. 6:16, III.129). Ambrose urges his priests to support their friends in need, to be the first in doing kindness, to bear one another's burdens (Gal. 6:2, III.129) and be ready to endure hardship and enmity on their friend's behalf.

So, my sons, take good care of the friendship you have entered into with your brothers: in the whole range of human life, there is nothing more wonderful than this. It really is a comfort in this life to have someone to whom you can open your heart, someone with whom you can share your innermost feelings, and someone in whom you can confide the secrets of your heart . . . who will always be faithful to you, someone who will rejoice with you when things are going well, sympathize with you when circumstance are hard, and encourage you in times of persecution. (III.132)

With a friend, "you join your spirit to his, . . . your aim is to be no longer two, but one. You entrust yourself to him as to another self, you fear nothing from him, and you do not ask anything dishonourable from him" (III.134). Friendship is expressed in goodwill and respect and is often more genuine among the poor than the rich; for "friendship is a virtue, not a means to material gain . . . " (III.134). Ambrose is the first Christian writer to name friendship unequivocally "a virtue." In so doing he comes closer than any writer before his own protégé Augustine, to calling love itself "a virtue."

"Is there anything more precious than friendship?" Ambrose asks. (III.136) It is common to humans and angels. "God himself makes us his friends, though we are really the very lowliest of his servants" (III.136; John 15:15). In his treatise on devout widowhood, Ambrose links celibacy, a "counsel of perfection," to friendship with God, because orders are given to subjects, but counsels to friends.[26] Christ gives us a pattern of friendship marked by oneness in spirit and mutual openness. How sharp then is the pain of betrayal. Ambrose applies the psalmist's sad reproach to a treacherous friend (Psalm 55:13) to Judas's betrayal of Jesus. But, as demonstrated by God's forgiveness to Job's unsympathetic "comforters" in response to Job's prayer for them, forgiveness and reconciliation are possible. "Arrogance did them nothing but harm; friendship brought them nothing but good" (III.138). On that note, Ambrose closes his exhortation.

Augustine

Augustine (354–430), a prodigious scholar, was born and educated in Roman north Africa, taught in Rome, and rose to become professor of rhetoric in imperial Milan. In youth he had been attracted to Manichaeism but in Milan he attended Ambrose's sermons, returned to mainstream Catholic Christianity and was baptized in 387. Back in north Africa, becoming Bishop of Hippo, he made a monastery in his episcopal household and produced voluminous writings, laying down the essential philosophical framework for western Christian theology throughout the Middle Ages.

Augustine's theological system is structured on his doctrine of love, *caritas*. He named *caritas* not merely a virtue but "the great and true virtue" which contains all the classical virtues and scriptural commandments. He defines *caritas* as love directed to God, and to all else in God and for God, contrasting with *cupiditas*:

> I call *caritas* the motion of the soul toward the enjoyment of God for his own sake, and the enjoyment of one's self and one's neighbour for the sake of God; but *cupiditas* is a motion of the soul toward the enjoyment of one's self, one's neighbour, or any corporal thing for the sake of something other than God.[27]

This immensely influential doctrine gives *caritas* a linear trajectory, as a selfless desire reaching towards God, which was not wholly hospitable to mutual love and friendship—and yet friends and friendship were immensely important to Augustine. He longed, he says, to love and be loved. He discusses friendship in his autobiographical *Confessions,* in the *City of God,* in other works, and not least in his correspondence with friends, both men and women, but never wrote a treatise on friendship.

When Augustine looks back at his early friendships he remembers an ambivalent experience, characterized by enjoyment but also shame, confusion, and pain. As a boy, friendship led him astray. He recalls vandalising a neighbor's pear tree with a group of friends, just for fun. As a young man he had a close friendship, "sweet to me beyond all the sweetnesses of life that I had experienced" but was drowned in grief when his friend fell ill and died.[28] He found solace among his intellectual friends in Carthage, and with a faithful concubine whom he never names, but dearly loved. Some of his friends followed him to Milan, were also converted and baptized, and returned with him to his new monastic life in north Africa, sharing their possessions on the pattern of Acts 4:32.

Now Augustine begins to speak of true friendship that can never be lost, grounded in common commitment to Christ and the shared gift of love "poured into our hearts by the Holy Spirit that has been given to us" (Romans 5:5). He writes to Marcianus, joyful that this old friend is approaching baptism because now their relationship, previously resting on merely mortal grounds, will be real and eternal in Christ.[29] He remarks that before his own conversion he could have had no true friend, because anyone who then had wished for him the things he wished for himself, would not have been a true friend. He approves Cicero's definition of friendship as "agreement in all things human and divine, together with *caritas* and *benevolentia,*" but adds that the truth about things divine, and hence also things human, is found in Christ, so true friendship rests on agreement in Christ, who commands us to love God, and love our neighbor as our self. "If, together with me, you hold most firmly to these two, our friendship will be true and eternal; and it will bind us together not only with one another, but with the Lord as well."[30]

In principle, all the redeemed in Christ are therefore friends of one another. Augustine the bishop found his circle of friendship much widened, to embrace "ordinary" people and many who needed healing. All were to be lovingly accommodated. In a sermon he remarks that when Jesus chose his friends he picked "not senators but fishermen."[31] We should not judge, but seek the good in everyone.[32] The offer of Christ's friendship is universal. All can be loved, either in a practical way or inwardly in prayer.[33]

Augustine is acutely aware of the anxieties and sorrows, from illness to treachery, that friendships bring in this fragile life. He lists them in his great work *City of God*; but there he also looks forward to the perfection of friendship in heaven, the "perfectly ordered and completely harmonious fellowship in the enjoyment of God, and of each other in God."[34]

Cassian

John Cassian (ca. 360–435) probably hailed from present-day Romania. He left home as a youth with his friend Germanus, both intent on becoming monks in Bethlehem. While there they journeyed to Egypt to bring back wisdom from the desert fathers. Some years later, in 415, after a time in Constantinople, Cassian moved to Marseilles in southern Gaul. There he founded a complex of monasteries for men and women. Fluent in Greek and Latin, he conveyed the wisdom of desert monasticism to the west in two Latin books, the *Institutes* which provides rules for monastic life and the overcoming of vices, and the *Conferences* which conveys teaching on the spiritual life in the form of twenty-four talks by desert fathers. Both books were recommended by Benedict in his Rule, thus becoming permanently embedded in western monasticism.

Conference Sixteen, "On Friendship" (*De amicitia*) is given by Abba Joseph, a hermit in the Nile delta who came from a leading family, was well educated and spoke eloquently in Greek. His cue to speak on friendship comes when he asks Cassian and Germanus whether they are blood brothers. They reply that they are joined by "spiritual brotherhood" and a lasting bond of common commitment.

Joseph opens in classical style, reflecting on the many reasons that bonds of love may form: perhaps through kinship, a shared interest or occupation, or the attractiveness of a person of good reputation. Even robbers value their companions, and animals and birds cherish their young. But all these relationships are common to good and bad alike, and are impermanent. Only one love (*caritas*) is indissoluble, and that is based on similarity in virtue and depends on continued commitment by both partners.

Joseph lists six foundations for "true friendship," which are essentially basic rules for monastic life. First, contempt for worldly wealth and for all possessions and possessiveness; second, to restrain one's will, bow to that of others and not assume one is wiser than others; third, to set nothing above "the good of love and peace"; fourth, to "never be angered for any reason, whether just or unjust"; fifth, to seek to calm any anger that another may have conceived against one; and sixth, to reflect daily that one is going to depart from this world, which helps to prevent us both from annoying others and feeling annoyed. Anger at petty things is to be avoided and so too is dissension over doctrinal matters. This is what is meant by having one heart and soul, and loving one another according to Christ's commandment.

"Finally," says Joseph, "the virtue of love is so great" that John the Apostle says it is God himself, so when Paul says God's love has been poured out in our hearts by the Holy Spirit, "it is as if he were saying that God has been poured out in our hearts" (XIII). It is possible to show this love (*caritas*), which is *agapē*, to all, even our enemies; but we love our kin, and the virtuous, with added "affection" (*diathesis, adfectio*), as Jesus loved John, and this is perfectly "ordered" love (XIV).

Some stubborn brothers, Joseph adds, refuse to reconcile, rejecting Christ's command not to let the sun go down on their anger (XV–XVI) and feigning patience with a resentful silence (XVIII). Some even refuse to eat, but are merely feeding their pride, sacrificing to demons and not to God (XIX). But a monk should aim for genuine tranquillity of heart (XXII). When mistreated or annoyed, monks practice deep forbearance and patience, not taking revenge but loving from an enlarged heart, looking forward to reconciliation (XXIII–XXVII). Cassian ends by saying all who heard Joseph speak on friendship were inspired "all the more ardently to make enduring the love (*caritas*) of our companionship" (XXVIII).

CONCLUSION

Friendship acquired a new meaning in the NT as God's open friendship in Christ, offered to all. God's friendship transcends the limits of human friendship, reconciles human beings to God and transforms them into friends of God and of one another. Early Christian writers emphasized how love (*agapē, caritas*) had become the great virtue and a divine gift, containing within itself all the earlier virtues and the scriptural commandments. They understood friendship as true and eternal, grounded in common commitment to Christ. In our own day, the Christian emphasis lies on friendship in Christ as a sign of human unity and a source of friendship-love that reaches out to those in need, irrespective of faith or any other difference, seeking to heal the wounds of this world.

NOTES

1. Bible quotations are from the New Revised Standard Version (NRSV).

2. John Burnaby, *Amor Dei. A Study of the Religion of St Augustine* (London: Hodder & Stoughton, 1938; reprinted with corrections, Norwich: Canterbury Press, 1991), 21.

3. For a fuller discussion see Liz Carmichael, *Friendship: Interpreting Christian Love* (London: T&T Clark, Continuum [now Bloomsbury] 2004, corrected 2006), 7–67.

4. Cicero, *De amicitia* 24, trans. W.A. Falconer; Loeb Classical Library (London: Heinemann, 1923, repr. 1964).

5. For example, Pontius Pilate, the Roman governor of Judea, owed his position to the patronage of the Emperor Tiberius; hence in John's account the leaders were able to threaten Pilate: "If you release this man, you are no friend of the emperor" (John 19:12). Luke remarks that until that day Pilate had been at enmity with Herod Antipas, ruler of Galilee, but after Pilate sent Jesus to Herod for questioning, the two became "friends" (Luke 23:12). Whether personal or political is not specified. John the Baptist is described at John 3.29 as the "Friend of the Bridegroom," a "best man" appointed to prepare for the arrival of the bridegroom, Jesus.

6. Aristotle, *NE* 8.11, 1161b5.

7. Aristotle, *NE* 8.2, 1155b19.

8. Cicero, *De amicitia,* 20.

9. Plutarch, summarizing classical literature, names these pairs in "On Having Many Friends," in *Moralia* (Cambridge, MA: Harvard University Press, 1928), LCL 222: 50–51.

10. Aristotle, *NE* 8.11, 1161a24–25; 8.12, 1162a16–34.

11. Aristotle, *NE* 8.8, 1159a27–33.

12. Xenophon, *Symposium* iv.49.

13. Plato, *Symposium* 212A.

14. J. M. Rist, *Epicurus: An Introduction* (Cambridge: Cambridge University Press, 1972), 158.

15. Plato, *Lysis* 207D.

16. These verbs alternate at John 21:15–17, probably simply for stylistic reasons (Carmichael 2004, 37).

17. During the early twentieth century the argument was popular among German-speaking biblical scholars that *agapē* had been coined specifically to denote strong, disinterested divine love, contrasted with *eros* as weak, self-interested human love (*philia* being dismissed as a mere subset of *eros*). This view was expounded in Anders Nygren's influential book, *Agape and Eros* (1930–36). English-speaking scholarship challenged it, and by the 1980s it was overtaken by a renewed interest in friendship.

18. *De Abraham* II.ii.5, PL14, 458.

19. Ambrose, *Expos. Evang. Sec. Luc.*1.12. PL15 1538C.

20. Ambrose, *De off.* I.38–9; III.136.

21. Philo, *Mos.*2.171; *Spec.*1.317, 3.155.

22. Gregory of Nyssa, *The Life of Moses* (trans. and notes by A. J. Malherbe and E. Ferguson), CWS, New York: Paulist Press, 1978, 320.

23. *In Cant. Hom.*13, PG 44.1044B-C.

24. *Ep.* 168.

25. *De off.* III.124–138. Quotations are from Ambrose, *De Officiis*, edited with an Introduction, Translation, and Commentary by Ivor J. Davidson, 2 vols, (Oxford: Oxford University Press, 2001). See also Carmichael (2004), 41–51.

26. *De viduis* 72, PL16.

27. *On Christian Doctrine*, III.x.16, trans. D. W. Robertson, Jr., Library of Liberal Arts (Indianapolis: Bobbs-Merrill, 1958; repr. 1978).

28. *Confessions* IV.iv.7 trans. H. Chadwick (Oxford: Oxford University Press, 1992).

29. *Ep.* 258, to Marcianus. PL33.

30. *Ep.* 258.4, PL33.1073.

31. *Sermo* 87.x.12, PL38.536–7.

32. *De div. quaest.* 83 q.71.5–6, PL40.81–3.

33. *Ep.*130.vi.13, to Proba, PL33.499.

34. *City of God* XIX.8, 17, trans. H. Bettenson (Harmondsworth: Penguin, 1972).

BIBLIOGRAPHY

Note: PG, PL, refer to Migne, Patrologia Graeca, and Patrologia Latina.

Ambrose, *De Officiis*. Edited, with an Introduction, Translation, and Commentary, by Ivor J. Davidson. 2 vols. Oxford: Oxford University Press, 2001.

Aristotle. *Nicomachean Ethics.* Translated by H. Rackham. Loeb Classical Library 73. Cambridge, MA: Harvard University Press, 1926.

Augustine, *City of God*. Translated by H. Bettenson. Harmondsworth: Penguin, 1972.

Burnaby, John, *Amor Dei. A Study of the Religion of St Augustine*. London: Hodder & Stoughton, 1938; reprinted with corrections, Norwich: Canterbury Press, 1991.

Augustine, *Confessions*. Translated by H. Chadwick. Oxford: Oxford University Press, 1992.

Augustine, *On Christian Doctrine*. Translated by D. W. Robertson, Jr. Library of Liberal Arts. Indianapolis: Bobbs-Merrill, 1958; repr. 1978.

Cassian, John, *The Conferences*. Translated by B. Ramsey, OP. Ancient Christian Writers, 57. New York: Paulist Press, 1997.

Carmichael, Liz, *Friendship: Interpreting Christian Love*. London: T&T Clark, Continuum (now Bloomsbury) 2004, corrected 2006.

Cicero, M. Tullius, *De Amicitia*. Translated by W. A. Falconer. Loeb Classical Library. London: Heinemann, 1923, repr. 1964.

Gregory of Nyssa, *The Life of Moses*. Translated and notes by A. J. Malherbe and E. Ferguson. CWS. New York: Paulist Press, 1978.

Plutarch. *Moralia*, Translated by Frank Cole Babbitt. 15 vols: Loeb Classical Library 222. Cambridge, MA: Harvard University Press, 1928.

Rist, J. M., *Epicurus: An Introduction*. Cambridge: Cambridge University Press, 1972.

Chapter 9

Seeking God Together in Christ
Friendship in the Christian Life

Paul J. Wadell

It is impossible to be a Christian without friends. Don't even try. That is not only because a good and happy life—a genuinely human life—is impossible without friends, but also because no one becomes a Christian all on her own any more than one grows, develops, and flourishes all on her own. There is no self-made Christian, no solitary disciple. Christianity is a wholly absorbing, difficult but abundantly hopeful, way of life that requires companions who guide, support, love, challenge, and encourage one another (just as good friends do) as *together* they strive to grow in the love, goodness, and holiness of God.

This chapter will explore why friendship matters for Christians—why it is integral to the Christian life—but also why Christians think somewhat differently about friendship than ancient Greek, Roman, and Chinese philosophers did, and perhaps significantly differently than we think about friendship today. Christians can learn from, and be enriched by, what Plato, Aristotle, Cicero, Confucius, and our contemporaries think about friendship, but their understanding of friendship will differ in important ways because Christians tell another story, they are part of a different narrative. For Christians, friendship has a different trajectory because for Christians the goal of friendship goes beyond a virtuous life in this world to seeking fullness of joy with God and the saints. Augustine, the great theologian of early Christianity, knew this; the twelfth-century monk Aelred of Rievaulx certainly did as well; and so did Thomas Aquinas, the thirteenth-century theologian whose writings on the Christian life remain stunningly relevant eight centuries later. Because friendship was at the core of their theologies, Augustine, Aelred, and Aquinas are trustworthy guides for helping us grasp the central importance of friendship in the Christian life as well as what is distinctive about a Christian theology of friendship. Because Aelred and Aquinas built on Augustine's foundational theology of friendship, more extensive analysis will be given to what Augustine thought about the role of friendship in the Christian life.

Thus, the first part of the chapter will introduce Augustine. Friendship played a pivotal role in his understanding of himself and his understanding of what it means to be human. Augustine was deeply influenced by classical philosophies of friendship, but, as we shall see, his understanding of the meaning, purpose, and responsibilities of friendship notably changed after he became a Christian. In the second part of the chapter, we'll turn to Aelred of Rievaulx and consider what his classic work *Spiritual Friendship* contributes to a Christian theology of friendship. We'll discover that although Aelred's view of friendship was undoubtedly influenced by Cicero and Augustine, he goes beyond them by giving more attention to false forms of friendship, relationships that should never be called "friendships" because they are morally and spiritually corrupting. Finally, the chapter will conclude with an analysis of Thomas Aquinas' description of the theological virtue of charity as a life of friendship with God that unfolds in an ever expanding love and friendship for others, including some of the ways Aquinas says friends of God are called to do God's work in the world.

AUGUSTINE

Augustine was born in northern Africa in 354. A man of tremendous intellect and talent, passion and energy, and a superb speaker and writer, Augustine's legacy has indelibly marked the substance and development of Christian theology.[1] One cannot dip their toe in the waters of Christian theology without soon reckoning with Augustine. But Augustine is also an apt mentor for appreciating the place of friendship in the Christian life.[2] Augustine did not become a Christian until 387 when he was thirty-three years old, but we would be mistaken to think that Augustine only became interested in friends the day he was baptized. Augustine was formed by a tradition that understood friendships to be the key personal relationships of our lives. Yes, friendships are comforting and reassuring, they bring pleasure and joy to our lives. But, even more, Augustine insists, it is impossible to take even our first steps on our life's journey without friends. We should never see friends as lifestyle options we can either accept or reject as we wish because human beings are inescapably social creatures who are fashioned to be in relationship with one another and who, from the beginning to end of our lives, absolutely need and depend on one another. Augustine taught that human beings are created *for friendship* and that the deep meaning of life is that people should live together as friends. This is why there is no happiness, no peace, and no lasting satisfaction in our lives without good friends. It is also why he believed that we never outgrow our need for friends. At every stage of life, we need people who want our good, who agree with us on what matters most in life, and who are joined with us as together we pursue what we love and believe will fulfill us.[3]

Consider the *Confessions*, Augustine's spiritual autobiography of the first thirty-three years of his life leading to his conversion to Christianity. Even a casual reading of the *Confessions* reveals that Augustine is hardly ever alone. He is almost always with friends, talking and joking with them, remembering things they did together as children, imagining future adventures with friends, or, in one memorable scene, blaming his friends for persuading him to join them the night they stole pears from a neighbor. Friendship pervades Augustine's life; it is impossible to understand who he is apart from his friends.

Augustine offers the fullest account of his understanding of friendship in Book IV of the *Confessions* when Augustine, now a teacher in Thagaste, the town where he was born, recalls the death of a friend, a death that throws Augustine into a prolonged depression and wrenching desolation. "As a boy he had grown up with me; we had gone to school and played together," Augustine tells us. He was a friend "who shared my interests and was exceedingly dear to me," so much so that Augustine declares that it was "a friendship sweeter to me than any sweetness I had known in all my life."[4] These passages highlight some of the fundamental characteristics of the classical understanding of friendship that significantly informed Augustine's own view of friendship.[5]

First, like Cicero and Aristotle, Augustine emphasizes that friendships are formed around shared interests and activities. Friends share similar values, beliefs, and purposes, and they enjoy similar activities. Second, when Augustine writes that his friend was "exceedingly dear to me," like his philosophical predecessors, he reminds us that friendship is a bond of mutual love and affection. Friends obviously like one another and enjoy one another's company, but they also love and care for one another, and thus are devoted to one another's good. This is why friends have good will (benevolence) toward one another and are actively committed to seeking one another's good (beneficence). Third, when Augustine says that they had been friends since youth, he recognizes friendships need time to grow and develop, and that the deepest and most lasting friendships are often ones that span notable periods of our lives. There are no "instant friendships" because the intimacy that lives at the heart of good friendship deepens the longer the history that is shared between the friends. This is one reason friends want nothing more than spending time together and why people who do not have time for one another can never really be friends.

A fourth characteristic of the classical understanding of friendship that Augustine mentions when recounting the death of his friend is that because of all friends share between them and the deep love that unites them, a friend can rightly be described as "another self."[6] The unity that the love of friendship creates is so penetrating and resilient it is as if one soul lives between the friends.[7] Augustine movingly describes this aspect of friendship when he says that when his friend died he felt that part of him had died with his friend, but also that something of his friend would continue to live in him. "I was . . . still more amazed that I could go on living myself when he was dead—I, who had been like another self to him," Augustine recalls. "It was well said," he continues, "that a friend is half one's own soul. I felt that my soul and his had been but one soul in two bodies, and I shrank from life with loathing because I could not bear to be only half alive; and perhaps I was so afraid of death because I did not want the whole of him to die, whom I had loved so dearly."[8] How is Augustine finally able to move beyond his sorrow and grief? How is he able to find healing and to reconnect with life? Not surprisingly, it is through the comfort, support, and encouragement of other friends.[9]

Friendship in the Christian Life

What Augustine says about friendship in the *Confessions*—as well as the numerous letters he wrote throughout his life to friends—indicates how extensively classical understandings of friendship, particularly Cicero's *De Amiticia*, shaped his own understanding of friendship and provided a framework for developing his theology of friendship once he became a Christian.[10] And yet, after he converted to Christianity, his understanding of the meaning and purpose and practice of friendship radically shifted.[11] As Coleman Ford notes in *A Bond Between Souls—Friendship in the Letters of Augustine*, "Augustine uniquely transformed classical notions of friendship in service to the Christian life."[12] Rather than abandoning what he had learned about friendship from philosophers, he reformulated "classical notions of friendship into a deeply theological and spiritual relationship"[13] by considering how friendship among Christians, rather than distracting them from their life in Christ, might be an especially salutary means of serving that life.[14]

Augustine initially reveals how he came to a different understanding of friendship in the *Confessions*. Book VIII of the *Confessions* concludes with the story of Augustine's conversion, an event which occurs with his good friend Alypius, who is worried about Augustine, nearby.[15] Augustine is baptized that Easter by his friend and mentor, Ambrose, bishop of Milan. He leaves his position as a teacher of rhetoric, suffers through a terrible toothache that renders the usually chatty Augustine silent for a few days, and then begins to live the Christian life in a small community, a household of friends, that includes his mother, Alypius, his son Adeodatus, his brother Navigius, two of his cousins, and two of his students.[16] Like any real community (and like any real friends), these unique individuals hardly agree on everything, but they are able to live well together—to be happy and flourish together—because they are joined as one in what they take to be the fundamental calling of their lives: to help one another make their way to God by growing together in Christ.

If every friendship is built around shared goods, for the newly baptized Augustine, the deepest and most lasting friendships are centered around the highest and most excellent good, which now for him is loving God and helping one another on their journey to God. For the Christian Augustine, that's happiness, that's a life truly worth living.[17] And it beautifully illustrates the shape of the Christian life: coming together in relationships and communities with people who want what is best for one another, who share a common vision of life, who are united in the convictions and commitments that form them, and who help one another grow in love and goodness and holiness through friendship with God and one another. Ten years after his baptism, Augustine expanded on this idea when he wrote a short rule of life. Inspired by the passage in the Acts of the Apostles that describes the early Christians as being of "one heart and mind,"[18] Augustine envisioned a community of friends in which each one strove to love God and be united in mind and heart on their mutual journey to God.

Augustine's understanding of friendship and community can sound odd to us today because we live in societies that are often so fragmented and polarized that it can be exasperatingly hard to get people to be of "one heart and mind" about anything. Nor do we live in societies where people necessarily support one another, seek the best for each other, and help one another along. There is something countercultural—and some would say hopelessly naïve—about Augustine's vision of the Christian life. But, Christians believe, there is also something compelling and highly attractive about it because it shows that genuine community is possible, that we are happiest when we come together in pursuit of things that matter, and that when we make love for God and one another the center of our lives we can, despite all that can potentially divide us, live together in peace. These are the deepest longings of our hearts.

Augustine was a realist. He did not think getting people to be of "one heart and mind" would be easy, any more than he believed friendships and communities inspired by that desire would ever be perfect. But he did believe they were worth aspiring to because such friendships and communities exemplify what God wants for us and what God's grace makes possible for us. Instead of collapsing in on ourselves, valuing ourselves over others, seldom bothering to love, and living for nothing more than calculated self-interest, which is a sure path to despair, Augustine believed that the power of God's grace is to draw us out of ourselves into friendship and community with others. He believed this because he had taken to heart the passage in Romans 5:5 where Paul proclaims that "the love of God has been poured out into our hearts through the Holy Spirit that has been given to us."[19] Augustine held that God was no stingy lover. God had not poured that love into the hearts of a carefully chosen few, but into the hearts and souls of every person who had ever lived. That divinely given love is something every person shares together. It is a binding force that draws women and men across the ages into the deepest solidarity possible. And since friends share things in common, and since this extravagant grace marks every human being, Augustine could rightly claim that to live in friendship and community is to live in harmony with the deepest truth of our nature.

But there is more. Once he became a Christian, Augustine gave an intriguing twist to how he believed friendships began. We typically think that we choose our friends. They begin when, after some consideration, we take the initiative to reach out to another in friendship, or they take the initiative to reach out to us. But Augustine disagreed. He claimed that we do not carefully select our friends; rather, they are brought into our lives by God.[20] Friends are God's gifts to us, God's providential blessings through which God cares for us, watches over us, guides and sustains us, comforts and challenges us, and brings us more fully to life.[21] We do not seek these relationships; we receive them and are entrusted with them.[22] Friends are the specially chosen people that God brings into our lives so that we might experience God's love through them and grow in God's love with them. For Augustine, God loves us in and through our friends.

Augustine came to this understanding of friendship because he was convinced that what Paul wrote in 1 Corinthians 4:7 was undeniably true: "What do you possess that you have not received?" Like Paul, after his conversion Augustine came to see everything as a gift, everything as a gracious manifestation of God's personal and insightful love for us, including our friends. Friends are gifts of God's merciful and compassionate love, expressions of God's abiding care and goodness, and memorable examples of how God can sometimes take us by surprise. Most of all, in the life of real friendships, we discover that God loves us, reaches us, prods and blesses us not apart from our friends, but through them. God ministers to us through our friends. For Christians, behind the gift of the friend is the Gift-giver.

Remembering that friends are God's gifts to us can prevent us from ending too quickly relationships in which we further learn what it means to love God and our neighbors, and thus fulfill what Jesus taught are the two greatest commandments: "You shall love the Lord, your God, with all your heart, with all your soul, and with all your mind. This is the greatest and the first commandment. The second is like it: You shall love your neighbor as yourself"

(Mt 22:37–39). Rather than seeing these two commandments in unyielding opposition, as if to love God was to neglect to love our neighbors or ourselves, just as to love our neighbors or ourselves was to take time away from loving God, Augustine joined them together. For Christians, Augustine came to see, loving our friends should always lead to a deeper love for God not only because we recognize that our friends are gifts from God, but also because to love our friends is to want for them the very thing that we want for ourselves, namely that they love God more than anything else because God is the supreme good of every creature. This is why for Augustine, Marie Aquinas McNamara notes, "God is the end as He is the beginning of all true friendship."[23] Friendships begin as gifts of God's love for the sake of seeking God and growing in love of God.[24] But loving God should always lead to a deeper and more grateful love for our friends not only because God lives in them and in some unique way they image the goodness and loveliness of God, but also because our friends are the specially chosen neighbors God has brought into our lives to love in ways we cannot love everyone. In this way, Augustine avoids seeing love for God and love for others as rival loves locked in endless competition. Quite the contrary, he intimately connects them so that each love mutually enhances and strengthens the other.[25] This is why it is completely fitting to speak of Christian friendships as "schools of love."[26] Augustine knew that Christians grow in love and goodness and holiness not in imaginary relationships where loving is always easy and fulfilling, but in the very real relationships of our lives that are often uplifting and immensely gratifying, but can sometimes ask more of us than we think we can give.

What does this sketch of Augustine's theology of friendship tell us? First, Christian friendships can only rightly be understood when seen in light of the story of God's boundless and unending love. That makes all the difference. If Aristotle believed the highest form of friendship—and really the only true friendship—was among virtuous friends who sought happiness and well-being for one another through a virtuous life in this world, the *telos* or ultimate purpose and goal of friendship among Christians is the truly transcendent good of everlasting life and happiness with God and the saints.[27] To be a Christian is to continually orient one's life to God and to see that life as an ongoing journey to God. As they took that journey, friends helped one another remember *who they are, what they are about*, and *where they are going*. They are children of God and disciples of Christ who are called to the heavenly banquet, the everlasting feast with God and all the friends of God in heaven. They make their way to the feast by helping one another grow in friendship with God through their love and friendship with one another.

Second, Augustine shows us that for Christians friendship is a morally and spiritually transformative relationship that is integral to the Christian life. No one becomes a Christian alone. The Christian life is a wholly social enterprise that requires friends who help one another grow in gospel virtues and in the love and goodness of God. These friends *teach* one another about the love of God, *form* one another in the love of God, and help each other *practice* the love of God.[28] They do so through the love and kindness, care and concern, generosity and compassion they show not only to one another, but also to all the neighbors they pass along their way. They do not hoard their love, carefully parceling it out only to those in their tightly closed inner circle, but extend it liberally and lavishly in any way they can whenever they can because nobody loves like Christ by being stingy with love. And, Augustine insisted, Christians must extend the circle of love to their enemies not only because Christ commanded that they love their enemies, but also because all human beings share a common human nature, and especially because all have been loved and befriended by God.[29] Augustine urged his fellow Christians to love their enemies in the hope that by doing so they would change from being enemies to friends and would come to know and love God.[30]

Third, because the Christian life is a journey to God, if a friend sees her friend developing attitudes and behavior at odds with the example of Christ and detrimental to growing in goodness and holiness, she has the responsibility, Augustine insists, to call this to the attention of her friend.[31] Yes, friends should comfort and encourage and support one another, but sometimes they must correct one another. If the heart of friendship is to seek the good of a friend, how could we do that if we saw a friend developing ways of thinking and acting that were hurting her and others, and said nothing? In the Christian life, love does not always mean accepting the other person as she is; rather, love sometimes means exhorting and challenging her to become what God's love calls her to be and what God's grace helps her to be. For Augustine, a friend is different from a flatterer. Anyone can flatter us, anyone can tell us what we want to hear. But only someone who truly loves us will have courage enough to speak uncomfortable but necessary truths to us.

Fourth, despite the high value Augustine placed on friendships, he believed friendships will never give us the intimacy, love, peace, and joy we hope for in life. No friendship will ever be perfect. This is partly because we are finite, limited creatures who live in time and whose strongest desires can never be completely satisfied in this world. It is partly because even best friends fall short, hurting and disappointing one another no matter how hard they try to love one another. But it is also because we can never know and love—or be known and loved by—our friends as deeply and wholly and lastingly as we would wish. Even at their best and most intimate, Augustine believed, friendships are shadowed by a longing and incompleteness that can only be fulfilled in everlasting communion with God and the saints in heaven.[32] There is an *eschatological* character to Augustine's theology of friendship.[33] This does not mean the love and affection, the joy and delight that we experience with

our friends is unreal; rather, it means such friendships strain for and antici-
pate a fullness and perfection that can only be found in the "city of God"
where all will know and love God as they fully know and love one another.[34]
For Augustine, friendships are inherently hopeful because they point to, and
already share in, even if imperfectly and incompletely, the shimmering intimacy and unbreakable love that abound in friendship with God and the saints
in heaven.

AELRED OF RIEVAULX

The son of a married Catholic priest, Aelred was born in northern England in
1110.[35] As a young man, he served for a short time in the court of King David
of Scotland.[36] In 1134, Aelred entered the Cistercian abbey in Rievaulx and
thirteen years later was elected abbot.[37] Shortly after he was elected abbot,
Aelred began writing *Spiritual Friendship*, a short work composed of three
books, each of which is a dialogue between Aelred and one or more of his fellow monks at Rievaulx.[38] Aelred did not complete *Spiritual Friendship* until
shortly before his death in 1167.[39]

Even a cursory reading of *Spiritual Friendship* reveals that Aelred's understanding of friendship was highly influenced by Cicero and Augustine.[40]
Aelred wrote *Spiritual Friendship* to show his fellow monks how their
friendships could be integrated into their religious vocation, so that rather
than impeding, weakening, or competing with their relationship with Christ,
friendships could serve and strengthen that relationship.[41] Like Augustine,
Aelred believed that Christ is the center of spiritual friendships; indeed,
the friends are not only joined together by their mutual love for Christ, but
Christ is also actively part of their friendship. *Spiritual Friendship* opens
with Aelred telling his fellow monk Ivo: "Here we are, you and I, and I hope
a third, Christ, is in our midst."[42] A bit later, he says: "For what more sub-
lime can be said of friendship, what more true, than that it ought to, and is
proved to, begin in Christ, continue in Christ, and be perfected in Christ?"[43]
Thus, through spiritual friendship, the friends journey to God by imitating
Christ. Furthermore, like Augustine, Aelred said that love of God must be
the foundation of spiritual friendships,[44] so that through their friendship with
one another they become true friends of God.[45] And, as Augustine believed,
Aelred taught that a friend is "the companion of your soul, to whose spirit
you join and attach yours," so that eventually it is as if two had become one.[46]
In their life together, such friends comfort and support one another, bear one
another's burdens, confide in one another, and openly confess their failings
lest they stray from the path to God.[47] Finally, like Augustine, for Aelred

spiritual friendships are perfected "in the life to come" where all are joined in friendship and "God shall be all in all."[48]

But Aelred goes beyond Augustine by giving much more attention to relationships that are counterfeit versions of friendship, relationships that ought not be described as friendships at all because they are morally and spiritually harmful. The first he calls *carnal friendships*. Although the term might be strange to us, the reality of carnal friendships certainly is not. These are relationships in which each person plays on the other's weaknesses, encouraging one another in behavior that is morally and spiritually corrupting. Unlike true friendship, carnal friendships are built around shared weaknesses; they spring "from mutual harmony in vice."[49] In these relationships, each person has found someone with whom they will be comfortable doing wrong as together they develop habits by which they increasingly diminish themselves and harm others. Such relationships should never be described as friendships, first because true friendships should always make us better, not worse. And second because the quintessential quality of friendship is that friends have good will toward one another and help one another seek what is best, which is hardly the case with these corrupting relationships.[50]

The other counterfeit expression of friendship Aelred names *worldly friendships*. At first glance, they seem less worrisome than carnal friendships, but in some respects they are more dangerous because their corrupting effects can be harder to spot. Aelred says worldly friendships are characterized by a "desire for temporal advantage or possessions," and are "always full of deceit and intrigue."[51] Unlike true friendships in which each friend focuses on the good of the other, worldly friendships are essentially self-serving relationships whose fundamental aim is the promotion and advancement of oneself. The question lurking behind every worldly friendship is "What's in it for me?" Today we might call these relationships "friends with benefits." Thus, even though the term "worldly friendship" comes from a twelfth-century monk, these relationships are hardly relics of a bygone age. Quite the contrary, worldly friendships can be found almost everywhere: in high school and college, in business, in politics, in academic life, in churches, and certainly on social media.

For Aelred, worldly friendships endanger the Christian life because through them one becomes excessively focused on the goods of this world—money, possessions, status and recognition, comfort and pleasure—so that he grows gradually unmindful of God. He becomes overly attached to—and ambitious about—the things of this world so that he increasingly neglects his spiritual life and eventually even forgets that his life concerns God. Immersed in worldly friendships, flittering from one relationship to another, he becomes too at home in the world, too settled, so that he no longer recognizes that he is a pilgrim on a journey to God, a journey that promises far more joy and peace and satisfaction than all the world's goods could ever provide. Aelred's warning is clear: if we surrender to worldly friendships, we forget *who we are*, *what we are about*, and *where we are going* because something other than God has become the object of our hope.

THOMAS AQUINAS

Thomas Aquinas was born near Aquino, a small town between Rome and Naples, around the year 1225. When he was nineteen, Aquinas entered the Dominicans, a religious community he admired for their life of poverty, prayer, and preaching. After he was ordained a priest in 1250, he was sent to teach in Paris. In 1265, Aquinas was sent to teach in Rome. It was there that he began his *magnum opus*, the *Summa Theologiae*, which is widely considered the most significant theological work ever written, even though Aquinas considered it a "beginner's book" in theology! Aquinas worked on the *Summa Theologiae* over the next eight years as he moved from Rome back to Paris and from Paris to Naples, where, after a mysterious experience early on the morning of December 6, 1273, he abruptly stopped writing.[52] Aquinas never finished the *Summa Theologiae*, but his treatise on the theological virtue of charity in the *Summa* lifts up an important element to a Christian theology of friendship.[53]

Aquinas described charity as a life of friendship with God that continually unfolds in love for others. If we describe someone as "charitable," we typically mean that she is kind and thoughtful, generous and considerate. All that is right, but, for Aquinas, charity means so much more. For him, God befriends us so that we can live in friendship with God, and from that friendship reach out in an ever expansive friendship of others.[54] Aquinas realized that if friends refuse to open their friendship to others, including those they might initially feel comfortable avoiding, that friendship risks becoming dangerously self-centered. As Jesus suggested, should we really be content with a love that doesn't venture beyond those who love us (Mt 6:46)? In his account of charity, Aquinas showed that Christians avoid this risk when they realize that friendship is not an end in itself, but exists to serve a larger purpose, namely, to participate in the creative and redemptive activity of God in the world. Christian friendship is completed in the call to do God's work in the world. Without this outward direction, friendships can become "clubby" and exclusive, thereby narrowing the horizons of our world so that we become increasingly picky about whom we decide to love. Aquinas's understanding of charity pushes against the temptation to shrink our circle of concern by arguing that since God has loved and befriended everyone, true friends of God should reach out to "all those put on the path alongside us"[55] with a love that cuts across the social, economic, ethnic, racial, national, and religious boundaries that typically circumscribe our lives.

How are Christians in their friendship with God called to contribute to the work of God? There are many ways, but in Aquinas's analysis of the six "acts" or "effects" of charity, three may be most pertinent for a Christian theology of friendship: mercy, kindness, and almsgiving. Mercy or compassion is the act of love by which we befriend those "put on the path alongside us" who are suffering and in pain, broken, burdened, discouraged, and disillusioned, perhaps barely hanging on.[56] With mercy, the sufferings of another person touch us, drawing us out of ourselves to be with them in their sorrow and affliction, and to do what we can to help them. Instead of turning away from someone who is suffering, with compassion we move toward him so that he does not have to suffer alone. A life of charity compels Christians to be grieved by the suffering of others precisely because true friends of God see all persons not as strangers, but as fellow human beings who are loved and befriended by God. A Christian theology of friendship summons friends to be ministers of mercy and compassion to all. Indeed, Aquinas wrote that God "shows forth his almighty power" principally through his compassion, and that it is compassion that makes us most like God.[57]

Kindness is the act of charity by which we do good for another. It is not thinking about doing good, but doing it in all the ways it can be done whenever the occasion arises for whomever the neighbor is who crosses our path, even if that neighbor is our enemy.[58] As a practice of charity and Christian friendship, kindness fights the temptation to turn in on ourselves by summoning us to be on the lookout for ways to do good. With kindness, Christian friends carry on the work of God by being continually attuned to opportunities to bless, encourage, support, comfort, and affirm not only those closest to them, but also any person they may encounter on any ordinary day. As Aquinas observed, a person of kindness is intentionally poised to do good "if the occasion arises and whoever the person in need may be."[59]

Finally, almsgiving is the practice of Christian friendship that responds to the bodily needs of others, particularly the most destitute and vulnerable members of society.[60] Aquinas broadened almsgiving beyond its customary meaning of giving money to the poor by linking it with the traditional corporal works of mercy outlined in Jesus' parable of the Last Judgment (Mt. 25:31–46): feeding the hungry, giving drink to the thirsty, clothing the naked, sheltering the homeless, visiting the sick, visiting the imprisoned, and burying the dead.[61] Clearly, Aquinas could not fathom how one could live in friendship with God if she ignored the bodily needs of her neighbors. In a world where millions are starving and homeless, everyday struggling to survive; in a world where migrants and refugees are often turned away rather than welcomed; in a world where violence and war leave far too many dead needing to be buried, the calling to practice the corporal works of mercy could not be more urgent. Moreover, given the evidence of global climate change, the growing extinction of species, and the depletion of natural resources, it is clear that the body we call Earth is also suffering and in pain. A Christian theology of friendship summons us to extend mercy and compassion not just to human bodies, but to the whole of creation.

CONCLUSION

This chapter has explored the role of friendship in the Christian life. Augustine, Aelred of Rievaulx, and Thomas Aquinas each insists that human beings cannot have a genuinely good human life without friends. But they also claim that Christians think differently about friendship because their lives are guided by the story of God's creative and redemptive love. In a Christian theology of friendship, friends are companions on a journey to God. As they take that journey, these friends help one another grow in the love and goodness of God through their mutual imitation of Christ. But as they take that journey they also reach out in befriending love to all they pass along the way. Instead of turning in on themselves, their love for God unfolds in active and insightful love for others. In this way, they do the work of God and give thanks for having been blessed with such a joyous way of life through and with their friends.

NOTES

1. For a superb account of the life of Augustine, see Peter Brown, *Augustine of Hippo: A Biography* (Berkeley: University of California Press, 1967).

2. For how other contemporary Christian scholars interpret Augustine's understanding of friendship, each in ways that support the analysis offered in this chapter, see Carolinne White, *Christian Friendship in the Fourth Century* (Cambridge: Cambridge University Press, 1992), 185–217; Brian Patrick McGuire, *Friendship and Community: The Monastic Experience 350–1250* (Kalamazoo, MI: Cistercian Publications, 1988), 47–57; Liz Carmichael, *Friendship: Interpreting Christian Love* (London: T&T Clark International, 2004), 55–68; Victor Lee Austin, *Friendship: The Heart of Being Human* (Grand Rapids: Baker Academic, 2020), 76–79; and Coleman M. Ford, *A Bond Between Souls: Friendship in the Letters of Augustine* (Bellingham, WA: Lexham Academic, 2022). For an excellent but slightly different interpretation, see Gilbert C. Meilaender, *Friendship: A Study in Theological Ethics* (Notre Dame, IN: University of Notre Dame Press, 1981), 16–24.

3. White, *Christian Friendship*, 85. See also Austin, *Friendship*, 76–77.

4. Augustine, *The Confessions*, trans. Maria Boulding, OSB (Hyde Park, NY: New City, 1997), IV.7.

5. For an overview of the principal characteristics of good friendships, see Paul J. Wadell, *Becoming Friends: Worship, Justice, and the Practice of Christian Friendship* (Grand Rapids: Brazos, 2002), 55–65.

6. White, *Christian Friendship*, 194.

7. White, *Christian Friendship*, 188.

8. Augustine, *Confessions*, IV.11.

9. Augustine, *Confessions*, IV.13.

10. Ford, *Bond Between Souls*, 15.

11. Ford, *Bond Between Souls*, 54.

12. Ford, *Bond Between Souls*, 10.

13. Ford, *Bond Between Souls*, 53.

14. For a more extensive analysis of Augustine's theology of friendship, see Wadell, *Becoming Friends*, 77–95.

15. Augustine, *Confessions*, VIII.19.

16. Augustine, *Confessions*, IX.7.

17. Paul J. Wadell, *Happiness and the Christian Moral Life: An Introduction to Christian Ethics*, 3rd ed. (Lanham, MD: Rowman & Littlefield, 2016), 8–15.

18. Acts 4:32. Scripture references are taken from Jean Marie Hiesberger, general editor, *The Catholic Student Bible* (New York: William H. Sadlier, 1995). Subsequent references will be cited in the text.

19. White, *Christian Friendship*, 196. See also Augustine, *Confessions*, IV.4.

20. White, *Christian Friendship*, 196. See also Austin, *Friendship*, 77.

21. Marie Aquinas McNamara, OP, *Friendship in Saint Augustine* (Fribourg: University Press, 1958), 202.

22. Augustine, *Confessions*, IV.7.

23. McNamara, *Friendship in Saint Augustine*, 206.

24. White, *Christian Friendship*, 201.

25. White, *Christian Friendship*, 202.

26. On this point, see Meilaender, *Friendship*, 17–22.

27. Wadell, *Becoming Friends*, 83–84.

28. Wadell, *Becoming Friends*, 84.

29. Ford, *Bond Between Souls*, 20.

30. White, *Christian Friendship*, 207.

31. White, *Christian Friendship*, 193.

32. White, *Christian Friendship*, 204.

33. Wadell, *Becoming Friends*, 92–94.

34. Wadell, *Friendship and the Moral Life* (Notre Dame, IN: University of Notre Dame Press, 1989), 100.

35. For other studies of Aelred of Rievaulx's view of the role of friendship in the Christian life that support the interpretation offered in this section of the chapter, see McGuire, *Friendship and Community*, 296–338; Carmichael, *Friendship*, 70–100; and Austin, *Friendship*, 82–92.

36. McGuire, *Friendship and Community*, 302.

37. Austin, *Friendship*, 83.

38. For a more extensive account of Aelred of Rievaulx's *Spiritual Friendship*, see Wadell, *Becoming Friends*, 97–118.

39. McGuire, *Friendship and Community*, 308.

40. McGuire, *Friendship and Community*, 299.

41. McGuire, *Friendship and Community*, 297.

42. Aelred of Rievaulx, *Spiritual Friendship*, trans. Mary Eugenia Laker, SSND (Kalamazoo: Cistercian, 1977) I.1.

43. Aelred of Rievaulx, *Spiritual Friendship*, I.9.

44. Aelred of Rievaulx, *Spiritual Friendship*, III.5.

45. Aelred of Rievaulx, *Spiritual Friendship*, II.14.

46. Aelred of Rievaulx, *Spiritual Friendship*, III.6.

47. Aelred of Rievaulx, *Spiritual Friendship*, II.11–12.

48. Aelred of Rievaulx, *Spiritual Friendship*, III.134.

49. Aelred of Rievaulx, *Spiritual Friendship*, I.38.

50. Wadell, *Becoming Friends*, 102–03.

51. Aelred of Rievaulx, *Spiritual Friendship*, I.42.

52. The material for this biographical sketch of Aquinas is from Paul J. Wadell, *The Primacy of Love: An Introduction to the Ethics of Thomas Aquinas* (New York: Paulist), 7–16. For a more comprehensive account of the life of Aquinas, see James A. Weisheipl, OP, *Friar Thomas D'Aquino: His Life, Thought, and Works* (Garden City, NY: Doubleday, 1974).

53. For other contemporary studies of Aquinas on charity that support and expand on what is offered here, see Daniel Schwartz, *Aquinas on Friendship* (Oxford: Oxford University Press, 2007); Mary Ann Fatula, OP, *Thomas Aquinas, Preacher and Friend* (Collegeville, MN: Liturgical), 154–180; Edward Collins Vacek, SJ, *Love, Human and Divine: The Heart of Christian Ethics* (Washington, DC: Georgetown University Press, 1994), 319–330; Eberhard Schockenhoff, "The Theological Virtue of Charity," trans. Grant Kaplan and Frederick G. Lawrence, in *The Ethics of Aquinas*, ed. Stephen J. Pope (Washington, DC: Georgetown University Press), 244–58; Bernard V. Brady, *Christian Love: How Christians Through the Ages Have Understood Love* (Washington, DC: Georgetown University Press, 2003) 164–79; Carmichael, *Friendship*, 101–28; and Stephen J. Pope, "Christian Love as Friendship: Engaging the Thomistic Tradition," in *Love and Christian Ethics: Tradition, Theory, and Society*, ed. Frederick V. Simmons with Brian C. Sorrells (Washington, DC: Georgetown University Press, 2016), 210–25.

54. Aquinas, *Summa Theologiae (ST)*, II-II.23.1.

55. Schockenhoff, "Theological Virtue of Charity," 252.

56. Aquinas, *ST*, II-II.30.1. "Indeed the Latin word for mercy, *misericordia*, comes from one's heart being miserable (*miserum cor*), at the sight of another's distress."

57. Aquinas, *ST*, II-II.30.4.

58. Aquinas, *ST*, II-II.31.1.

59. Aquinas, *ST*, II-II.31.2.1.

60. Aquinas, *ST*, II-II.32.1.

61. Aquinas, *ST*, II-II.32.2.

BIBLIOGRAPHY

Aelred of Rievaulx. *Spiritual Friendship*. Translated by Mary Eugenia Laker, SSND. Kalamazoo: Cistercian, 1977.

Aquinas, Thomas. *Summa Theologiae*, vol. 34. Translated by R.J. Batten, OP. New York: McGraw-Hill, 1975.

Augustine. *The Confessions*. Translated by Maria Boulding, OSB. Hyde Park, NY: New City, 1997.

Austin, Victor Lee. *Friendship: The Heart of Being Human*. Grand Rapids: Baker Academic, 2020.

Brady, Bernard V. *Christian Love: How Christians Through the Ages Have Understood Love*. Washington, DC: Georgetown University Press, 2003.

Brown, Peter. *Augustine of Hippo: A Biography*. Berkeley: University of California Press, 1967.

Carmichael, Liz. *Friendship: Interpreting Christian Love*. London: T&T Clark International, 2004.

Fatula, Mary Ann, OP. *Thomas Aquinas, Preacher and Friend*. Collegeville, MN: Liturgical, 1993.

Ford, Coleman M. *A Bond Between Souls: Friendship in the Letters of Augustine*. Bellingham, WA: Lexham Academic, 2022.

Hiesberger, Jean Marie, general editor. *The Catholic Student Bible*. New York: William H. Sadlier, 1995.

McGuire, Brian Patrick. *Friendship and Community: The Monastic Experience 350–1250*. Kalamazoo: Cistercian, 1988.

McNamara, Marie Aquinas, OP. *Friendship in Saint Augustine*. Fribourg: University Press, 1958.

Meilaender, Gilbert C. *Friendship: A Study in Theological Ethics*. Notre Dame, IN: University of Notre Dame Press, 1981.

Pope, Stephen J. "Christian Love as Friendship: Engaging the Thomistic Tradition." In *Love and Christian Ethics: Tradition, Theory, and Society*, edited by Frederick V. Simmons with Brian C. Sorrells, 210–25. Washington, DC: Georgetown University Press, 2016.

Schockenhoff, Eberhard. "The Theological Virtue of Charity." Translated by Grant Kaplan and Frederick G. Lawrence. In *The Ethics of Aquinas*, edited by Stephen J. Pope, 244–58. Washington, DC: Georgetown University Press, 2002.

Schwartz, Daniel. *Aquinas on Friendship*. Oxford: Oxford University Press, 2007.

Vacek, Edward Collins, S.J. *Love, Human and Divine: The Heart of Christian Ethics*. Washington, DC: Georgetown University Press, 1994.

Wadell, Paul J. *Becoming Friends: Worship, Justice, and the Practice of Christian Friendship*. Grand Rapids: Brazos, 2002.

Wadell, Paul J. *Friendship and the Moral Life*. Notre Dame, IN: University of Notre Dame Press, 1989.

Wadell, Paul J. *Happiness and the Christian Moral Life: An Introduction to Christian Ethics*, 3rd ed. Lanham, MD: Rowman & Littlefield, 2016.

Wadell, Paul J. *The Primacy of Love: An Introduction to the Ethics of Thomas Aquinas*. New York: Paulist, 1992.

Weisheipl, James A., OP. *Friar Thomas D'Aquino: His Life, Thought, and Works*. Garden City, NY: Doubleday, 1974.

White, Carolinne. *Christian Friendship in the Fourth Century*. Cambridge: Cambridge University Press, 1992.

Chapter 10

Love, Friendship, and Solidarity

A Christian Theology of Friendship

Marcus Mescher

Religious teachings repeatedly stress moral obligations to one's neighbors—especially those in great need—much more than the moral demands of friendship. Perhaps this is because virtuous friendships are marked by the natural expression of *philia* love that is attentive and responsive to the needs of our friends. Christianity's "Great Commandment" to love God and neighbor does not delineate how to navigate competing duties to family, friends, neighbors, and strangers, to say nothing of how a preferential concern for the poor and vulnerable should be integrated into preexisting relationships and roles. This chapter examines contributions from a number of key figures whose perspectives can enhance our moral perception and reasoning in how to discern how to balance friendships with other dimensions of the moral life. It proceeds in three steps: first, by considering the merits and limits of partiality in loving others; second, by exploring how to integrate friendships into moral duties bound to other proximate relationships; third, by proposing a constructive model of friendship for advancing inclusive solidarity and liberative praxis.

WRESTLING WITH PARTIALITY IN LOVE: FROM ARISTOTLE TO OUTKA

The philosophy of friendship is indebted to Aristotle, who ranks these relationships in increasing value according to utility, pleasure, and virtue. Aristotle contends that friends ought to be social equals who mutually share common interests or endeavors, and will the good of the friend (loving the friend as another self, not for one's own benefit).[1] Taking a different approach,

Augustine pays less attention to the moral quality of friendship, which is not a significant factor in the *ordo amoris* (the ordering of love) he develops to navigate the duties to love God, others, and oneself. For Augustine, since God is love (1 Jn 4:8), all love is love for God and for union with God.[2] God alone is to be enjoyed, whereas the world is to be used as an instrument for loving God.[3] Love of God, according to Augustine, means loving God who is present in the neighbor. Since everyone is to be considered a neighbor— i.e., there are no non-neighbors—all are worthy of our love and "All people should be loved equally."[4] Love is a discipline that requires firm commitment of the will and depends on God-given continence and justice.[5] In Augustine's view, the heart of the moral life is loving the right things in the right way for the right end, which is union with God.[6] Moral virtue requires overcoming the impulses of the body, concupiscence, passions, and disordered desires to keep our primary focus on loving God.[7] When we love ourselves and others well, we honor the command to love God.[8]

Thomas Aquinas builds on Augustine's framework to develop a more nuanced ordering of love. Aquinas defines love of God as friendship with God.[9] He uses the word "charity," translated from the Latin word *caritas*, to describe this theological virtue that comprises love, benevolence, mutuality, and communication.[10] Love of God should order all our other loves; Aquinas argues we should love ourselves and all others in friendship for God's sake and for union with God.[11] Whereas Augustine says we should love all neighbors equally, Aquinas notes this is not actually possible. Instead, Aquinas contends that our love of God and self come before our proximate bonds to parents, children, and a spouse (who rely on us more than strangers) and then more generally those closer to us before others who are more distant. However, Aquinas argues that as a matter of justice, the gravity of others' need should supersede proximity when discerning how to honor the moral demands of our relationships.[12]

Martin Luther proposes the human relationship with God in terms of faith rather than love. While Augustine and Aquinas present love of self as necessary, Luther warns that this can become a sinful violation of the *kenotic* and cruciform Christ-like love that ought to mark Christian discipleship.[13] Luther presents love not as friendship or union but as an expression of faith through service to others. He claims, "as Christians we do not live in ourselves but in Christ and the neighbor . . . As Christians we live in Christ through faith and in the neighbor through love. Through faith we are caught up beyond ourselves into God. Likewise, through love we descend beneath ourselves through love to serve our neighbor."[14] Luther's contribution to the ordering of love is to de-center the self and strive for a countercultural practice of love that puts the needs of others first, just as Paul writes to the church in Philippi: "Do nothing out of selfishness or out of vainglory; rather, humbly regard others as more important than yourselves, each looking out not for his own interests, but [also] everyone for those of others" (Phil 2:3–4).

Danish philosopher Søren Kierkegaard adopts Luther's position to contrast the Christian love of neighbor with lesser "natural" loves like the desiring love of *eros*. Like Augustine, Kierkegaard emphasizes the radically universal demands of Christian neighbor love: it should break all bonds and distinctions to show the equality of all persons. In contrast to Aquinas, Kierkegaard opposes partiality or preferential love. Whereas in love of neighbor "God is the middle term," in friendship love (*philia*), the middle term is preference, which is a form of idolatry.[15] Kierkegaard concludes that reciprocal love—including friendship—is reducible to self-love: "I intoxicated in the-other-I."[16] He finds *eros* and *philia* ultimately incompatible with Christian love, the "essential form" of which is "self-renunciation."[17] Going even further, Kierkegaard's view of universal neighbor love suggests that we should actually ignore the unique qualities of the persons we encounter; he insists, "one sees his neighbor only with closed eyes or by *looking away* from all distinctions."[18] This gives us a view of Christian neighbor love that puts greater stress on extending love to others than on being attentive and responsive to the needs (to say nothing of the abilities) of our neighbors. Kierkegaard argues for this blanket, static concern because it avoids the temptation to compare or judge one's neighbor, a "moment" when love could be expressed, but is lost.[19]

A blanket, *agapic* other-regard long served as the dominant paradigm for Christian neighbor love. Swedish bishop Anders Nygren describes this *agape* love in terms of its Godlike qualities: it is spontaneous and "unmotivated," "indifferent to value," and "given without limit."[20] What is more, *agape* is not only Godlike, but God is the "acting subject" of this love.[21] Since all love is love of God, then "all love seems to be set upon a common object," to the point of disregarding the persons involved, since our neighbors are "given to us to be used as means and vehicle for our return to God."[22] Nygren's position risks distorting our neighbors into passive objects of our duty to love God. What is more, Nygren's hierarchy contests human agency in general, since he describes *agape* descending as a gift from God and the Christian is "merely the tube, the channel, through which God's love flows."[23]

Protestant moral theologian Gene Outka uses both Kierkegaard and Nygren's views on *agape* to more closely scrutinize how Christian neighbor love can be simultaneously universal and also sensitive to the needs of each unique neighbor. His conception of *agape*, which he labels as "equal regard," is characterized in terms of its universality, stability, and impartiality while also serving as regard for the neighbor's own sake.[24] Outka restores the connection between love and justice, stating that *agape* requires more than justice, but also never less.[25] Outka also points out that fulfilling the demands of *agape* is more complex and conflictual than acknowledged by many previous contributors to the ordering of love, since we encounter a countless number of neighbors and are limited by finite time, energy, and resources in trying to love others well. Outka retrieves the virtue of prudence (the practical reasoning championed by Aquinas) to weigh our responsibilities among competing relationships and levels of need. Outka departs from Kierkegaard in arguing that instead of turning a blind eye to the differences in our neighbors, the moral task is to determine which differences in others' identities, abilities, and circumstances do and do not matter. This, Outka advises, "gives particular trouble for agape."[26]

Friendship poses a moral challenge to the "equal regard" of *agape*. The time, concern, and even money we dedicate to friends can keep us from tending to the needs of those who are poor and vulnerable. In a departure from Kierkegaard and Nygren, Outka claims that *agape* is better expressed through mutuality rather than unilateral care: "love is absent when one party does all the giving and the other all the taking."[27] However, Outka warns that *philia* love tends to fluctuate, is prone to contingencies, mixed motives, and can become exclusionary. The more we invest ourselves in *philia* love, the more daunting it seems to live up to the demands of *agape* that is "deeply conjoined" but not interchangeable with "equalitarian justice."[28] For this reason, we need more guidance on how friendship fits into the ordering of love.

INTEGRATING FRIENDSHIPS INTO THE ORDERING OF LOVE: THREE CATHOLIC PERSPECTIVES

Philosopher Jules Toner adopts Aquinas' framework to investigate the moral valence of friendship and how it fulfills the command to love one's neighbor. Toner avoids distinctions between *eros*, *philia*, and *agape*, preferring a phenomenological examination of love as cognitive, affective, volitional, and enduring commitment. Toner presents dimensions of "radical love" reflecting a number of possibilities, like a polyhedron that contains desire and joy; care or responsibility; union; presence; affirmation; benevolence; and communion. Echoing Aquinas, Toner describes radical love as an affective act of affirming the loved one in and for the beloved that constitutes "actual union of the lover and beloved."[29] Toner believes friendship is crucial to moral formation because it requires practice in being present and sharing in mutual exchange. This is a dynamic wherein those who share love participate in a "double experience" of cross-identification and affirmation.[30] By analogy, one cannot offer one's hand without also—or even first—accepting the other's hand. But Toner is not content to highlight how friendship is rooted in mutuality or reciprocity. Rather, Toner observes how love is transformational: "the lover is the loved as other and is more fully oneself," meaning that the more one enters into the union of love with other persons, "the more I am myself."[31] Looking at this longitudinally, love becomes "richly differentiated, constantly varying" in an "amazing kaleidoscopic flowing [of] expressions of love."[32] In contrast to Kierkegaard's claim that we should close our eyes when looking upon a neighbor and departing from Outka's blanket "equal regard," Toner offers a view of love that embraces a relational anthropology, showing how we are formed by the persons we love. It follows that we fail to be formed by the people we never bother to love.

Toner's contribution to the ordering of love is to highlight how the experience of loving others shapes our identity, agency, and capacities. Friendship is not only co-affirmation but a kind of liberation into greater self-realization: "I become I in the way that only you can make me be."[33] Later, he expounds, "By sharing their conscious lives, each friend in some measure experiences life and the universe not only from his or her own perspective but also from the friend's unique perspective. Each friend, therefore, to some extent takes on the other's ways of perceiving, understanding, and affectively responding to the world they live in."[34] Toner challenges the idea that friendship must be exclusive or buffers dyads from the wider community. Instead, friendship becomes a pathway toward more inclusive—if not aspirationally universal—communion, as he explains: "To begin a personal friendship with one person is to take a step on the road toward ever greater communion and sharing lives in a community of universal personal friendship, in which each friend lives all personal life as it grows ever richer by reason of each friend's growth."[35] Here we begin to see the connections between friendship and solidarity.

Catholic moral theologian Edward Vacek embraces this vision of friendship as communion, describing it as a process of being loved by God, responding to God's love with love, and then together with God forming a community of cooperation between God and ourselves. Vacek is especially interested in the relationship between freedom and friendship, where the person's choice to cultivate friendship "codetermines, though in a dependent way, the manner and form of God's involvement in the world."[36] Vacek is wary of conflating love with benevolence, desire, joy, delight, other-identification and shared feelings, respect and shared interests. He contends that love is better understood as active readiness, intentional movement, affective perception of higher value, reception of goodness, affirming response, and an ever-new freedom to love more; he attests, "the more we love, the more we are *able* to love."[37] Each person's expression of love is a uniquely free act for God, family, and friends, and also for society in general: "the contribution that each of us makes to justice or peace is irreplaceable. It is not an empty tautology to assert that without me God cannot do what God does through me" since "only I can love as I love."[38] While *agape* might stretch one's concern to neighbors in need, Vacek privileges *philia* as the way to communion, "the foundation and goal of Christian life."[39] Vacek notes that while the Great Commandment instructs disciples to "love God and neighbor as oneself," Jesus calls his disciples friends (John 15:13), a call to mutual relationship with one another that leads toward communion as partners in mission. To give *philia* pride of place, Vacek appeals to Jesus calling his disciples friends (John 15:13). Vacek adds that *philia* is more interested in deep, mutual, and long-term commitments than self-sacrificial *agape*, which risks being reduced to episodes of benevolence.[40]

Here it is appropriate to turn to the work of Catholic ethicist Paul Wadell, who cogently frames friendship as the "crucible for the moral life."[41] Friendships are where we become our true selves, where we deliver or fall short of making moral choices, and where we make an impact on others. Wadell builds a bridge between *agape* and *philia*, pointing to the ways they are mutually-reinforcing. He states, "With agape, we come, like God, to make friends with the world" and then continues, "Friendship is the love in which agape is learned," before concluding that "agape is not something other than friendship, but describes a friendship like God's, a love of generous vision that it looks upon all men and women not as strangers but as friends."[42] Many friendships are provisional, opportunities to gradually grow in love; they are also avenues to connect with even wider circles (the friends of our friends), a direction that moves from particular toward universal love. Wadell synthesizes the work of both Augustine and Aquinas in claiming that the point of our friendships—both with God and one another—is to become more like God by loving what and whom God loves. Friendships at their best teach us about what is good, right, true, and just while at their worst, they reveal the immorality of being dishonest and disloyal or selfish and stingy. Wadell sums up his vision of the centrality of friendship for the moral life: "What we learn in the moral odyssey is that our moral deliverance, our wholeness and completion, ultimately come not from ourself, but from those we allow to become part of our life . . . We have to learn to acknowledge the other because they are the key to our moral wholeness."[43] Wadell summarizes friendship as an emancipatory experience of reception and recognition of another, respect for one another, and response to loving self-gift. Like Vacek, Wadell sees one of the key merits of friendship is that it flows out of the exercise of freedom, as he explains, "The Christian moral life is what happens to us when we grant God, and others, the freedom to be our friends."[44]

Thanks to Toner, Vacek, and Wadell, we can more easily recognize that Christian neighbor love is not sufficed by loving people—even if generously—from a distance; it means drawing near to others and allowing ourselves to be reached by others, practicing the authenticity and vulnerability that make moral growth possible. To view the demands of discipleship only through the lens of *agape* is to miss the way that mutuality makes it possible to share life together by being people not just *for* others but *with* others. In this way, friendship leads us from encountering others and exchanging parts of ourselves with others to accompanying one another on the road toward solidarity, justice, and peace. This requires that we intentionally cultivate friendships with and among those on the margins of social status, security, privilege, and power.

FRIENDSHIP ON THE MARGINS: INCLUSIVE SOLIDARITY AND LIBERATIVE PRAXIS

Gustavo Gutiérrez, one of the founding figures in liberation theology, insists that there can be "no authentic commitment to liberation" in the pursuit of justice without friendship with the poor and "sharing of the life of the poor."[45] Gutiérrez, drawing from his own experience living among the poor in Lima, Peru, points out that poverty entails more than economic deprivation or social alienation; poverty results in premature death. For this reason, poverty stands in direct opposition to the will of God whose signature deed is liberation (Exod 3:7–8) and who desires life in abundance for all (John 10:10). The goal of justice and peace is to advance the fullness of life for all. These efforts require more than philanthropy or policy reform; they also demand humanizing those made to question if they count, matter, or belong. Friendship can heal social separation, stigma, and shame. It can also forge bonds that transform people from docile witnesses or indifferent bystanders to invested allies and vocal advocates. As friendship grows, the problems of my friend become my own. Yet friendship resists the paternalism of exercising power over others or trying to fix their problems; friendship honors the dignity and agency of one's friends. Friendship is about power-sharing and partnership united by common values and goals. Gutiérrez explains, "Without friendship there is neither authentic solidarity nor a true sharing. In fact, [the promotion of justice] is a commitment to specific people . . . Only the closeness that makes us friends allows us to profoundly appreciate the values of the poor today, their legitimate desires, and their own way of living the faith."[46] Whereas *agape* might orient our hearts and minds to others in need, *philia* keeps us from seeing our neighbors as a faceless group or as passively waiting for help. Gutiérrez envisions friendship as a social expression of love, but not love as blanket other-regard. Instead, friendship is a social manifestation of love that spurs a willingness to share life "with those who suffer despoliation and injustice. The solidarity is not with 'the poor' in the abstract but with human beings of flesh and bone. Without love and affection, without—why not say it?—tenderness, there can be no true gesture of solidarity."[47] Friendship only takes root when people are recognized as unique individuals with their own hopes and dreams, affirmed as agents of their own destiny.

Virtuous friendships provide vital training in moral formation by practicing sacrificial love, the ability to give and receive truth-telling, mutual respect and long-term fidelity, compassionate support and reliable accountability, as well as the process of forgiving and being forgiven. But friendships can also become possessive, overly demanding, and even toxic.[48] Although Aristotle claimed that friendship could only be shared by social equals, friendships often have to account for asymmetries in power, resources, and opportunities. Friendships are not confined to shared interests or similar backgrounds; they can bring people together across differences, disrupt categories of "otherness," and upend assumptions we have about others. While he envisions friendship as a practice of liberation and solidarity, Gutiérrez never acknowledges how friendship with the poor should be integrated into the ordering of love, or how to reconcile a special concern for the marginalized with one's preexisting roles and relationships—to say nothing of the pitfalls lurking in these dynamic, complex, and sometimes fragile relationships.

Methodist moral theologian Christine Pohl pairs friendship with hospitality as necessary ingredients to build community through understanding and acceptance. This orientation toward investing in relationships often stands in stark contrast with secular demands for change at the individual and structural levels of society. Friendship and hospitality—especially with the poor and to strangers—provide stability in a time of social distrust and division.[49] Friendships humanize people, break down labels, and urge us in the direction of lifelong conversion toward greater transparency and accountability. For those who enjoy a high degree of comfort and convenience, friendships with people on the peripheries of status, security, and power can be transformative. Such friendship gives rise to reflection on connections between one's personal lifestyle choices and how this benefits from or exacerbates unjust inequalities. For example, an image or story shared on social media that one person finds funny or harmless could be rightly called out as insensitive by someone who has experienced sexual violence. In the context of a virtuous friendship, this exchange is not about being "woke" or part of "cancel culture" but the duty to share perspectives that help us discover and dismantle bias or blind spots, especially when they result from cultural norms that may desensitize us to human degradation or exploitation. Friendship requires continuous efforts to grow in authenticity, integrity, humility, curiosity, and compassion. What is real or true for one person may not be for their friend and vice versa. Relationships between marginalized and nonmarginalized persons inevitably give rise to questions about asymmetries in power and agency.[50] Friendship resists tokenizing any person or situation by incarnating fidelity to persons in their concrete reality. It seeks understanding across difference and celebrates difference rather than pressuring others to distort or contort who they are for the sake of conformity or uniformity. In a social context marked by widespread suspicion and scorn, Pohl's call to combine friendship and hospitality as communal practices can break open new possibilities for personal and social transformation.

However, these shared relational practices can be taxing, and the Christian moral life means balancing demands to family and friends as well as to neighbors and strangers. While Gutiérrez envisions friendship on the margins as empowering, they can also prove daunting if not paralyzing for those already feeling stretched thin or failing to measure up to what they owe to their most proximate bonds. Feeling overwhelmed can cause psychological stress, persistent shame, and social alienation, making it harder to love oneself and others, even as people sometimes overcompensate by trying to act even more selflessly.[51] It also should be noted that friendships at the margins can be susceptible to exploitation, targeted by those seeking to take advantage of others' generosity or vulnerability. Here it is instructive to return to Aquinas, who champions prudence for ordering the pursuit of what is good, right, true, and just. Aquinas calls prudence "right reason in action" that is "caused by love."[52] Prudence provides the guide for calibrating how to balance friendships with our obligations to others near and far. It also helps us discern how we embrace our lifelong vocation to advance solidarity, justice, and peace. While each person is called to love and do justice, this does not look the same for everyone. In other words, there is no universal ordering of love. By virtue of each person's conscience, everyone has the ability to discern what is within and beyond one's capacity to love God, self, and others. What is more, etymologically, "conscience" means "to know together," a reminder that no one stumbles upon moral wisdom alone; moral growth finds traction in and through our relationships, especially in those relationships where we experience safety and trust, mutual respect and care, equality and co-responsibility.

When we fall short of loving well, reflecting on our experiences can teach us how to better love ourselves and others in the future. True friends are willing to share this journey of discovery, even when it involves remorse and repentance. Gutiérrez describes how conversion is a necessary part of this maturation process: "A spirituality of liberation will center on a *conversion* to the neighbor, the oppressed person, the exploited social class, the despised ethnic group, the dominated country . . . To be converted is to know and experience the fact that, contrary to the laws of physics, we can stand straight, according to the Gospel, only when our center of gravity is outside ourselves."[53] The work of liberation and solidarity move at the speed of friendships, which cannot be delivered on-demand. Friendships evolve over time. They are at least bilateral and often multilateral, weaving new bonds together and sometimes mending broken ties, as well. Friendship is not outcome-based, but ultimately ordered more toward fidelity than achieve-ment or success. In a time when many people focus on return-on-investment, maximizing efficiency, or enhancing comfort, the gifts and tasks involved in friendship can seem profoundly countercultural. Gutiérrez presents friendship as a corrective against self-indulgence, distraction, and deception; it plays a pivotal role in spirituality and praxis to be ever more attentive and respon-sive to the joys and hopes, fears and needs of others. *Philia* establishes one's center of gravity outside the self and friendship—especially with those on the margins—makes real the inclusion and interdependence of solidarity.

Friendships reveal our identity and values, personally and collectively. In a social context where "friends" are sometimes simply acquaintances, co-workers, neighbors, people we meet just once, or those who send a request to share social networks online, this Christian theology of friendship offers a vision of virtuous friendship. A virtue, says Aristotle, can be under-stood as a golden mean between the extremes of deficiency and excess (*NE* 1105b–1119b). For example, a lack of courage looks like the vice of coward-ice whereas too much courage would be foolishly brazen, so the moral task is to prudently discern the midpoint between these extremes. Analogically, virtuous friendships avoid both deficient and excessive concern or commit-ment. Friendships should not tolerate ignorance, indifference, or inaction in the face of unmet needs. Neither should friendships be so consuming that they make it harder for us to love God, self, and others well. Virtuous friendships help us seek wisdom and grow in our capacity to love and be loved. Virtuous friendships give us practice in self-awareness and the cycle of building—and sometimes having to rebuild—trust as necessary ingredients to social cohesion. When we share in friendships on the margins, we can experience conversion from beliefs and practices that insulated us from degradation or deprivation. When our friendships cross lines of religious belief and practice, they can serve as interpersonal and transpersonal avenues for interfaith dia-logue, cultural exchange, a broader sense of belonging, and a richer sense of purpose.[54] When we enter into relationships that help us identify our true self and shed our false self, to be freely and fully the person God created us to be, we can savor the blessing of friendship and create the conditions for personal and collective flourishing. Friendship is not only an essential dimension of the Christian moral life; it is what social holiness looks like.

NOTES

1. Aristotle, *Nicomachean Ethics*, ed. Richard McKeon (New York: Random House, 2001), 1155a–57b.

2. Augustine, *Confessions*, trans. Henry Chadwick (Oxford: Oxford University Press, 2008), XI.xxix.39.

3. Augustine, *On Christian Doctrine*, trans. R.P.H. Green (Oxford: Oxford University Press, 1999), I.iv.4, 10.

4. Augustine, *On Christian Doctrine*, I.xxx.31–32; I.xxviii.29.

5. Augustine, *Confessions*, X.iv.5–X.vi.8.

6. Augustine writes, "Descend that you may ascend to God" (*Confessions*, IV. xii.19).

7. This is a simplistic summary; it should be noted that Augustine's view of love is entangled with descending mind-soul-body distinctions as well as many temptations to sin; see *Confessions* I.vii.12 and VII.xvii.23, for example.

8. Augustine, *On Christian Doctrine*, I.xxvi-27–I.xxvii.28.

9. Thomas Aquinas, *Summa Theologiae*, II.II.25.1. All citations in this chapter are from the *Secunda Secundae*.

10. Aquinas, *Summa Theologiae*, II.II.23.1. Charity is not identical to love but a supernatural habit that perfects the natural inclination, ability, and delight in loving. Charity is the most excellent of the virtues and no virtue exists without it (II.II.23.6–7); it is a grace-conferred gift of the Holy Spirit, who alone decides its measure (see 1 Cor 12:11) and progression throughout life (II.II.24.9).

11. Aquinas, *Summa Theologiae*, II.II.25.4; 27.3,7; 28.1.

12. Aquinas, *Summa Theologiae*, II.II.31.3; 32.9; 32.5.

13. Martin Luther, *The Freedom of a Christian*, trans. Mark D. Tranvik (Minneapolis: Fortress, 2008), 82–84.

14. Luther, *The Freedom of a Christian*, 88, 92.

15. Søren Kierkegaard, *Works of Love*, trans. H. V. Hong and E. H. Hong (Princeton: Princeton University Press, 1995), 70.

16. Kierkegaard, *Works of Love*, 59.

17. Kierkegaard, *Works of Love*, 65–68. In fact, Kierkegaard contends that the most Christian of all loves is love for the dead, since they cannot reciprocate (see *Works of Love*, 317–329).

18. Kierkegaard, *Works of Love*, 79.

19. Kierkegaard, *Works of Love*, 178.

20. Anders Nygren, *Agape and Eros*, trans. Philip P. Watson (London: SPCK, 1953), 75–77.

21. Nygren, *Agape and Eros*, 129.

22. Nygren, *Agape and Eros*, 498; 505. This is not the only problematic claim Nygren makes; he also asserts that the Christian Scripture's emphasis on *agape* renders justice "obsolete and invalidated" (see pp. 89–90, 456).

23. Nygren, *Agape and Eros*, 737.

24. Gene H. Outka, *Agape: An Ethical Analysis* (New Haven, CT: Yale University Press, 1972), 13.

25. Outka, *Agape*, 80.

26. Outka, *Agape*, 270.

27. Outka, *Agape*, 36.

28. Outka, *Agape*, 309.

29. Jules J. Toner, *Love and Friendship* (Milwaukee, WI: Marquette University Press, 2003), 195.

30. Toner, *Love and Friendship*, 117, 122.

31. Toner, *Love and Friendship*, 124.

32. Toner, *Love and Friendship*, 144.

33. Toner, *Love and Friendship*, 175.

34. Toner, *Love and Friendship*, 249.

35. Toner, *Love and Friendship*, 301–302.

36. Edward Collins Vacek, *Love, Human and Divine: The Heart of Christian Ethics* (Washington, DC: Georgetown University Press, 1994), 26.

37. Vacek, *Love, Human and Divine*, 64.

38. Vacek, *Love, Human and Divine*, 104.

39. Vacek, *Love, Human and Divine*, 280.

40. Vacek, *Love, Human and Divine*, 311.

41. Paul J. Wadell, *Friendship and the Moral Life* (Notre Dame: University of Notre Dame Press, 1989), xiii.

42. Wadell, *Friendship and the Moral Life*, 74, 81, 96.

43. Wadell, *Friendship and the Moral Life*, 148.

44. Wadell, *Friendship and the Moral Life*, 167.

45. Gustavo Gutiérrez, *A Theology of Liberation: History, Politics, and Salvation*, trans. Caridad Inda and John Eagleson (Maryknoll, NY: Orbis Books, 1988), xxxi.

46. Gustavo Gutiérrez, "The Option for the Poor Arises from Faith in Christ," trans. Robert Lasselle-Klein, James Nickoloff, and Susan Sullivan, *Theological Studies* 70 (2009): 325.

47. Gustavo Gutiérrez, *We Drink From Our Own Wells: The Spiritual Journey Of A People*, trans. Matthew J. O'Connell (Maryknoll, NY: Orbis Books, 2003), 104.

48. In this chapter friendships have been presumed to be virtuous, leading to shared fulfillment and flourishing. But this is not always the case; friends sometimes prove bad influences and lead us astray and it is also true that we can fail in our duties to love our friends as they deserve. Augustine reflects on an episode of laying waste to a fruit tree, something he never would have done if he had been walking alone (*Confessions* II.vi.12). Alternatively, he shares a moving tribute to a friend who dies, a person he describes as "my 'other self'" and "half my soul" (*Confessions* IV.vi.11).

49. Christine D. Pohl, *Making Room: Recovering Hospitality as a Christian Tradition* (Grand Rapids: Eerdmans, 1999).

50. See, for example, the work of Traci West, who analyzes the loss of autonomy and constrained agency of incarcerated women who are sexually abused in *Disruptive Christian Ethics: When Racism and Women's Lives Matter* (Louisville: Westminster John Knox, 2006), 62–71.

51. See, for example, Mario Mikulincer and Philip Shaver's edited volume, *Prosocial Motives, Emotions, and Behavior: The Better Angels of our Nature*, ed. Mario Mikulincer and Phillip R. Shaver (Washington, DC: American Psychological Association, 2010). Insofar as doing good for others has real and perceived implications for status and power, this can lead to excessive altruism or dependency rather than inclusive participation and empowerment.

52. Aquinas, *Summa Theologiae*, II.II.47.1–2.

53. Gutiérrez, *A Theology of Liberation*, 118.

54. See, for example, the dialogue, friendship, and collaboration modeled by the "Interfaith Amigos": http://interfaithamigos.com/Home.html.

BIBLIOGRAPHY

Aquinas, Thomas. *Summa Theologiae*. Translated by R. J. Batten, OP. Vol. 34, New York: McGraw-Hill, 1975.

Aristotle. *Nicomachean Ethics*. Edited by Richard McKeon. New York: Random House, 2001.

Augustine. *Confessions*. Translated by Henry Chadwick. Oxford: Oxford University Press, 2008.

Augustine. *On Christian Doctrine*. Translated by R.P.H. Green. Oxford: Oxford University Press, 1999.

Gutiérrez, Gustavo. "The Option for the Poor Arises from Faith in Christ." Translated by Robert Lasselle-Klein, James Nickoloff, and Susan Sullivan. *Theological Studies* 70 (2009): 317–26.

Gutiérrez, Gustavo. *A Theology of Liberation: History, Politics, and Salvation*. Translated by Caridad Inda and John Eagleson. Maryknoll, NY: Orbis Books, 1988.

Gutiérrez, Gustavo. *We Drink from Our Own Wells: The Spiritual Journey of a People*. Translated by Matthew J. O'Connell. Maryknoll, NY: Orbis Books, 2003.

Kierkegaard, Søren. *Works of Love*. Translated by H. V. Hong and E. H. Hong. Princeton: Princeton University Press, 1995.

Luther, Martin. *The Freedom of a Christian*. Translated by Mark D. Tranvik. Minneapolis: Fortress, 2008.

Mikulincer, Mario, and Phillip R. Shaver. *Prosocial Motives, Emotions, and Behavior: The Better Angels of Our Nature*. Edited by Mario Mikulincer and Phillip R. Shaver. Washington, DC: American Psychological Association, 2010.

Nygren, Anders. *Agape and Eros*. Translated by Philip P. Watson. London: SPCK, 1953.

Outka, Gene H. *Agape: An Ethical Analysis*. New Haven, CT: Yale University Press, 1972.

Pohl, Christine D. *Making Room: Recovering Hospitality as a Christian Tradition*. Grand Rapids: Eerdmans, 1999.

Toner, Jules J. *Love and Friendship*. Milwaukee, WI: Marquette University Press, 2003.

Vacek, Edward Collins. *Love, Human and Divine: The Heart of Christian Ethics*. Washington, DC: Georgetown University Press, 1994.

Wadell, Paul J. *Friendship and the Moral Life*. Notre Dame: University of Notre Dame Press, 1989.

West, Traci C. *Disruptive Christian Ethics: When Racism and Women's Lives Matter*. Louisville: Westminster John Knox, 2006.

Chapter 11

A Path through the Hell of War Trauma

Pavel Florensky's Theology of Friendship

Adam Tietje

War is hell. Coming home is hell, too.[1] After war, the survival and potential flourishing of many veterans turns on friendship. There is a path through the hell of trauma.[2] But, you cannot walk it alone, it can only be walked with a friend. Or so my reading of Russian polymath[3] and Orthodox Christian theologian Pavel Florensky (1882–1937) suggests. Florensky's most well-known book, *The Pillar and Ground of the Truth*, is framed as a series of twelve letters to his best friend, Sergei Troitsky.[4] These letters bear witness to the possibility of surviving hell through friendship. It is Troitsky who accompanies Florensky through his own experience of hell. Drawing on two of these letters, *Gehenna* (Letter 8) and Friendship (Letter 11), this chapter traces the movement out of hell made possible through friendship and makes the case for friendship as a source of healing after the trauma of war.[5]

Florensky's account of the damned in *Gehenna* provides the starting point.[6] I first argue that key features of Florensky's account of the self in hell echo the hell of trauma after war. Next, I examine Florensky's own experiences of hell and the possibilities for a way through it. While Florensky is not a combat veteran, his exploration of the spirituality of friendship has much in common with veterans' experience of combat trauma. I then home in on Florensky's account of friendship as both a participation in the divine life and in the life of a wider community. I close by suggesting that friendship offers the conditions for the possibility of the reconstitution of the self after war.

I should say before continuing that my interest in the role of friendship as a healing balm after war flows out of my own experience. I served as an active duty US Army chaplain from 2009–2018 and continue to serve as a chaplain in the US Army Reserve. I know the hell of war, both personally and in my role as a chaplain. I am a Christian chaplain and theologian and this chapter is written primarily from within and for that particular tradition and from the particularity of my own experiences of war trauma and as a caregiver. However, my hope is that the particularity of what I write here will be the occasion for resonances across religious traditions and diverse experiences of trauma and war.

FLORENSKY'S *GEHENNA* AND THE HELL OF COMBAT TRAUMA

Combat trauma provokes a hell-like loss of relationship. Similar loss is depicted in *Gehenna*, Florensky's eighth letter. He begins with this tantalizingly poetic imagery:

> My *starets*! I cannot tell you with what apprehension I approach the writing of this letter. Do I not see how difficult it is to find the right words here? The skeleton of our obtuse concepts is too rough and, in covering it with the almost-intangible tissue of experience, it would be easy to tear this tissue to shreds. Perhaps your hands alone will receive it as not torn. Your hands alone.[7]

The skeleton of obtuse concepts does indeed follow. As obtuse and skeletal as it may be, Florensky's account is fascinating.[8] More fascinating still is that Florensky wraps this skeleton with his own flesh, his own experience, however thin and seemingly intangible. Florensky bookends this letter with his own experiences of hell. I want to give these stories their due. I think they are pivotal for understanding the relationship between hell and friendship. But, before I go there, I want to start from the inside out. That is, I want to start with the skeleton. In particular, I want to start with the most frightful aspect of these obtuse concepts, Florensky's imaginary of the damned.

Florensky's damned—to be fair, damned is my word here—are "husks," "empty 'skin[s],'" "mask[s] . . . without any substantiality."[9] The damned are subjects without subjectivity or better yet, subjectivities without subjects. They are "pure illusion," existing only for themselves. In themselves—that is the damned as the self existing only for itself—the damned are locked in eternal desire without satisfaction. Hell is a "place of excruciating and insatiable desires."[10] It is the intensification and eternal forestalling of desire. In passion, hell runs hot. While, at the same time, hell freezes over and solidifies the self. Hell is also the desire of the self to be for itself coming to rest. Or as Florensky puts it:

Selfhood has received what it has desired and what it continues to desire: to be a kind of absolute, to be independent of God, to assert itself against God. To selfhood is given this independence, this absolute negative freedom of egotism. It desired to be alone, and it became alone; it desired isolation, and it became isolated. Henceforth neither God nor anything else except it itself will affect it.[11]

The damned are eternally *incurvatus in se*. There is a catatonic quality to hell. In reaching their goal, the damned have come to a standstill. Time itself is contracted to an "eternal, frozen 'now,' which never becomes the past."[12] The damned have "become frozen in a terrible and disgusting vision."[13] The eternal now is the past that refuses itself as past. Thus, "Hell is the home for the insane of the universe, where people will be persecuted by memories."[14] Hell is the eternal recurrence of the "was" as ever-present now such that the damned no longer know (what is knowing in hell?) the difference. Florensky writes: "The horror lies precisely in the fact that insane selfhood, selfhood that has lost its mind, will not be able to understand what is happening to it: all is only 'here and now.'"[15] For Florensky, this all adds up to "a foul dream without a dreaming subject pierced by God's burning gaze, a nightmare seen by nobody."[16]

Florensky's account suggests there are two aspects of nonrelation in hell. First, the self's relation to itself collapses in on itself. The damned self has something like the gravitational pull of a blackhole with everything pulled inward and nothing allowed to escape the event horizon of the self. Time (and here I leave behind the physics of blackholes) itself is frozen under the sway of the eternally inwardly curved ego. The loss of relationship to others that follows—most significantly, loss of relationship to God—is ultimately the loss of relationship to oneself. World-loss is self-loss. The self is only ever constituted in relation and these relationships are mediated through time, a time now undone.

For many, combat trauma is a kind of living hell. Florensky's account of the experience of the damned is quite near—if not in degree, certainly in kind—to the experience of those who come home from war. Horrific trauma freezes time in ways not unlike what Florensky describes. After trauma, the happening never quite happened, it is always happening. The perceived linear flow of time is disrupted by overwhelming traumatic violence. Trauma creates a new relationship to time in which the trauma threatens to break in to any given moment. The past refuses to be past. The event of trauma exceeds its own moment, refuses containment, and forcefully reemerges. This reemergence can take the form of nightmares, intrusive thoughts and memories, and daytime hallucinations or flashbacks.[17] This new relation to time is also a new relation to space.[18] In a moment, one can be taken from relative safety "here" and forced to relive violence, failure, and death back "there." Time after trauma is characterized by such episodic eruptions, but eruptions that characterize one's relation to all other times.

The rupture between the self and the world as well as the self and itself that occurs after an encounter with overwhelming violence and death is akin to a gaping wound. The self itself is the site of this wound. The self becomes an open chasm between order and chaos and past and present. Hope fades as the past refuses itself as past and becomes an ever-present future. The protective boundaries between the self and world (for it was from the world that the threat first came) are often thickened while one's internal boundaries disintegrate. Trauma is not "in your head." It is in your body.[19] It is visceral and uncontrollable. It is elevated blood pressure and sweat. It is in your soul. It is spiritual. It is darkness and doubt and despair and God-abandonment.[20] It unites body and soul under its tyranny, even as it sets the self against itself, body against soul, soul against body, body against body, and soul against soul. For many, the only imaginable end to this living nightmare is a purgative act of violence through which the self in its final moment regains control. Yes, hell is like combat trauma.

FLORENSKY'S EXPERIENCE OF *GEHENNA*: FRIENDSHIP AS A WAY THROUGH HELL

Florensky, thankfully, does not remain in the torturous depths of hell. He writes of how he himself came through by way of the love of his friend, and in so doing, illumines the possibility of surviving other forms of hell through friendship. Returning, then, from the skeleton to the flesh, the story that begins the letter on *Gehenna* describes Florensky's own nightmarish experience of the second death (the description in the book of Revelation of eternal spiritual death):

> Once in a dream I experienced the second death in all its concreteness. I did not see any images. The experience was a purely interior one. Utter darkness, almost materially dense, surrounded me. Powers of some kind dragged me to the edge and I felt this to be the edge of God's being, that beyond it is absolute Nothing. I wanted to scream but could not. I knew that in one more moment I would be expelled into the outer darkness. The darkness began to flow into my whole being. Half my consciousness of self was lost, and I knew that this was absolute, metaphysical annihilation. In ultimate despair I cried with a voice that was not my own: "Out of the depths have I cried unto thee, O Lord. Lord hear

my voice!" My whole soul was in those words. Someone's hands gripped me, a drowning man, powerfully and threw me somewhere, far from the abyss. The jolt was sudden and powerful. Suddenly I found myself in my usual surrounds, my room. From mystical nonbeing, I was thrown back into ordinary, every-day life. Here at once I felt myself in the presence of God and then I awoke, drenched in a cold sweat.[21]

Here Florensky recounts a dream, an experience of mystical darkness "at the edge of God's being." He is "dragged" there and unable to cry out. He perceives himself to be on the threshold of the outer darkness. He is under threat of losing himself ("Half my consciousness of self was lost"), losing the world, and losing God. This is an overwhelming experience of the absence of God, where "Nothing," nonbeing, and darkness surround him. There on the very edge of "metaphysical annihilation" a voice within him cries out to God with the words of Psalm 130. What follows is the fulfillment of the cry of the Psalmist for redemption from the depths. Florensky, drowning in the abyss, is grabbed and "thrown back into ordinary, everyday life." Returned to his room, he once again feels the presence of God and awakens.

In his dream, Florensky narrates himself as a passive recipient of this expe-rience. The powers *drag* him. The darkness *flows* into his being. Florensky himself is paralyzed. He wants to scream, but cannot. His cry for salvation is in "a voice that was not my own" and it is "someone's hands" that grip him and cast him out of the abyss. In his confession at the end of the letter, Florensky is seemingly unable to act in the face of "the fire of *Gehenna*" ignited in his soul, "an unbearable burning."[22] At the end of the letter, Florensky recounts a different experience where he is beset by the fiery passion of the undying worm. He mentions "lust," but in a quote from St. Macarius the Great and after his description of the temptation itself.[23] Through another St. Macarius quote that does occur during his description of "this fall," he writes: "There is an impure fire which inflames the heart: runs through all the members and incites people to obscenity and thousands of evil deeds."[24] Here it seems that Florensky is being overcome with sexual lust. But, he is more than tempted. "In despair," he *surrenders* his "soul to the destructive simoon."[25] "In *vain*," he tries to resist.[26] He *cannot* "cast off [his] slavery."[27] In this experience, he is physically taken to near death. Florensky is unable to eat or sleep, loses weight, and "would have been happy to die."[28]

This second experience blows over him like a hot desert wind, a simoon. Although he stands under the threat of death and is even succumbing to it, he lies down before the icon of Jesus. He cries out to God for mercy. He recog-nizes his "slavery," even as he worries he "might soon stop being conscious of [it]."[29] Yet, he has not been lost completely to the outer darkness. In this story, he is *losing* his mind and *losing* himself in a similar way that "half [his] consciousness of self is lost"[30] in his dream. He is similarly *losing* his body and his care for it. He finds no peace or respite either before the icon or in his cell. But, all is not lost. Against the wisdom of St. Issac the Syrian ("do not leave your cell"[31]), he leaves his cell in the midst of his darkness. He does his best to put on the appearance of calm while he is out and among the others. It is there—outside the hot and torturous solitude of his cell—that he finds the calming air of friendship.

Florensky's friend—I presume Sergei Troitsky—makes the sign of the cross over him. His hand hovers over his body and gently touches him—Father—as he draws him—Son—body and soul—and the Holy Spirit—back into the triune fellowship. He sings to him. He sings Florensky's favorite hymn, an annunciation hymn. He draws Florensky out of burning passion by taking him back to a time and a place in which he can stand firm. In song he reminds Florensky, "the Lord is with Thee."[32] He leads him to vespers—perhaps hand in hand—and back into the beloved community. It is there during evening prayer, through the prayers of his friend ("I felt your prayers had been heard") that "a freshening wind blew from somewhere."[33] The simoon dissipates. Florensky is set to rest somewhere solid within his soul and is at peace, a peace that flows with his tears. In that moment, the Spirit descends, "like a drop of fragrant myrrh, quietly dripping on the earth,"[34] bringing coolness to his soul.

Florensky survives his brush with death and hell, but not, this time, by being dragged to safety. This time, Florensky's friend applies, so to speak, a cold compress to his fevered forehead. He wipes the sweat away, brushes his hair back, holds his hand, and sings to him. Through the care of his friend, the fever breaks. Florensky concludes that "it was through you, my Friend, that I received my peace, through you, my Friend, that I was saved from the undying worm. It was by your friendly prayers that I saw the 'spiritual dawn' of triumphant heaven."[35] As depicted by Florensky, hell is a lonely place, yet through the presence of another, through breath and touch, and through song and prayer the Spirit descends and the oppressive heat of hell dissipates. There is a path through hell, but it cannot be walked alone.

Salient features of Florensky's account of the damned and of his own experience of hell are like the experience of combat trauma, especially one's relationship to oneself, others, God, and even time. In one key way, Florensky's account is *not* like the experience of trauma. Neither his dream at the beginning of the chapter, nor his temptation and "fall" at the end have their genesis in an encounter with overwhelming violence. Neither are the result of violence of the sort that evades understanding in its initial unfolding, i.e., unbearable violence, the kind of violence that the self cannot take into itself and comprehend as it occurs. In the first instance, trauma is an unbearable event. But, it is also "the unbearable nature of its survival."[36] Florensky's account of hell does not so much illuminate trauma in the first sense, but it is helpful to understand trauma as the hell of bearing of the unbearable in survival.[37] Florensky's letter on *Gehenna* bears witness to the possibility of surviving hell through friendship. This is, in some way, the story of every combat veteran who comes home, the story of surviving hell. Yet, for many, it is precisely survival that becomes a descent still further into the depths. It is in this space of survival as its own hell that the possibility of surviving hell once again becomes an urgent, existential question. Florensky suggests that it is a question that cannot be answered alone.

FLORENSKY ON FRIENDSHIP

Each of Florensky's letters unfold in the context of friendship. The task of following this thread through the whole book exceeds the scope of this chapter, but fortunately, Florensky devotes an entire letter to friendship. If it is a friend that makes hell bearable, even makes a way through hell itself possible, it is necessary now to be clear, *what is friendship?*

Florensky opens the letter on friendship by reminiscing. It is a cold and windy winter day. A snowstorm rages outside. His thoughts are drawn to the candle he has just lit for the icon-lamp. He writes: "We brought this candle from *there*, that is, from where you and I wandered together."[38] His "Distant Friend," Sergei Troitsky, is brought near ("Again I am with you"[39]) as he remembers their journey to the Paraclete hermitage. Florensky recalls them fasting and praying together and trudging together through deep snow. This journey, culminating in taking communion together, was "the seed" of their friendship.[40] As with his letter on *Gehenna*, Florensky begins with his own experience, *their* experience, their friendship itself.

This is the penultimate letter of the book, but should really be understood as its climax.[41] In his introduction to the book, Richard Gustafson writes: "Florensky's most controversial theological teaching is his notion of love as friendship, the lyrical center and culminating idea of the book."[42] Everything leads to friendship, to *this* friendship even. Within this letter, Florensky moves from the beginning of their friendship in communion to making the case for *adelphopoiesis* (brother-making).[43] Florensky's argument for *adelphopoiesis* unfolds in the context of his own *adelphopoiesis* with Troitsky,[44] the solemnization of which is perhaps the memory of their time at the Paraclete hermitage. For Florensky, then, the dyad of friendship, exemplified by *adelphopoiesis*, is the most basic unit of Christian life.

Friendship is nothing less than participation in the divine life. Florensky sees *adelphopoeisis* as the sacramental form of such friendship. Through it friends are joined for "co-ascesis, co-patience, and co-martyrdom."[45] Friendship "makes of two a particle of the Body of Christ."[46] Christ is "in the midst of them," Florensky says, "like a soul is in the midst of every member of the body that it animates."[47] Christ himself binds—one could also say "mates"—together the souls of friends "in an intimate unity."[48] This is not a "psychic" phenomenon, but one that plumbs the "noumenal depths."[49] For, "friends form a dual-unity, a dyad. They are not they, but something greater: one soul."[50]

Through friendship, one discovers an "I" that is "not-I" in an intimacy that reorders and reorients one's own "I."[51] Florensky writes:

> Between lovers the membrane of selfhood is torn. And, in a friend, one sees oneself as it were, one's most intimate essence, one's *other* I. But this other I is not different from one's own I. A friend is *received* into the I of the lover. . . . A friend is admitted into the organization of the lover, is not alien to him in any way, is not expelled from him.[52]

There is a "limitlessness" to the unity of friendship. Friends bear the joys and sorrows of a friend "in mutual patience, mutual forgiveness."[53] The "I" that is "not-I" becomes a new "I" as "each of the friends obtains a foundation for his own person, finding his own I in the I of the other."[54] "What is friendship?" Florensky writes, it is "self-contemplation through a Friend in God. Friendship is the seeing of oneself with the eyes of another, but before a third, namely the Third."[55] This interpenetration in the life of friends bound together by Christ in the Spirit is nothing short of a *perichoresis*. This is not a given, but the task of friendship.[56]

Florensky finds ample scriptural and traditional warrant for the centrality of the dyad of friends. There is, of course, David and Jonathan. Florensky also sees this dyad at work in the sending of the seventy "two by two," among the apostles in the early church, and among the saints of the church. In the Gospel of John, while Jesus addresses all the disciples as friends (John 15:14), Jesus and John, "the disciple whom he loved," shared a unique and intimate bond. It is not surprising, then, that John remained with Jesus at the cross and that Jesus entrusted John with the care of his mother (John 19:26–27). Friendship is a faithfulness unto death or perhaps worse, even in the midst of faithlessness. In these examples, friendship always exists in the context of the wider community.

Friendship fosters agapic love in particular communities of faith. The philic love of friends is not simply something that blossoms in the midst of community, but is indeed the most basic building block of ecclesial or communal agapic love.[57] Florensky's account of friendship amounts to a "sociology of the church."[58] The life of agapic love is not the life of an individual or "human atom"[59] for whom the world is her neighbor. Agapic love is found and formed in particular communities of faith in which the dyad of friendship *is* the "community molecule."[60] Florensky over accepts the scientific grammar of the Enlightenment in order to turn it on its head. If Enlightenment rationality had atomized human persons, Florensky's turn to friendship as a molecule resists that reduction. Moreover, friends are not just free floating, but community molecules. For Florensky, friendship is the basic building block of society itself. Political communities, religious or otherwise, are not a collection of individual atoms, but molecules, at the heart of which is a relationship of friendship.[61] Likewise, friends need the community to draw out and deepen their love and life together.[62]

One final and important note, Florensky published this letter after Sergei left their covenantal friendship and married Florensky's sister (1909) *and* after Sergei was stabbed to death (1910).[63] So it is that he addresses the letter to his "*Distant* Friend."[64] As he thinks of Sergei he writes: "my life slides toward 'the other shore' so that I could look at you at least from there."[65] He writes knowingly of David's grief over Jonathan and turns to Psalm 88 in sorrow:

> The tremendous moans of the 88th Psalm break off with a wail—for a friend. Words can be found for all other sorrows, but the loss of a friend and dear one is beyond words. It is the limit to sorrow . . . "To be without a friend" has a mysterious relation to "to be without God." The deprivation of a friend is a kind of death.[66]

He concludes that "only my friend can smile, speak, and comfort as he does, no one else. Yes, no one and nothing in the world can compensate me for his loss."[67] Florensky's tears—the "cement of friendship"[68] binding them together even in death—no doubt, stained this letter as he wrote. The letters are riven with traumatic grief at the sudden loss of Troitsky, first to marriage, then to death. In the communion of saints, the faithful love of friendship abides after death in grief and, yes, even in hope.

If "to be without a friend" is related to "to be without God," it is surely also related to "to be without oneself." For, it is in the "I" of another that one discovers his own "I." After horrific trauma, the connective tissue of the self is badly damaged, even torn. It is in connection with another, a friend, that one's "I" can know itself as loved on the other side of the violence of war. The "being with" of a friend is intimately connected to the "being with" of God.

A PATH WHERE THERE WAS NO PATH:
FRIENDSHIP AFTER WAR

The aim of this chapter is not to contest the value of various forms of therapy and professional care after war trauma.[69] After trauma, therapeutic intervention is often necessary. But, it is never sufficient. Life after war depends on the renewal or development of relationships that precede and extend beyond any given therapeutic relationship. Foremost, I would suggest, is one's relationship with God. Elsewhere, I have written on war trauma as an experience of God-abandonment.[70] The hell of trauma is precisely the shattering of the bonds of love and trust, with potentially the most profound among them being one's relationship with God.

Florensky attends to hell as an experience that threatens to break in and overwhelm life in this world. No matter how overwhelming, Florensky knows love to be more powerful and decisive for human life than death and hell. This is not a matter of dogma, but a form of knowledge that is deeply experiential and relational.[71] The theology explored in each letter unfolds in the context of friendship. Truth is known in relationship.[72] God is known in and through loving relationships with friends and brothers. Likewise, the truth—that we are not abandoned in hell after war—can only be known relationally. After war, the self as open wound can only be held, contained, and cared for as it is received into the life of another and thereby received into the life of God.

This reception is bodily and embodied. Florensky's account of the simoon is an interior drama, but not disembodied. His passions are bodily passions, running through his "members." The "unbearable burning" begins to consume his very body as he loses weight. Friendship, too, is fully embodied. It is Sergei's subtle, yet sure bodily presence that mediates the presence of the Spirit. After war trauma, one's very self is an open wound and one's body accursed. As one is received into the "I" of another, a friend, one is given back oneself, not as wound, but gift. In friendship, Gene Rogers concludes: "The Spirit does not float free from concrete human bodies, but rests upon, inspires, and takes embodied life from them."[73] As one's body is held and caressed by another as beloved, one's body is given back as gift. Through friendship after war, one receives oneself, one's very body as a gift.

In his dream, Florensky cries out in a voice that is not his own. This is surely the work of the Spirit who cries out to God when we cannot (Rom. 8:26ff).[74] In his dream, a hand grabs Florensky and pulls him out of the abyss. It is Jesus who rescues sinners who are drowning (Matt. 14:31). In the famous icons of the *anastasis*, Jesus similarly grips the hands of Adam and Eve as he pulls them up from their graves. Word and Spirit work together, crying from deep to deep, grabbing hold of us, and leading us out of the depths. The dyad of Word and Spirit works in and through the dyad of friendship. Through friendship we are gifted by the Spirit to the Son. This is at the center of Florensky's account of friendship. Florensky's letters are addressed to a friend, but ultimately to Christ. Through friendship we are made friends of God.

Friendship makes a path where there is no path. In a Holy Saturday sermon, the Swiss Catholic theologian Hans Urs von Balthasar suggests: "He it is who walks along paths that are no paths, leaving no trace behind, through hell, hell which has no exit, no time, no being; and by the miracle from above he is rescued from the abyss, the profound depths, to save his brothers in Adam along with him."[75] The dead Christ, our friend and brother, becomes the path where there are no paths. The body of Christ entombed is the occasion for the resurrecting work of the Spirit. Through the dyad of friendship, the dyad of Word and Spirit continues to make a way through hell, even the hell after war.

Friendship is by no means a cure-all for the trauma of war, but it can make a way where there was no way, a path where there was no path. The hell of trauma can be lifelong, but so too can the faithfulness and love of a friend. Through friendship, the Spirit rests upon and among us, and draws us into the divine life as friends of God. This life of love, Florensky says, "can only be attained by a long (O how long!) ascesis."[76] In the church, ascesis came to mean a form of spiritual discipline or training in virtue. Yet, before it meant training for spiritual battle, ascesis referred to the discipline and training undertaken by athletes preparing for physical contests and soldiers in preparation for war. Coming home from war requires a new and different sort of ascesis, but one which friends forged on the battlefield may be uniquely poised to undertake. In this new ascesis, the wounds and intimacy of the old ascesis are transfigured through sharing together at the altar.

NOTES

1. This is a nod to the title of the first chapter in my book *Toward a Pastoral Theology of Holy Saturday* (Eugene, OR: Wipf and Stock, 2018)—"War is Hell. Coming Home is Hell, Too."—which is itself a nod to Tyler Boudreau's account in *Packing Inferno: The Unmaking of a Marine* (Port Townsend, WA: Feral House, 2008).

The views expressed in this chapter are those of the author and do not reflect the official policy or position of the US Army, Department of Defense, or the US Government.

2. When I refer to trauma in this chapter, I am referring to combat trauma more broadly understood and inclusive of moral injury. Trauma, clinically understood, is usually considered a fear-based stress response. See Judith Herman's *Trauma and*

Recovery: The Aftermath of Violence—From Domestic Abuse to Political Terror (New York: Basic, 1997 [1992]), for an introduction to trauma. War trauma can be what happened, an explosive encounter with death, but it can also be associated with events bound up with moral agency and killing in particular. Jonathan Shay, a VA psychiatrist, first used the term moral injury to capture that excess in light of the experiences of betrayal the Vietnam veterans he worked with named. Shay defines moral injury as "a betrayal of what's right, by a person who holds legitimate authority (e.g., in the military—a leader) in a high-stakes situation." See his "Moral Injury," *Psychoanalytic Psychology* 31, no. 2 (2014): 183. In the work of Brett T. Litz et al., "Moral Injury and Moral Repair in War Veterans: A Preliminary Model and Intervention," *Clinical Psychology Review* 29 (2009): 695–706, moral injury is used to name violations of deeply held moral beliefs or failures to act in accordance with one's deepest conception of what is right and good that lead to psycho-social impairment and maladaptive behaviors. Moral emotions like guilt and shame feature prominently in these more clinical discussions of moral injury. For a theological account of moral injury, see Warren Kinghorn, "Combat Trauma and Moral Fragmentation: A Theological Account of Moral Injury," *Journal of the Society of Christian Ethics* 32, no. 2 (2012): 57–74. See also my "*Contra* Rambo's Theology of Remaining: A Chalcedonian and Pastoral Conception of Trauma," *Pro Ecclesia* 28, no. 1 (2019): 22–38.

3. See Loren Graham and Jean-Michel Kantor, *Naming Infinity: A True Story of Religious Mysticism and Mathematical Creativity* (Cambridge, MA: Harvard University Press, 2009).

4. To whom the letters are addressed seems to be the source of much confusion. Robert Slesinsky seems unaware of Sergei Troitsky and suggests they are written to "a friend." See "Fr. Paul Florensky: A Profile," *St. Vladimir's Theological Quarterly* 26 (1982): 20. He similarly leaves Troitsky out of his *Pavel Florensky: A Metaphysics of Love* (Crestwood, NY: St. Vladimir's Seminary, 1984). Richard Gustafson, in his introduction to the book, also leaves the friend unidentified, but suggests that it is ultimately Christ. See "Introduction to the Translation" in *The Pillar and Ground of the Truth: A Essay in Orthodox Theodicy in Twelve Letters*, trans. Boris Jakim (Princeton: Princeton University Press, 1997 [1914]), xi–xii. Avril Pyman, in his recent biography of Florensky, makes it clear that Sergei Troitsky is the one addressed. See *Pavel Florensky: A Quiet Genius: The Tragic and Extraordinary Life of Russia's Unknown Da Vinci* (New York: Continuum, 2010), 57–58, also 66. Of course, that Florensky writes for Troitsky, the reader as an unspecified friend, or Christ need not be mutually exclusive. The ambiguity is, no doubt, intentional. This debate, to be clear, is bound up with debates about Florensky's sexuality and the nature of his friendship with Sergei. There is a good deal of evidence that their relationship was romantic and that the *adelphopoiesis* I make the case for later in the chapter, was in fact a solemnization of that relationship.

5. Stephanie Arel has rightly pointed out to me that my account of friendship as a source of healing for trauma is not universally applicable. Friendship may be a long way off for those whose very capacity to form bonds of attachment has been traumatically impaired.

6. *Gehenna* is a New Testament Greek word used as a synonym for hell. It is derived from the Hebrew *Ge Hinnom* which means the valley of Hinnom, a place outside of Jerusalem. In the Hebrew Bible, It is referenced in 2 Chronicles 28 in connection with Ahaz's idolatry and the practice of child sacrifice in fire. In Jesus' day, it was a place where trash was continually burning.

7. Florensky, *The Pillar and Ground*, 151.

8. Florensky makes the case for what he takes to be an antinomic account of hell, bringing together the thesis and antithesis of what might be called a traditional view of hell and universal salvation, what he calls "Vulgar Origenism." See Florensky, *The Pillar and Ground*, 153. The traditional view of hell takes seriously sin and evil, God's justice, and human freedom, while universal salvation leans into forgiveness and God's "unthwartable" will to "be all in all" (1 Cor. 15:28). He affirms both "eternal torments" and "universal restoration," not as both/and, but as antinomy. Florensky argues that the final judgment splits the person in two. For the I "in itself" this is experienced as purgative, while the I "for itself" is cast into the outer darkness. For a great summary of his argument see Erica Ridderman, "The Antinomy of Gehenna: Pavel Florensky's Contribution to Debates on Hell and Universalism," *Scottish Journal of Theology* 74, no. 3 (2021): 235–51.

9. Florensky, *The Pillar and Ground*, 160–61.

10. Florensky, *The Pillar and Ground*, 181.

11. Florensky, *The Pillar and Ground*, 177.

12. Florensky, *The Pillar and Ground*, 180.

13. Florensky, *The Pillar and Ground*, 180.

14. Florensky, *The Pillar and Ground*, 181.

15. Florensky, *The Pillar and Ground*, 176.

16. Florensky, *The Pillar and Ground*, 171.

17. See American Psychiatric Association, *Diagnostic and Statistical Manual of Mental Disorders: DSM-V* (Washington, DC: American Psychiatric Association, 2013), 271–80.

18. Shelly Rambo names this a "middle space" of survival between death and life. See her *Spirit and Trauma: A Theology of Remaining* (Louisville, KY: Westminster John Knox, 2010). It might also be called a middle time.

19. See Bessel van der Kolk, *The Body Keeps the Score: Brain, Mind, and Body in the Healing of Trauma* (New York: Penguin, 2014).

20. For further explorations of the theological dimensions of trauma see Serene Jones, *Trauma and Grace: Theology in a Ruptured World* (Louisville, KY: Westminster John Knox, 2009), Rambo's *Spirit and Trauma*, and her more recent *Resurrecting Wounds: Living in the Afterlife of Trauma* (Waco, TX: Baylor University Press, 2017), and my *Holy Saturday*.

21. Florensky, *The Pillar and Ground*, 151.

22. Florensky, *The Pillar and Ground*, 187.

23. Florensky, *The Pillar and Ground*, 187.

24. Florensky, *The Pillar and Ground*, 187.

25. Florensky, *The Pillar and Ground*, 187.

26. Florensky, *The Pillar and Ground*, 187.

27. Florensky, *The Pillar and Ground*, 187.

28. Florensky, *The Pillar and Ground*, 188.

29. Florensky, *The Pillar and Ground*, 187.

30. Florensky, *The Pillar and Ground*, 151.

31. Florensky, *The Pillar and Ground*, 187.

32. Florensky, *The Pillar and Ground*, 188.

33. Florensky, *The Pillar and Ground*, 188.

34. Florensky, *The Pillar and Ground*, 188.

35. Florensky, *The Pillar and Ground*, 189.

36. Cathy Caruth, *Unclaimed Experience: Trauma, Narrative, and History* (Baltimore: Johns Hopkins University Press, 1996), 7.

37. Deborah Hunsinger describes surviving trauma this way in *Bearing the Unbearable: Trauma, Gospel, and Pastoral Care* (Grand Rapids: Eerdmans, 2015).

38. Florensky, *The Pillar and Ground*, 284.

39. Florensky, *The Pillar and Ground*, 285.

40. Florensky, *The Pillar and Ground*, 285.

41. The final letter on jealousy is the working out of what protects the love shared between friends. See Florensky, *The Pillar and Ground*, 331–48.

42. Gustafson, "Introduction to the Translation," xviii. Gustafson's claim that Florensky's account of love as friendship is controversial can be seen as much in its absence as its presence. A recent article on Florensky's account of love fails to mention either *adelphopoiesis* or Sergei. While friendship is mentioned, it is tangential. See Oleg Pavenkov and Mariia Rubtcova, "El amor como concepto en la filosofia religiosa de Pavel Florensky," *Anales del Seminario de Historia de la Filosofia* 33 (2016): 163–80. Gustafson fails to mention *why* Florensky's account is so controversial. It is controversial because it is so deeply entangled with Florensky's relationship with Sergei.

43. For more on *adelphopoiesis* see John Boswell, *Same-Sex Unions in Premodern Europe* (New York: Villard, 1994). See also Claudia Rapp, *Brother-Making in Late Antiquity and Byzantium* (New York: Oxford University Press, 2016). *Adelphopoiesis* is a rite akin to marriage and hence why Sergei's marriage to Florensky's sister was felt as such a deep betrayal. See Pyman, *A Quiet Genius*, 68.

44. See Pyman, *A Quiet Genius*, 66.

45. Florensky, *The Pillar and Ground*, 296.

46. Florensky, *The Pillar and Ground*, 303.

47. Florensky, *The Pillar and Ground*, 303.

48. Florensky, *The Pillar and Ground*, 298.

49. Florensky, *The Pillar and Ground*, 311.

50. Florensky, *The Pillar and Ground*, 311.

51. Florensky, *The Pillar and Ground*, 314–15. His account of friendship is grounded in his rejection of the rationalistic "law of identity" (A=A), the notion that beings are self-contained, unrelated, isolated units. See Florensky, *The Pillar and Ground*, 22–24. Florensky sees identity established precisely in and through relation. Florensky's account of friendship is exactly that: A=A and ~A (or I = I and ~I). This

relational account of identity is grounded in God's own being. See Florensky, *The Pillar and Ground*, 39–42.

52. Florensky, *The Pillar and Ground*, 310.

53. Florensky, *The Pillar and Ground*, 310.

54. Florensky, *The Pillar and Ground*, 312.

55. Florensky, *The Pillar and Ground*, 314.

56. Florensky, *The Pillar and Ground*, 320.

57. Florensky examines the various Greek categorical distinctions around love between *erōs, storgē, agapē*, and *philia* toward the beginning of his friendship chapter. Florensky's account of friendship combines aspects of *philia, erōs*, and *agapē*. See Florensky, *The Pillar and Ground*, 289. Florensky's account of friendship is infused with passion, desire, and the erotic.

58. Eugene Rogers, "Florensky: Maximus Meets Russian Romanticism" (lecture, The University of North Carolina at Greensboro, Greensboro, NC, October 17, 2019). See also Eugene Rogers, *After the Spirit: A Constructive Pneumatology from Resources outside the Modern West* (Grand Rapids: Eerdmans, 2005), 189–91.

59. Florensky, *The Pillar and Ground*, 301.

60. Florensky, *The Pillar and Ground*, 301.

61. Before, during, and after war, the sacrificial virtues of friendship among soldiers are taken up by the state and often directed toward corrupt ends. I suggest that the virtues of friendship also make possible truth-telling, protest, and the building of movements for peace. Friendship is precisely where the virtues needed for such politics are cultivated, because at its root politics is built upon relational practices. As Luke Bretherton argues, politics, at its most basic level, is the relational practices and prudential judgments that enact the good of association. See his *Christ and the Common Life: Political Theology and the Case for Democracy* (Eerdmans, 2019), 32–34. The political agency of soldiers is severely attenuated, both legally in the context of politics as statecraft and in the absence of relational practices of democracy available to them in the context of military hierarchy. This attenuation of agency is the context for the betrayal of moral injury. See my "War, Masculinity, and the Ambiguity of Care," *Pastoral Psychology* 70 (2021): 1–15. Soldiers need personal and political healing and I see friendship as key for enabling both. My exploration of friendship as a source for healing after war, then, is not a turn away from the political, but toward it. My article with Joshua Morris should be read as complementary to the work of this chapter. I look forward to bringing these two streams of thought together more directly in the future. See Adam Tietje and Joshua Morris, "Shifting the Pastoral Theology Conversation on Moral Injury: The Personal Is Political for Soldiers and Veterans, Too," *Pastoral Psychology* (2023), https://doi.org/10.1007/s11089-023-01059-x.

62. Friends and brothers run parallel for Florensky and even, to some extent converge. Both friends and brothers bear each other's burdens. Still, these relations remain distinct in the ecclesial *oikonomia*. Florensky sum it up this way: "In order to live among brothers, it is necessary to have a Friend, if only a distant one. In order to have a Friend, it is necessary to live among brothers, at least to be with them in spirit. In fact, in order to treat everyone as oneself it is necessary to perceive in this one person an already achieved—even if only partial—victory over selfhood. The

agapic love of ecclesial life flows from the bonds of friendship." See Florensky, *The Pillar and Ground*, 297.

63. Pyman recounts that "Florensky felt betrayed and abandoned when Troitsky entered into a betrothal with his [Florensky's] younger sister" and suggests that "the trauma, for Florensky, had been his friend's deviation to his sister rather than the bloody shambles of his murder." See Pyman, *A Quiet Genius*, 68.

64. The Friendship letter was not part of the original eight sent to Troitsky. The first draft was likely composed in 1909 after Troitsky's marriage and before his death. See Pyman, *A Quiet Genius*, 81–82. However, it was not published until April 1911, five months after Troitsky's death. See Pyman, *A Quiet Genius*, 190. Therefore, I find my suggestion that this letter reflects Florensky's grief over the loss of Troitsky, through marriage and ultimately death, plausible.

65. Florensky, *The Pillar and Ground*, 285.

66. Florensky, *The Pillar and Ground*, 299–300.

67. Florensky, *The Pillar and Ground*, 313.

68. Florensky, *The Pillar and Ground*, 318.

69. The title of this section is taken from Hans Urs von Balthasar's Holy Saturday radio sermon "We Walked Where There Was No Path." See his *You Crown the Year with Your Goodness: Sermons Through the Liturgical Year*, trans. Graham Harrison (San Francisco: Ignatius, 1989), 87–92.

70. See my *Holy Saturday*.

71. Florensky begins *The Pillar and Ground of the Truth* by stating: "Living religious experience as the sole legitimate way to gain knowledge of the dogmas—that is how I would like to express the general theme of my book." See *The Pillar and Ground*, 5.

72. Florensky writes: "The spiritual activity in which and by which knowledge of the Pillar of Truth is given is love." See *The Pillar and Ground*, 285.

73. Rogers, *After the Spirit*, 191.

74. For more on the Holy Spirit and human prayer see Rogers, *After the Spirit*, 172, also 212ff.

75. Balthasar, *You Crown the Year*, 91.

76. Florensky, *The Pillar and Ground*, 285.

BIBLIOGRAPHY

American Psychiatric Association. *Diagnostic and Statistical Manual of Mental Disorders: DSM-V*. Washington, DC: American Psychiatric Association, 2013.

Balthasar, Hans Urs von. "We Walked Where There Was No Path." In *You Crown the Year with Your Goodness: Sermons Through the Liturgical Year*, 87–92. Translated by Graham Harrison. San Francisco: Ignatius, 1989.

Boswell, John. *Same-Sex Unions in Premodern Europe*. New York: Villard, 1994.

Boudreau, Tyler. *Packing Inferno: The Unmaking of a Marine*. Port Townsend, WA: Feral House, 2008.

Bretherton, Luke. *Christ and the Common Life: Political Theology and the Case for Democracy.* Eerdmans, 2019.

Caruth, Cathy. *Unclaimed Experience: Trauma, Narrative, and History.* Baltimore: Johns Hopkins University Press, 1996.

Florensky, Pavel. *The Pillar and Ground of the Truth: A Essay in Orthodox Theodicy in Twelve Letters.* Translated by Boris Jakim. Princeton: Princeton University Press, 1997 [1914].

Graham, Loren and Jean-Michel Kantor. *Naming Infinity: A True Story of Religious Mysticism and Mathematical Creativity.* Cambridge, MA: Harvard University Press, 2009.

Gustafson, Richard. "Introduction to the Translation." In *The Pillar and Ground of the Truth: A Essay in Orthodox Theodicy in Twelve Letters,* ix–xxiii. Translated by Boris Jakim. Princeton: Princeton University Press, 1997 [1914].

Herman, Judith. *Trauma and Recovery: The Aftermath of Violence—From Domestic Abuse to Political Terror.* New York: Basic, 1997 [1992].

Hunsinger, Deborah. *Bearing the Unbearable: Trauma, Gospel, and Pastoral Care.* Grand Rapids: Eerdmans, 2015.

Jones, Serene. *Trauma and Grace: Theology in a Ruptured World.* Louisville, KY: Westminster John Knox, 2009.

Kinghorn, Warren. "Combat Trauma and Moral Fragmentation: A Theological Account of Moral Injury." *Journal of the Society of Christian Ethics* 32, no. 2 (2012): 57–74.

Kolk, Bessel van der. *The Body Keeps the Score: Brain, Mind, and Body in the Healing of Trauma.* New York: Penguin, 2014.

Litz, Brett T., et al. "Moral Injury and Moral Repair in War Veterans: A Preliminary Model and Intervention." *Clinical Psychology Review* 29 (2009): 695–706.

Pavenkov, Oleg and Mariia Rubtcova. "El Amor como Concepto en la Filosofia Religiosa de Pavel Florensky." *Anales del Seminario de Historia de la Filosofia* 33 (2016): 163–180.

Pyman, Avril. *Pavel Florensky: A Quiet Genius: The Tragic and Extraordinary Life of Russia's Unknown Da Vinci.* New York: Continuum, 2010.

Rambo, Shelly. *Spirit and Trauma: A Theology of Remaining.* Louisville, KY: Westminster John Knox, 2010.

Rambo, Shelly. *Resurrecting Wounds: Living in the Afterlife of Trauma.* Waco, TX: Baylor University Press, 2017.

Rapp, Claudia. *Brother-Making in Late Antiquity and Byzantium.* New York: Oxford University Press, 2016.

Ridderman, Erica. "The Antinomy of Gehenna: Pavel Florensky's Contribution to Debates on Hell and Universalism." *Scottish Journal of Theology* 74, no. 3 (2021): 235–51.

Rogers, Eugene. *After the Spirit: A Constructive Pneumatology from Resources outside the Modern West.* Grand Rapids: Eerdmans, 2005.

Rogers, Eugene. "Florensky: Maximus Meets Russian Romanticism." Lecture at The University of North Carolina at Greensboro, Greensboro, NC, October 17, 2019.

Shay, Jonathan. "Moral Injury." *Psychoanalytic Psychology* 31, no. 2 (2014): 182–91.

Slesinsky, Robert. "Fr. Paul Florensky: A Profile." *St. Vladimir's Theological Quarterly* 26, no. 1 (1982): 3–27.

Slesinsky, Robert. *Pavel Florensky: A Metaphysics of Love.* Crestwood, NY: St. Vladimir's Seminary, 1984.

Tietje, Adam. "*Contra* Rambo's Theology of Remaining: A Chalcedonian and Pastoral Conception of Trauma." *Pro Ecclesia* 28, no. 1 (2019): 22–38.

Tietje, Adam. *Toward a Pastoral Theology of Holy Saturday: Providing Spiritual Care for War Wounded Souls.* Eugene, OR: Wipf and Stock, 2018.

Tietje, Adam. "War, Masculinity, and the Ambiguity of Care." *Pastoral Psychology* 70 (2021): 1–15.

Tietje, Adam and Joshua Morris. "Shifting the Pastoral Theology Conversation on Moral Injury: The Personal Is Political for Soldiers and Veterans, Too." *Pastoral Psychology* (2023), https://doi.org/10.1007/s11089-023-01059-x.

Chapter 12

The Project of Friendship

Biblical, Butlerian, and Beer-Brewing Reflections

Brandy Daniels and Shelly Penton

This is my commandment, that you love one another as I have loved you. No one has greater love than this, to lay down one's life for one's friends. —John 15:12–13

This chapter theorizes friendship as a model, or paradigm, that human beings employ as they attempt to live into Christian love. It is hard to argue with the long line of Christian theological tradition when it comes to the type of love the church must embody. Neighbor-love (*agape*) dominates Christian discourse, not necessarily (though, occasionally) to the exclusion of all other kinds of love, but as their foundation.[1] Within theological and Biblical (not to mention philosophical) scholarship, there is a great deal of literature that challenges the elevation of *agape* at the expense of other forms of love. For instance, Biblical scholars have challenged the distinction between *agape* and *philia*, pointing to how there is a great deal of overlap in use in Second Testament Greek, to how the terms are often deployed interchangeably.[2] Theologians have emphasized the entanglements between *agape* and *eros*, have wrestled with the relationship between divine and human love, and have debated extensively about the political character of love.[3] Despite these Biblical and theological interventions and debates that speak to the complexity of Christian love and the forms it takes, a great deal of attention is focused on the universal, unconditional, and self-sacrificial love identified as *agape*. As Swedish theologian Anders Nygren put it in *Agape and Eros: The Christian*

Idea of Love, which became perhaps the most influential theological treatise on love in the twentieth century, *agape* "is the centre of Christianity; the Christian fundamental motif *par excellence,* the answer to both the religious and the ethical question." Without *agape,* Nygren concludes, "nothing that is Christian would be Christian."[4]

In this chapter, we aim to add to the literature that complexifies the character of Christian love by turning to *philia,* friendship love, as, again, a model for Christian love—not so much to counter *agape,* but to frame it. Drawing on modern philosophical literature on the formation of subjectivity and community, we highlight how interrelationality is pivotal for such formation. It is through relation that we become who we are, and that we learn how to exist in relation.[5] Turning to the work of Jean-Paul Sartre, Hannah Arendt, and Judith Butler in order to elucidate the dynamics at play in the ethical, formational, and intentional intersubjectivity that is friendship, we propose the heuristic of "project": friendship *as* project, and friendship *through* project.

In reviewing these existentialist and political philosophies, key qualities emerge as central for, and via, the project of friendship: particularity, mutuality, and reciprocity. Strikingly, these key qualities are also characteristic of love in the Gospel of John's invocation of friend. A scene from John 15 is the theological register upon which our argument stands. Taking our cue from Jesus' last words to his friends, we concretize our theory of project with a case study of our own friendship in beer-brewing. We conclude by plotting out a theological path for friendship to be recognized as a paradigm of Christian love.

THE PROJECT OF FRIENDSHIP: DIALOGUING WITH SARTRE AND ARENDT

The language of project may invoke a kind of instrumentalism for some, such as a task to be completed or a thing to be fixed. While our turn to the language of project is by no means divorced from use or utility, our own purpose for the term has deeper connotations and draws on a range of theoretical resources.[6] In the following theoretical sections on the project of friendship, we argue that friendship is an intersubjective project in which the other is the self's self-project. This definition lends itself to our framing of friendship as a viable paradigm for Christian love and ethical formation.

Our use of the language of project draws on existentialist thought, particularly that of Jean-Paul Sartre. For Sartre, project is the unifying factor of the authentic subject; a projection of the self into existence; and the goal and fulfillment of the self through action in the world. Our proposal of "friendship *as* project" arises out of Sartre's work. Friendship is an example of project as Sartre understands it, i.e., a unifying projection of the subject into the world.

When Sartre speaks about project, however, he emphasizes its importance to the individual self. This emphasis does not quite fit with the relational matrix presented in friendship.[7] Thus, our delineation of "friendship as a project" limits and subtly diverges from Sartre's concept of project. In friendship, the self does not simply project itself into the world. Instead, the self's project is—in the words of Aristotle—"another self" (*allos autos*).[8] The *self-reflective* intersubjective nature of the friendship relation, as well as its governing focus on the other, makes friendship a unique project. Through friendship, the self, through the project of knowing another, also becomes aware of and develops the self, becoming "otherwise" in the process. It is, a becoming through "unbecoming." As we note below in our brief examination of John 15, the nature of the friendship relation presupposes subjects who are on equal terms. Ideally, the relation's formational quality is equal and reciprocal. It is a kind of "virtuous circle" of relation as selves grow together through dynamic knowledge of and love of one another and themselves. The friendship relation itself is a fused whole of equal and self-reflective intersubjectivity; it is the co-self-project of the friends.

Our understanding of friendship as project, and as accomplished through project, also draws from Hannah Arendt. Her perception of the embeddedness of human beings in society and her keen sense of human plurality take us beyond Sartre's conception of the individual, pointing toward a more capacious understanding of human relationality and (self)transcendence. In *The Human Condition*, Arendt offers a theory of human action based on public speech in the ancient Greek polis. Action, Arendt says, is political, egalitarian, unifying, and open-ended. It is not aimed at the necessity of preserving life. Thus it is not guided by self-interest, and could play out in a gathering of free and equal members. This coming together of diverse, equal members creates something new (beginnings). It leads to new knowledge, not of the self alone but of the self in relation to others, in terms of what it means to be human. The action taken leads to new futures, which in turn prompts new gathering and therefore new concerted action. Action, for Arendt, is not individual, conservative, or bound to the mechanistic necessity of life. It is, in a sense, "transcendent." It transforms the world, leading to futures uncontrolled and unpredicted by those taking action.

Arendt characterizes action as different from thinking. Thinking is an activity strictly played out within oneself in the form of a dialogue. It requires the splitting of the self in dialogue. Engaging in communication with others, however, requires the unity of the self in relation to others. But, talking with a friend is a special case, that counts as a kind of thinking. With a friend who holds common thoughts, one can carry out a dialogue honest enough to qualify as dialogue with oneself. This brings Arendt to the concept of friend as an "other self," again echoing Aristotle.[9] Yet the commonality and equality shared between friends does not make them the same. On the contrary, their differences make equality and dialogue possible. Their commonality does not lie in their sameness but in their ability to see the truth in each other's view of the world, thereby rendering the world "in common."[10] Friendship illuminates the complex nature of the thinking self and its constitution in relation. Ideally, the equality and commonality of the friends broadens both of their worldviews, permitting the growth of both the individuals and their relationship in turn. We argue that this kind of friendship is the locus for building (Christian) community.[11]

Inspired by Arendt's discussion of thinking and action, we speak of the "project" of friendship. We connect "friendship *through* project" with "friendship *as* project." On the one hand, a shared project is the site of the friendship; on the other hand, the friendship itself is a project. Like action, friendship *through* project has a provisional goal beyond the friendship relation. But reaching the external goal does not entail the dissolution of the friendship. Like thinking, friendship *as* project opens up the potential for dialogue within the self, and between friends who are close enough to become a common self. To draw more closely on Arendt's language, in the project of friendship, action is carried out by free, equal, and differing selves who transcend their own lives. In doing so, they transform the original conditions that brought them together. To drawn on existentialist language, the project of friendship both constitutes the particular ground or field of the relationship and transcends the relationship. The constitutive project itself changes continuously and dialectically with the changing friendship relation, reformulated by the friends as they "become" together. This transformation of both the project and the relation cannot be separated. Friendship *as* project depends on friendship *through* project, and friendship *through* project is meaningless without friendship *as* project.

But what does it mean, in light of John 15, for the interrelation of friendship to form one in a way that one might lay down one's life for a friend? What might it mean to consider the kenotic thrust of Christian discipleship, of becoming *undone*, of unbecoming, by and through friendship to the ends of love? What might it mean to practice Christian discipleship via friendship in light of Christ's kenotic action?[12] Here, a turn to the work of Judith Butler is helpful.

(UN-)BECOMING TOGETHER? THE PROJECT OF FRIENDSHIP: BUTLERIAN CONSIDERATIONS

In *Giving an Account of Oneself,* critical theorist Judith Butler emphasizes the importance of relationality, of particularity, in and as ethics. In her Spinoza-lectures-turned-book, Butler considers the problem of subjectivity and subject formation in the context of ethics and responsibility. Drawing on a range of psychoanalytic and poststructuralist thinkers, Butler refocuses ethical analysis by arguing that the subject is not simply the ground for ethics, but also the problem for ethics. Because the subject is constituted in and by relationships—because relationality both "conditions and binds the self"—relationality is central to and "an indispensable resource for" ethics.[13] Butler's primary focus is that of *challenging* accounts of the ethical subject that presume and/or reinforce a kind of moral autonomy of the ethical agent. The "I" is formed and constituted by relation, and it is done so within the context of social norms. When giving an account of one's self, the self is always addressing an Other while at the same time being interpellated as a self through moral norms and that other. Which is to say, inherent in the sense of one's self is the recognition of the limits and the opacity of that self—we are deprived of giving an account of ourselves outside of these limits.

Yet these limits, Butler argues, also provide an opportunity for a "new sense of ethics" that can emerge from the "willingness to acknowledge the limits of acknowledgment itself."[14] An ethics that is "based on our shared, invariable, and partial blindness about ourselves," where the self only emerges by and in relation to the other, means for Butler that the self can become responsible, but only by acknowledging that it cannot be without the other—only in the very space of relationality. *Giving an Account of Oneself* vitally highlights the ways in which our relationships are central to and constitutive of our ethical lives. Butler's insights offer something for theological reflection here. As becomes clear in the following section, Jesus' words in John 15 that we lay down our lives for our friends point in a very direct way that we might be ultimately undone by another, undone to the point of death. Butler emphasizes the ways in which that undoneness occurs not only in death, but in the course of our relationships—that it is part of the ethical possibilities of our relationships.

Yet, just as Butler offers us something for theological reflection on friendship, John 15 too offers something to Butler's account of relational (un)becoming—that of the lens of friendship. Interestingly, unlike the word *family*, the word *friend* appears only sparingly in *Giving an Account of Oneself*—only in the acknowledgments, as the book is dedicated to her "friend and interlocutor Barbara Johnson" and in the story of Georg, where the reference is to an imaginary friend, a mirror-fragment of himself.[15] Georg's father claims to have written to this "friend," Butler explains, "and it is finally unclear whether the friend even exists or whether he is the point of struggle between what belongs to the father and what belongs to the son . . . the name for a boundary that is never quite clear."[16] What, though, of the *actual* friend? What might the kind of relationality that is friendship—that of equality and reciprocity—add to an ethical and epistemological consideration of the kind of (un)becoming that Butler speaks of?

While Butler does not invoke the language of "project" in these existential and post-Hegelian reflections we have outlined, there are clear echoes of Butler's ethical emphasis on relationality, ethics, and the (un)formation of the subject. Moreover, in considering the limitations of Foucault's account of subject formation with regards to "think[ing] the other," Butler turns briefly to Arendt, via the work of feminist philosopher Adriana Cavarero.[17] Addressing the notion of recognition, in a decidedly Arendtian (and less so Levinasian) vein, Cavarero pushes against the notion of asking "what" we are, "as if the task were to simply fill the content of our personhood."[18] Instead, Cavarero poses, the question most central to recognition is direct, and direct*ed* to the other: "Who are you?"[19] Butler builds on Caverero and thus on Arendt, in highlighting how this question is not one of strict direct moral accountability, but one that, in the Arendtian concept of the social, "affirms that there is an other who is not fully knowable to me." "For Cavarero," Butler continues, this "implies a critique of conventional ways of understanding sociality, and in this sense she reverses the progression we saw in Hegel." Whereas Hegel moves from the dyad to social recognition, "for Cavarero," and, by extension, for Butler, "it is necessary to ground the social in the dyadic encounter."[20] Butler reflects on how, in these socially grounded dyadic encounters that serve as the site of and for ethics, the norms by which we seek to make ourselves recognizable are not fully ours, how the "interruption and dispossession of my perspective *as mine*" takes place in a range of different ways, and thus it "is only in dispossession that I can and do give any account of myself."[21] Within Butler's reflections on the unformational work of relationality, there are resonances of the deeply rooted theological concept of kenosis, Jesus's act of self-emptying in the incarnation.

ON LOVE AND FRIENDSHIP: FRAMING AGAPE THROUGH PHILIA IN JOHN 15

Butler's theory of dispossession of the self is played out in sacred terms in the Gospel of John, chapter 15. In Christian terms, dispossession of self is often formulated as self-sacrificing love, paradigmatically referred to as "agape" love.[22] In verse 12, Jesus commands his disciples to love (*agapao*) each other as he has loved (again, *agapao*) them. The coupling of agape with the command of self-giving is definitive of Christian love. But something extraordinary happens in the verse immediately following, where Jesus goes on to say that the greatest love (*meizona agapen*) is to lay down one's life for one's *friends* (*philoi*):

> This is my commandment, that you love (*agapate*) one another as I have loved (*egapesa*) you. No one has greater love (*agapen*) than this, to lay down one's life for one's friends (*philon*). You are my friends (*philoi*) if you do what I command you. I do not call you servants (*doulous*) any longer, because the servant (*doulos*) does not know what the master is doing, but I have called you friends (*philous*), because I have made known to you everything that I have heard from my Father.[23]

There is much to unpack here. We dwell on this passage to draw out the implications for friendship as- and through-project that we have theorized in previous sections, finding three qualities that are characteristic of a paradigmatic Christian-love-as-friendship: equality, particularity/concreteness, and transformation/mutual (un)becoming.

First, this passage speaks to the self-sacrificing characteristic that is agape's traditional defining quality in the Christian story. Jesus is willing to lay down his life, traditionally understood as to die, to sacrifice himself, because of the love he holds toward and embodies for humanity. However, instead of its universal application that typically would include strangers, enemies, or the world—which we have in other places in the four gospels—we have a qualification of it vis-à-vis his friends. Jesus does not say, "A greater love has no person than this, that they lay down their lives for an [unmarked, unknown, suffering, and/or hostile] other," which would fit well within other such instances of the command given to the disciples.[24] The breadth of the commandments to love in the four Gospels is astonishing, ranging from uncontextualized others, to any person whose suffering you can relieve, to any person who would commit evil against you. The point of this breadth is that love should be applied to everyone, universally, as God loves everyone, universally. Thus, the application of this paradigmatic (*agape*) love to *friends* in this passage—and not only its application but its application as the preeminent instantiation of love—seems counterintuitive, especially in light of other gospel verses that contrast loving those who already love you to loving those who hate you.[25] It seems, contrary to other instances of the love command, that we love others for their *particularity*.

One might object in response that this is not counterintuitive or contrary at all, given that Christians are commanded to love all people, regardless of particularities, such as class or tribe, and therefore, friends—despite (not because of) their particularity—fall within the category of all people. This is, in effect, what St. Aquinas was getting at when he described the relationship between God and human beings as charity (communicative, self-giving love) which could be called friendship (via modification of Aristotle's definition), and by extension, we love all others whom God loves because of our friendship *with God* (and *not* our friendship with *them*).[26] In this way, *agape*/charity subsumes friendship as a renaming of itself with no fundamental change to the nature of *agape*, whose effects are to love everyone because God loves everyone. This objection, however, sidesteps the issue of the qualifier of the act of self-giving in this passage: "no one has *greater* love than this, *to lay down one's life for one's friends*." The introduction of gradation into the conversation is not a delimiting one; in other words, it does not dictate that all loves fall within a hierarchy, nor would we (the authors) wish to argue such a thing. However, it serves to highlight rhetorically what is unique about this moment for Jesus: he is speaking with his *friends*, not with strangers, his family, or his executioners. The word marks the relationship between Jesus and those who listen in the moment, contextualizing and concretizing it. Out of that concretization, a genuine call to self-sacrifice arises.

Instead of an abstracted description of love in the form of beatitude or parable that he would offer to quibbling lawyers, we have a particularizing of it: Jesus tells his friends—whom he has lived, eaten, worked, and suffered with—to love as he does, by sacrificing themselves for each other. In this passage, there is no escape from the command to love, not because it is universally applicable or abstracted from all conditions, but quite the opposite: the command to love fully and selflessly is inescapable because the one whom you are called to love is in the room, is next to you, and has known you intimately. The face of the beloved is not veiled or imagined but instead fully rendered in the lines and imperfections of a friend's countenance. Jesus was talking to *his* friends, *his* particular and chosen companions, describing a love he would embody with *his* crucifixion. To put it differently, a call to self-sacrifice is meaningless without a genuine "for what?," or taken at its deepest level, "for whom?"

Moving beyond the *particularizing* of the command to love, the second point of focus is the imbued *equality* of those who are included within the friend-relation. It is important to note here how friendship differs from other relationships in Jesus' context. Scholars have explored the context of friendship in the Gospel of John, which draws on Greco-Roman conceptualization of friendship. Foundational to this conceptualization is that friends form a community of equals, as opposed to relationships formed between social superiors and their inferiors, and that the motive for the friendship bond is the good of the other, not of the self.[27] Equality was important in Aristotle's categorization of friendship and was reiterated in Roman thinkers, who extended the friendship relation to include patron-client relationships that were mutually beneficial and approached in good faith from both parties. New Testament scholar Gail O'Day highlights not only the self-sacrificial aspect of friendship that is present in Greco-Roman conceptualizations but also the aspect of *parresia*, or bold truthfulness. What distinguishes friends from other people in society is that they are able to speak the truth to one another—including, vitally, criticism. Such speech is only possible among equals, and further, equals whose goal is the good of the other. This point is echoed in Arendt's assertion that speaking to a friend is like speaking to oneself, which would include self-critique, and coupled with Butler, ethical self-awareness through self-dispossession. Jesus enacted friendship in the way he spoke truthfully and boldly to his friends, thereby treating them as equals.[28] This is what is understood when Jesus speaks to them not as "servants" but as "friends," differentiating the two based on intimate knowledge, that of the Father, which has passed between them. Such knowledge is, in fact, knowledge of Jesus' self—relationally and theologically always incomplete—which finds its home in his friends and implies the possibility of good faith dialogue through bold truthfulness and, in its most potent form, *transformation* of the self.[29]

The *equality* of Jesus' friendships is therefore characterized by his ability to change his friends' orientation toward the world and toward each other, the ultimate goal of *parresia*, in which selves are dispossessed and repossessed in a more intentional, more capacious way. However, *parresia* cannot be a one-way street in friendship. In other words, for the friend-relation to be genuine, Jesus must not only be able to change his friends, but they must also be able to change him. Though not drawn out in John 15, the example of another friend of Jesus, Lazarus, reflects the reciprocity implicit in the word "friend." In John 11, word of Lazarus' illness led Jesus to change his travel plans, and his death deeply grieved Jesus, moving him to miraculous action.[30] Jesus' actions—flowing from the grief-reformed unity of his self— change in relation to his friend. Further, the giving of life *to* a friend mirrors the action of the giving of life *for* a friend. Both acts are embodied in Jesus' self-sacrifice, actions based in a love Jesus then asks his friends to replicate. The *reciprocal* and *transformational* nature of Jesus' relationships with his disciples frame the friendship relation as an ideal model for Christ-like love.

John's scene in chapter 15 can be mapped out through the theme of Jesus as an ideal friend, one who speaks honestly to and gives himself for his friends as equals. *Agape* and *philia* in this chapter are interchangeable, but the framing of *agape* within the friendship relation in this passage opens up possibilities for a differently accented theorization of Christian love, one in which particularity, equality, and reciprocal transformation (i.e., [un]becoming) are emphasized.

BREWING FRIENDSHIP: A PROJECT

And so, to pick up where our theory of the friendship project left off: what might it mean to consider Butler's relational (un)becoming as an intentional ethical act—as, in, and through project? What might it mean to not only inevitably always already be dispossessed by the other, but to *pursue* a kind of becoming that is an unbecoming through an other? What might it mean to pose the friendship project as the place where equality, particularity, and reciprocal (un)becoming are brought to the fore, as in John 15?

These are massive questions that answering with any kind of adequacy would far overrun the scope of this chapter. While the key aim is to highlight *the questions themselves* as a lens for which and through which friendship might offer us theo-ethical resources, we do want to begin to illustrate and to elaborate what friendship as and through project as an ethical pursuit might look like via our own friendship. Since the entirety of our friendship is, again, too broad a lens to approach the question within the bounds of this paper, we have chosen a case study of sorts: our friendship in the context of our home-brewing project.

Our acquaintance of four years became true friendship when we both landed in Hyde Park, Chicago, in the summer of 2016. Since neither of us knew many people in the area, we began visiting each other's apartments, helping each other with small projects, and generally having fun conversations about shared interests. One night, despairing about the viability of the academic job market, we started envisioning what we could do (together!) if our current plans fell through. Thus, Telos Brewing was born.

It was a simple idea, immediately embarked on: we would start brewing our own beer, beers which would seasonally align with the church calendar or thematically connect with current events through a theological hermeneutic. Our first beer survived a few minor catastrophes during the brewing process and was presented for tasting to a small group of friends in December 2016—our *Advent Ale*.

During the process, our friendship grew and changed (as we grew together and changed each other). We were surviving the Chicago winter, pedagogical and professional challenges (Shelly was a student and Brandy a postdoctoral fellow and lecturer at the time), personal mishaps and political disaster (remember: 2016)—and a part of that survival was our friendship and our brewing project.

To "zoom in" to the case study that is our project of friendship through the project of beer-brewing even further, we consider the process and project of one of our brews in particular—the third beer we brewed together, *Felix Culpa*, a bourbon barrel porter brewed in and for the season of Lent. How did the process of that project contribute to and reflect the project of our friendship? How did it move us more towards an ethical practice of reciprocal unbecoming? The short answer: In a *lot* of ways. Here are a few.

First, on the most quotidian level and as anyone who has done any kind of home-brewing has already viscerally surmised, the home-brewing process is one fraught with complications, especially for two humanities scholars with only a basic knowledge of chemistry. There is a great deal of literature out there—psychological, sociological, philosophical, theological—that reflects on the ways in which the mundane realities of marital and other familial relationships are sites for a kind of destabilizing growth. This happens in the differing approaches and experiences, as well as the rising frustrations that occur in the day-to-day where one learns better how to love one's partner or family. There is much less reflection, however, on how friendship—commonly touted as a more fluid and inchoate chosen form of relationship loosely tethered by a reciprocity rooted in mutual self-interest—serves as a site for such growth. Beer-brewing is not only its own laboratory setting of sorts, but also, at least for us, a relational laboratory setting for friendship.

As Butler argues, ethical responsibility is an avowal of the limits of self-understanding, as we are asked to recognize the ways in which the other is unknowable. We can only be ethical in and through this failure to fully see or understand the other. While Butler's examples are far more serious and substantive than the mundane realities of beer-brewing, through projects of friendship we are faced with the opportunity to practice and learn such ethical responsibility. Our biggest brewing errors, and our biggest tiffs and frustrations in the midst of them, occurred when one of us presumed or attempted to know or understand one another, and in doing so, didn't see the other. When we were brewing *Felix Culpa*, for instance, I (Brandy) presumed she (Shelly) was picking up the ice, because that is what she always did, yet I basically ignored her the night before our brew day as she was talking about how busy and stressful her day was going to be. This had thus led her to assume, based on what she knew about me, that I would take care of it. Again, a remarkably mundane example, but nonetheless a site, a project, through which we practiced—both intentionally and inevitably—disavowing our assumptions about one another (and, in and through that, about ourselves), and in doing so, learning how to love one another (and ourselves) better.

There are many ways that the mundanity of brewing serve as a profound laboratory of sorts, not just for beer-making, but for ethical responsibility, care, and (un)becoming: in being midbrew and realizing that you forgot to get the ice; in not watching the wort, the simmer turning into a overflowing boil that leaves a liter of sticky beer residue piling up on your stove and creeping down into the crevices of your kitchen counter; in realizing your brewmate printed the labels wrong and you now have to pay to expedite new label paper and manage to print them off again in less than 48 hours when your brew-release party is planned; etc. Beyond these, however, the process of brewing together also has led to *deeper* moments of such ethical praxis.

For instance, we brewed *Felix Culpa* following the months of the 2016 election and inauguration of Donald Trump, months filled with grief, fear, and horror. As Lent 2017 began and the nation was wracked with protests, we turned to brewing and to a beer that would reflect our despair, as well as the possibility of hope within it. We finished it in time for Holy Week and Good Friday, holding the tasting party on the most mysterious and contemplative of Christian holidays, Holy Saturday, when we were forced to dwell with death and sin's seeming victory.

While we were putting the labels on our Good Friday beer, a conversation began concerning the nature and moral status of state policing. Without knowing it, we had commenced the longest conversation of our friendship: a twelve-hour argument (in the mode of Arendt's dialogue of the thinking self) stretching from dusk on Good Friday to the dawn of Holy Saturday. Regardless of our intention, our brewing had brought us together to listen and to learn about each other and ourselves. And as we thought with and cared for each other within that conversation, we noticed how it changed us—not only our views about the subject, but also our perspective of each other and our friendship. This in turn opened within our friendship a deeper capacity to listen and to learn from each other in subsequent conversations and difficulties, a continuing becoming of the friendship itself. As we watched the sunlight scatter across the yard and creep up the stone walls of the University of Chicago's Disciples Divinity House, the last piece of our conversation was about our friendship, a reflection on what it takes to sustain conversation and trust through conflict, frustration, and doubt. We were undone, and our friendship reborn.

THEOLOGICAL DIRECTIONS:
PHILIA AS CHRISTIAN LOVE

What could this small fragment of our friendship mean for our theological reflection? Returning to the conversation between Jesus and his friends in John 15, we ask ourselves: How can one know how to love people, unless one knows how to love, and be loved, by a friend with all their particularities, needs, and imperfections? How can one learn humility and openness without becoming aware of the ultimate mystery of oneself and the other, realized through friendship? How can one speak of self-sacrifice for the other in terms of *agape* without the framing of *philia*, in which one recognizes the self who is sacrificed and the other who is saved?

We are coming to understand that friendship love is both the epistemological comprehension of love and ethical formation of how to love, which becomes the experiential model and affective cue for loving ever more others. Even love of stranger and enemy finds its lived basis, beyond abstractions, here: the object of one's love approached in dignity as an equal, one's response qualified by context and need, and one's modality characterized by humble openness to the potential transformation rendered by the stranger in one's self. This is how we, divine and human, from moment to moment, love; namely, we give ourselves to and for our friends—always imperfectly, yet straining for a perfection that we know we can never quite apprehend.

"As the Father has loved me, so have I loved you; abide in my love . . . I have said these things to you so that my joy may be in you and that your joy may be complete. This is my commandment, that you love each other as I have loved you."[31] We pose this scene, founded on the paradigm of love that binds Jesus Christ to his friends, as the first scene of Christian community. Jesus' project is his friends, and their friendship is his project.[32] Without their presence with him, there is no love, either. And without love fulfilled in his incarnation and sacrifice—his (un)becoming—and without their loving response in *their* sacrifice and *their* (un)becoming, the Christian church would never have come into being.[33] The "project" of Christ's church is, first, friendship *through* the project of Christ; in other words, how loving relationships are constituted in light of the person of Christ and Christ's friendship with humanity, the ground and the goal for such relationships. Second, it is friendship *as* project, i.e., how we come to know and love each other, as Christ knew and loved his friends, and they, each other; in other words, (un)becoming as Christians in relation to each other and to the world. *Friend* is the proper name for the common noun of *love*.

Times have changed since we began brewing together; so, too, have our friendship and our brewing, as well as the way we conceive of them. Of course, it is impossible to disentangle our friendship *as* project from our shared projects—brewing and otherwise—though theorizing our friendship (in many reflective conversations not limited to academic book chapters) sometimes demands it. Our latest beer, Philia, is our ninth, and our tasting parties have grown from a small group of friends to large gatherings, which now include friends of friends that, wonderfully enough, become friends in their own right. Transformed, too, is our perspective on what this project does, both for us and for the world. We have developed it as a theological window through which to view not only current events but also our responsibility toward those events, a species of public theology that you can taste. We chose to apply our brewing qua public theology lens to our own friendship in our Philia beer, a metareflection on what our friendship has been and is becoming—and, notably, how we, as ethical subjects, are (un)becoming through this project of friendship.

NOTES

1. See, for example, Pope Francis' latest encyclical, *Fratelli Tutti: On Fraternity and Social Friendship* (Vatican City: Libreria Editrice Vaticana, 2020), https://www .vatican.va/content/francesco/en/encyclicals/documents/papa- francesco_20201003_ enciclica-fratelli-tutti.html. In chapter 2, "Stranger on the Road" (§56–86), Francis offers an extended exposition on the Parable of the Good Samaritan and agape/neighborly love as the key to Christians' relationships with each other and with the world.

2. See, for instance, Gustav Stärhlin, "φιλέω, καταφιλέω, φιλία," in *Theological Dictionary of the New Testament,* volume 9, eds. Gerhard Friedrich, Geoffrey W. Bromiley (Grand Rapids: Eerdmans, 1974), 113–171; Frederick W. Danker, Walter Bauer, and William Arndt, "ἀγάπη," in *A Greek-English Lexicon of the New Testament and Other Early Christian Literature,* 3rd edition (Chicago: University of Chicago Press, 2001), 6–7.

3. See, for instance, Benedict XVI, *Deus caritas est* (Vatican City: Libreria Editrice Vaticana, 2005), www.vatican.va/holy_father/benedict_xvi/encyclicals/documents/ hf_benxvi_enc_20051225_deus-caritas-est_en.html; Werner G. Jeanrong, *A Theology of Love* (New York: T&T Clark, 2010); Eric Gregory, *Politics and the Order of Love: An Augustinian Ethic of Democratic Citizenship* (Chicago: University of Chicago Press, 2008).

4. Anders Nygren, *Agape and Eros: The Christian Idea of Love* (Chicago: University of Chicago Press, 1982), 48.

5. While there have been many efforts to explicate the nature of friendship love theologically, those efforts tend to find their sources (justifiably) almost solely within the Christian tradition: theologians cite other, canonical, theologians. Our turn to more modern and philosophical sources may therefore seem unexpected or uncalled for; however, we hope with this move to open up fruitful ground for discussion, facilitating dialogue across disciplines. Though our commitment in this chapter is to the Christian tradition broadly, our method could be described as Tillichian: we depend on the dialect and foci of our contemporary context (including our personal story) to clarify ultimate questions, including the nature of love, ethics, and friendship.

6. In the introduction to *Giving An Account of Oneself* (New York: Fordham University Press, 2005), Judith Butler notes that she "make[s] eclectic use of various philosophers and critical theorists in [her] inquiry. Not all of their positions are compatible with one another," she writes, and notes that she does "not attempt to synthesize them here" (21). Our turn to an eclectic array of theoretical resources on "project" is in line with this Butlerian move.

7. Though there are arguably ethical implications of the self in relation to the world within Sartre's framework (Simone de Beauvoir's work elaborates some of these implications).

8. Aristotle, in the *Nicomachean Ethics*, refers to a friend as "another self" in several places: in Book VIII, chapters 4 and 9, and in Book IX, chapter 4. Here is a representative example: "So, because each of these characteristics belongs to the good person in relation to himself, and he stands in the same relation to his friend as to himself (his friend being another self), friendship too seems to be one of these characteristics, and those who have them to be friends." See Aristotle, *Nicomachean Ethics*, trans. and ed. Roger Crisp, Cambridge: Cambridge University Press, 2004, Book IX, chapter 4, 1166a. For comparison to a Christian source, see this beautiful and profoundly moving sentiment from St. Augustine's *Confessions*, Book IV, concerning the death of his friend (and referencing Cicero): "I was surprised that any other mortals were alive, since he whom I had loved as if he would never die was dead. I was even more surprised that when he was dead I was alive, for he was my 'other self.' Someone has well said of his friend, 'He was half my soul.' I had felt that my soul and his soul were 'one soul in two bodies.'" Augustine, *Confessions*, trans. Henry Chadwick (Oxford: Oxford University Press, 1991), 59.

9. Hannah Arendt, *Responsibility and Judgment*, ed. Jerome Kohn (New York: Schocken Books, 2003), 98.

10. Rendering the world in common is the secret ingredient of co-creation through action, the reason that Arendt found friendship as the potential ground for political community.

11. Here we go beyond Arendt, whose writing dwells more on the failure of Socrates' public dialogue (attempting to forge community relations as friend relations) and Plato's reaction to it. See Hannah Arendt, "Philosophy and Politics," *Social Research: An International Quarterly*, 71, no. 3 (Fall 2004): 436.

12. For more on how kenosis might function as a paradigm for Christian discipleship, including within feminist theologies, and in a way that takes seriously the ways kenosis and self-emptying has been utilized to justify the oppression of women, see Anna Mercedes, *Power For: Feminism and Christ's Self-Giving* (New York: T&T Clark, 2011).

13. Butler, *Giving an Account of Oneself*, 40.

14. Butler, *Giving an Account of Oneself*, 42.

15. Butler, *Giving an Account of Oneself*, viii.

16. Butler, *Giving an Account of Oneself*, 47.

17. Butler, *Giving an Account of Oneself*, 20.

18. Butler, *Giving an Account of Oneself*, 31

19. Butler here cites Adriana Cavarero who herself cites *The Human Condition*: "Action and speech are so closely related because the primordial and specifically human act must at the same time answer to the question asked to every newcomer: 'who are you?'" (31, cf. en16). The Arendt reference is from *The Human Condition* (1958), 183, cited partially in Cavarero, *Relating Narratives: Storytelling and Selfhood* (New York: Routledge, 2000), 20.

20. Butler, *Giving an Account of Oneself*, 32.

21. Butler, *Giving an Account of Oneself,* 36, 37.

22. This paradigmatic love is related to and parallels the "kenotic" love of Christ, or the self-emptying of God toward the world in order to relate intimately to the world in its own terms. Kenosis and agape, both examples of self-dispossession, reflect the other-loving relationality that speaks to the essence of God (and reality) in Christian tradition, which is echoed in Butler's concept.

23. John 15:12–15, New Revised Standard Version Updated Edition.

24. Cf. Matthew 5:4345; Matthew 7:12; Matthew 22:37–39; Matthew 25:37–40; Mark 12:28–34; Luke 6:35–36; Luke 10:25–37.

25. Matthew 5:43–48.

26. Thomas Aquinas, *Summa theologica*, trans. Fathers of the English Dominican Province (New York: Benziger Brothers, 1911–1925), IIa-IIae, q. 23 "agape considered in itself."

27. See Takaaki Harguchi, "*Philia* as *Agape*: The Theme of Friendship in the Gospel of John," *Asia Journal of Theology* 28, no. 2 (2014), 252; Gail O'Day, "Jesus as a Friend in the Gospel of John," *Interpretation*, vol. 58, no. 2 (Jan. 2004), 144–157.

28. O'Day, "Jesus as a Friend in the Gospel of John," 155. Perhaps one of the most notable thinkers who writes on parrhesia, Michel Foucault, also highlights the connections between bold truth-telling and friendship in his lectures on the topic, published as *The Courage of Truth* (New York: Picador, 2008). For instance, to offer just one example, Foucault turns to Socrates and Plutarch, pointing to how it is *parresia* that distinguishes the friend from the flatterer (7, 70).

29. As Jesus charges his friends in John 15:4, "Abide in me as I abide in you."

30. For more on Jesus' friendship with Lazarus, see Dana L. Robert, *Faithful Friendships: Embracing Diversity in Christian Community* (Grand Rapids: Eerdmans, 2019), 24ff.

31. John 15:9, 11–12.

32. By extension, appropriate to Christ's divinity, we can say that Christ's love for the world is friendship with all people, in all times and places, with all their contingency and particularities. And, appropriate to his humanity, we can say that Christ's equality with us in our state made this friendship possible.

33. We find a repetition of this logic and model of love in Jesus' postresurrection conversation with Peter in John 21:15–18, in which Jesus asks Peter if he loves him (*agapao*) twice, and ends by asking "Simon son of John, do you love (*phileo*) me?" and then commands him again to "Feed my sheep," which has been interpreted as tending and expanding Christ's church.

BIBLIOGRAPHY

Aquinas, Thomas. *Summa theologica*, IIa-IIae, q. 23. Translated by Fathers of the English Dominican Province. New York: Benziger Brothers, 1911–1925.

Arendt, Hannah. *The Human Condition.* Chicago: University of Chicago Press, 1958.

Arendt, Hannah. "Philosophy and Politics." *Social Research: An International Quarterly* 71, no. 3 (Fall 2004): 427–454.

Arendt, Hannah. *Responsibility and Judgment*. Edited by Jerome Kohn. New York: Schocken Books, 2003.

Augustine. *Confessions*. Translated by Henry Chadwick. Oxford: Oxford University Press, 1991.

Benedict XVI. *Deus caritas est: On Christian Love*. Vatican City: Libreria Editrice Vaticana, 2005. https://www.vatican.va/content/benedict-xvi/en/encyclicals/documents/hf_ben-xvi_enc_20051225_deus-caritas-est.html.

Butler, Judith. *Giving An Account of Oneself.* New York: Fordham University Press, 2005.

Cavarero, Adriana. *Relating Narratives: Storytelling and Selfhood.* New York: Routledge, 2000.

Danker, Frederick W., Walter Bauer, and William Arndt. "ἀγάπη." In *A Greek-English Lexicon of the New Testament and Other Early Christian Literature,* 3rd edition, 6–7. Chicago: University of Chicago Press, 2001.

Foucault, Michel. *The Courage of Truth: The Government of Self and Others II.* Lectures at the Collège de France, 1983–1984. Edited by Frédéric Gros. Translated by Graham Burchell. New York: Picador, 2008.

Francis. *Fratelli Tutti: On Fraternity and Social Friendship.* Vatican City: Libreria Editrice Vaticana, 2020. https://www.vatican.va/content/francesco/en/encyclicals/documents/papa-francesco_20201003_enciclica-fratelli-tutti.html.

Gregory, Eric. *Politics and the Order of Love: An Augustinian Ethic of Democratic Citizenship.* Chicago: University of Chicago Press, 2008.

Harguchi, Takaaki. "*Philia* as *Agape*: The Theme of Friendship in the Gospel of John." *Asia Journal of Theology* 28, no. 2 (2014): 250–262.

Jeanrong, Werner G. *A Theology of Love.* New York: T&T Clark, 2010.

Mercedes, Anna. *Power For: Feminism and Christ's Self-Giving.* New York: T&T Clark, 2011.

Nygren, Anders. *Agape and Eros: The Christian Idea of Love.* Chicago: University of Chicago Press, 1982.

O'Day, Gail. "Jesus as a Friend in the Gospel of John." *Interpretation*, vol. 58, no. 2 (Jan. 2004): 144–157.

Robert, Dana L. *Faithful Friendships: Embracing Diversity in Christian Community.* Grand Rapids: Eerdmans, 2019.

Stärhlin, Gustav. "φιλέω, καταφιλέω, φιλία." In *Theological Dictionary of the New Testament,* volume 9, 113–171. Edited by Gerhard Friedrich and Geoffrey W. Bromiley. Grand Rapids: Eerdmans, 1974.

Chapter 13

Religion Has No Bo(u)nds?

Expanding the Dimensions of Religion to the Attachment of Spiritual Friendship

Sarah Ann Bixler

Where does friendship fit in conceptualizations of religion? Religious traditions are often described in terms of believing, behaving, and belonging. Yet this oft-invoked trifecta overlooks an important dimension of religion, bonding. The bonding dimension of religion makes room for friendship's importance as an integral part of religion. This chapter traces the origin of the traditional religion trifecta and joins Vassilis Saroglou in arguing for the addition of bonding, thus expanding the bounds of the traditional dimensions of religion. Drawing from the theological discipline of Christian spirituality and the psychosocial discipline of attachment theory, I explore how the bonding dimension of religion makes room for friendship. More specifically, I draw on the writings of a medieval Cistercian monk Aelred of Rievaulx and contemporary psychologists who developed and who critique attachment theory. Both Aelred's vision for spiritual friendship and critiques of attachment theory invite a redirected focus from isolated pairs of friends to a broader network of friendship, situated in the context of a religious community. As we will see, friendship and a network of attachment bonds are just as integral to the human experience of religion as religious beliefs, behaviors, and sense of belonging.

DIMENSIONS OF RELIGION

Religious traditions often self-identify or are described by analysts in terms of believing, behaving, and belonging—ordering and emphasizing these dimensions in different ways. These categories came into popularity through the work of Rabbi Mordecai Kaplan. In his *magnum opus* published in 1934, *Judaism as a Civilization,* Kaplan argues that belonging is the most important element that binds Jews together worldwide as a people.[1] For Kaplan, certain bounds of Judaism are too rigid, "a series of fixed and static ideas" that could be corrected by an emphasis on belonging.[2] He recommends moving emphasis from "outdated beliefs and behaviors" to the more adaptable and creative dimension of belonging.

Sixty years later, British sociologist Grace Davie picked up on these dimensions of religion in a new configuration. She observed the persistence of beliefs without belonging and published *Religion in Britain Since 1945: Believing without Belonging.* Davie describes persons who "persist in believing, but see no need to participate with even minimal regularity in their religious institutions . . . [and] express their religious sentiments by staying away from, rather than going to, their places of worship."[3] According to Davie, the bounds of belief can endure without an accompanying community of belonging or the repetition of behaviors within places of worship to sustain it.

Anabaptist historian Alan Kreider has also analyzed belief, behavior, and belonging. His research is situated in the historical experience of religious conversion to Christianity. He notes that by the fourth century, a four-stage Christian conversion process had solidified that sought to reshape behavior first, followed by the learning of orthodox beliefs, and conferring belonging last of all in the climactic rite of adult baptism with accompanying participation in the Eucharist.[4] Under Constantine's appropriation of Christianity, this scope became abbreviated, until in the sixth century the conversion of belief was reduced to self-examination of conscience, behavioral expectations were set by Catholic church officials, and belonging was unilaterally conferred across European societies in infant baptism.[5] Kreider concludes that Christianity in the Christendom era revolved around a prescribed set of beliefs, belonging that enveloped both civil society and the church, and behavioral coercion.[6]

While Kreider, Davie, and Kaplan analyze the bounds of religion in different ways, in reconfiguring these three dimensions of religion they fail to account for the emotional interpersonal bonds of religious experience. This dimension of bonding includes one of the most important human bonds, friendship, which is an important aspect of many religious traditions but does not neatly conform to the bounds of belief, behavior, or belonging. Believing, the cognitive religious dimension, finds expression in dogmas, truth, intellect, and meaning.[7] These beliefs identify beings and forces that exist as externally transcendent to humankind and the material world. Although philosophy of religion explores principles that help define beliefs about what constitutes true friendship, friendship is not limited to a series of beliefs. It must be practiced. Behaving is the moral dimension of religion, where specific human actions express a religion's norms, virtues, and understandings of right and wrong.

Where, then, does friendship fit in conceptualizations of religion? Practices of friendship reflect particular behaviors, and those behaviors deemed as immoral generally represent a violation of friendship. Yet, friendship cannot be reduced to practices; it is also experienced as a sense of belonging. Belonging is the affiliative dimension, an individual's claim to a social or group identity that exists across historical and geographical contexts. Friendship, however, is realized in a bond with a particular person or persons more than to a social or group identity that exists across time and place. In these ways, friendship relates to but is ultimately something beyond any of the three traditional dimensions of religion. Friendship pushes the bounds of these three dimensions.

In 2011, Belgian psychologist of religion Vassilis Saroglou proposed expanding the bounds of the traditional religion trifecta with the Big Four model. As I will explore, this expansion makes a legitimate place for friendship in religion. From Saroglou's cross-cultural research, he concludes that believing, behaving, belonging, and *bonding* are "universally present across religions and cultural contexts" and distinguish religion from other social constructs.[8] These four dimensions are distinct from one another, and their expression and interconnectedness differ based on religious context.[9]

Saroglou highlights the equal importance of emotional connectedness—bonding—in addition to beliefs, behaviors, and belonging for religiosity. The Big Four model expands the traditional definition of religion by affirming an emotional dimension, which calls attention to essential emotional human bonds such as friendship in religious studies. These emotional bonds represent an important but often overlooked dimension of religion.

Saroglou's understanding of bonding as the emotional dimension of religion includes rituals and emotions that elicit a sense of self-transcendence. These bond the individual with a transcendent reality—whether a divine being, others, or the inner self. Accordingly, the prototypical emotion of the bonding dimension is awe. After noting the distinction of each of these four dimensions of religion, Saroglou combines them in six pairings that each correspond to a different religious form or expression. While "all four dimensions are present in any religious form," each religious form emphasizes two dimensions more than the others.[10] The three religious forms that emphasize bonding are its pairing with (1) belonging, in charismatic communities; (2)

behaving, as in asceticism; and (3) believing, in spirituality. This last combination emphasizes both believing in a transcendent reality and bonding with it, which is characteristic of the spiritual expression of friendship as defined in the works of Aelred of Rievaulx.

HOW DOES FRIENDSHIP FIT IN RELIGION?

In northern twelfth-century England, the abbot of the monastic community at Rievaulx wrote two seminal works on spiritual friendship: *Mirror of Charity* and *Spiritual Friendship.* According to Aelred, Jesus calls his followers into a doubly-transcendent experience of spiritual friendship with one another that leads to union with God. Spiritual friendship holds the power of spiritual transformation. Aelred observes, "One can make a rather easy transition from human friendship to friendship with God himself [*sic*], because of the similarity between the two."[11] Indeed, bonding for Aelred is an irreplaceable dimension of religion. The process of union, or bonding, with God grows from this transcendent experience of bonding with a friend. Yet, this does not occur with just any friendship; it must have a spiritual quality—the presence of belief in the divine. As friends together immerse themselves in contemplation of God, "Aelred understands spiritual friendship as *carrying* one's soul to union with God."[12] This combination of an emphasis on believing and bonding is characteristic of the spiritual expression of religion that Saroglou describes.

Contextually, Aelred represents the perspective of his own medieval Christianity, which regarded friendship as the highest form of Christian love.[13] Aelred notes that friendship, *amicitia,* is derived from love, *amor.*[14] He therefore claims the bond of spiritual friendship as the highest form of human love. "Love is the source and origin of friendship," he writes, "for although love can exist without friendship, friendship can never exist without love."[15] The depths of love in spiritual friendship grow from an emotion into a transcendent bond with another person because of belief in a divine presence, and ultimately lead to a bond with that divine being.

Ultimately, Aelred defines spiritual friendship as an attachment—to the friend, and to God. In his expositions on spiritual friendship, Aelred frequently employs the Latin word *affectus,* translated into English as "attachment." He defines it as "a kind of spontaneous, pleasant inclination of the spirit toward someone."[16] This spontaneous arising of attachment is not the result of conscious reason, but instead develops within the unconscious dimension of the self. Aelred refers to *affectus,* for example, as "the charming bond of friendship,"[17] alternatively translated as "the welcome attachment of friendship."[18] In this spontaneity of the spirit, the loving bond of friendship emerges as affection grows for the friend, which leads to union with God.

Aelred goes into great detail to systematize the ways love is moved toward its object by attachment and/or reason.[19] He outlines five types of attachment, which he orders from highest to lowest.[20] First, *spiritual attachment* goes beyond the temporal realm and can arise either from the movement of the Holy Spirit or devil.[21] For Aelred, attachment nurtured by the Holy Spirit is the highest form. Next, *rational attachment* arises from appreciation for someone's virtue.[22] Sometimes, a friend may need to release the physical presence of a beloved friend if life calls them away. Reason makes this letting go possible even when the attachment is strong, which makes the attachment primarily rational.[23] Aelred notes that irrational attachment occurs when someone is attracted to a person's nonvirtuous qualities or coerces someone for personal gain.[24] Third, *dutiful attachment* occurs when someone serves another person.[25] Aelred warns that this form of attachment can pose danger to the person in the serving position, because attachment to the one served can be mistaken for attachment to the benefits they provide. Aelred counsels that reason is especially important in this case, helping to protect the person in the serving position.[26]

Fourth, *natural attachment* is familial attachment.[27] Aelred insists that natural attachment should not be allowed precedence over reason; though family bonds are strong, their negative and positive impact must be discerned. Finally, the lowest form of attachment for Aelred is *physical attachment*. This occurs in the case of physical attraction, which can lead to good or evil, so it should be carefully moderated.[28]

In Aelred's delineation of these five types, he recognizes categorical differences among them. He believes that love moved by reason is holier and more secure than love moved by *affectus*—often translated in English as attachment—because affection is transitory and not subject to free will.[29] Yet this distinction between reason and affection becomes lost in some English translations of Aelred's work, where Aelred's broader concept of attachment is conflated with the particular experience of affection. Yet Aelred argues that even where no *affectus* is felt, such as in the case of an enemy, love can be moved by reason.[30] Love that arises from both *affectus* and reason, however, is perfect—and this is what he calls spiritual friendship.[31] Spiritual friendship is the highest form of attachment.

In some ways, Aelred's twelfth-century conception of attachment is similar to the psychosocial concept of attachment found in twentieth and twenty-first century scholarship. Aelred's fourth type, natural attachment, is closest to the current psychosocial theory based on familial bonds that naturally arise between children and their caregivers. Love for one's blood relatives "is inherent in our very nature," Aelred writes, and this natural attachment lays the groundwork for spiritual friendship.[32]

Yet while a link exists between Aelred's spiritual friendship and the modern view of psychosocial attachment, they are not equivalent. A primary area of distinction among all five types is the role that affection and reason play. Psychosocial attachment bonds arise unconsciously and may be analyzed by reason only after they emerge. Human beings form natural attachments toward those on whom they depend for survival and emotional cues, whether or not their needs are met in the relationship. As people become conscious of their attachments, they can work intentionally toward more healthy relationships. Without forgetting the distinctions between Aelred's understandings of relational attachment bonds and the modern psychosocial theory, this chapter explores the parallels between spiritual friendship and attachment—connections that support the addition of bonding to the dimensions of religion.

SPIRITUAL FRIENDSHIP AS AN ATTACHMENT BOND

In describing the contours of the bonding dimension of religion in his Big Four model, Saroglou specifically names attachment security as a component of human bonding that plays an integral role in religion.[33] As in Aelred's "natural attachment," attachment as conceptualized by modern psychosocial theory initially arises from an emotional bond. Because of this inception point, I concur with Saroglou that attachment is best located within the emotional bonding dimension of religion rather than as belief, behavior, or belonging. This initial "spontaneous, pleasant inclination of the spirit toward someone" can grow and develop into Aelred's ideal form of friendship, spiritual friendship.[34]

Saroglou recognizes that depending on the type of transcendent connection one has, bonding may produce different qualities of emotion: positive, negative, or a combination of the two. Attachment, of course, can be secure or insecure, eliciting a range of emotions. Though Aelred cites only positive emotions associated with his ideal experience of Christian spiritual friendship, except to allow for negative emotions in grieving a friend who has died, Aelred does acknowledge lesser forms of friendship in his five types delineated above where negative emotions might be characteristic.[35] Aelred also accounts for the possibility that extenuating circumstances merit immediate withdrawal of friendship, proving the fact that it was never true friendship at all. In less dire circumstances, if a friendship proves to be untrue it may be gradually dissolved, but Aelred insists that love must remain.[36]

Attachment as a modern psychosocial theory emerged in the 1950s from the work of British psychoanalyst John Bowlby and Canadian American developmental psychologist Mary Ainsworth. Their theory describes a behavioral system embedded in dyadic interaction. During a time of distress, infants employ their agency to have their anxiety soothed by seeking proximity to a caregiver who is the "attachment figure" or partner.[37] If the caregiver is attuned to the infant's needs, soothing will successfully occur. As defined by Ainsworth, attachment bonds specifically provide the "experience of security and comfort obtained from the relationship with the partner, and yet the ability to move off from the secure base provided by the partner, with confidence to engage in other activities."[38] These two distinctive qualities are known as the safe haven and the secure base: the secure attachment bond provides a safe haven from anxiety, and the secure base assures a place of refuge that affords the confidence and freedom to explore the world. The caregiver's effectiveness in providing each of these is dependent upon their emotional attunement to the child.

Secure attachment thrives in the context of freedom and love, where the relationship offers a place of comfort and security that enables the other to explore the world with autonomy. This attachment bond stimulates positive affect and does not remain a hierarchical relationship; as an individual matures, secure attachments become mutual in adolescence and beyond. Following the maturation of the individual, then, the terminology in attachment theory moves appropriately from "caregiver" to "partner."

Three qualities of secure attachment—attunement, safe haven, and secure base—are evident in Aelred's descriptions of spiritual friendship. Aelred attentively observes his friend, Ivo, among conversing monks and notices that he may be holding back something he wishes to say.[39] Similarly, he notices that another spiritual friend, Walter, is troubled while Aelred is occupied "dealing with worldly men." Aelred comments, "Just now you were shooting glances this way and that, rubbing your forehead with your hand, and running your fingers through your hair, with your face itself betraying your anger that something has happened to you against your will."[40] Observation with such personal details reflects an attunement where Aelred is attentive to Walter's emotional states, and Aelred connects friendship with such attentive presence.[41] In secure human attachment, attunement to another's signals activates attachment behavior that enables a person to have the experience of loving and being loved.[42] Aelred describes this love as "a show of favor," which is what attunement is: special attention to another's emotional states that enables the experience of mutual love.

Aelred also describes the soothing he received from his own dear friend who represented a safe haven for him in times of distress. Aelred writes, "He was my spirit's resting place, a sweet comfort in times of grief; when I was tired with labors his loving heart received me, and his counsel refreshed me when I was sunk in sadness and lamentation. When I was stirred up he set me at ease, and when I became angry he calmed me."[43] Such calming and rest within a safe haven can be achieved, of course, because of the mutual attunement Aelred shared with his spiritual friends that enabled them to attend to one another's emotional needs during times of distress.

Finally, spiritual friendship develops in the spirit of freedom, offering a secure base. A coerced relation is never true friendship for Aelred, because it violates the God-given capacity for free choice. As humans exercise free choice, they may love well or badly. The right use of love is directing it toward God, neighbor, and self. Self-centeredness, on the other hand, is the abuse of love.[44] Thus, Aelred insists that he seeks to submit to his friends rather than rule over them, even as an abbot.[45] Such freedom is a sign of secure attachment; as Aelred quotes Aristotle, "An insecure friendship is not friendship at all."[46] There is immense freedom in knowing that a friend loves you and will not seek to manipulate or dominate you, and is even willing to let you go. Indeed, Aelred releases his dearest friends in their deaths. Even as he confesses, "I shall follow you with attachment," he commits these beloved friends into the presence of God.[47]

Aelred describes four components of spiritual friendship that are consonant with secure attachment relationships: love, affection, security, and delight. He explains each in turn:

> Friendship involves love when there is a show of favor that proceeds from benevolence. It involves affection when a certain inner pleasure comes from friendship. It involves security when it leads to a revelation of all one's secrets and purposes without fear or suspicion. It involves delight when there is a certain meeting of the minds—an agreement that is pleasant and benevolent—concerning all matters, whether happy or sad.[48]

Security, of course, is part of the ideal pattern of attachment. A person develops the expectation that their needs will be met and does not feel anxious, distant, or terrified in the relationship. The presence of love and affection result in mutual delight. Aelred's descriptions of spiritual friendship thus overlap in crucial ways with the characteristics of secure psychosocial attachment. The transcendent nature of these relationships affirms the importance of the bonding dimension as an integral part of religion. Every human being develops attachment bonds, and those secure bonds that are particularly characteristic of spiritual friendship facilitate transcendent emotional connection to others and to God. Indeed, as Saroglou proposes, attachment and other types of emotional bonds are "universally present across religions and cultural contexts" and play a role in distinguishing religion from other social constructs.[49]

EXPANDING THE BOUNDS OF ATTACHMENT THEORY

In what types of human relationships, then, can the emotional bond of friendship facilitate the experience of religion? Critiques of modern attachment theory resonate with Aelred's own monastic context in which attachment was not only operative in one-on-one relationships, but across a broader network of friends in religious community. Such critiques challenge modern attachment theory's traditional bounds in a Western-biased dyadic framework. In contrast to the Eurocentric assumption that takes a single, primary attachment figure as normative, a broader social network of attachments is present in many cultures. This has important implications for envisioning friendship in the bonding dimension of religion.

The modern psychosocial theory of attachment as conceived by Bowlby and Ainsworth centers the bond between two persons. In this conceptualization, a child bonds individually with each caregiver and has a normative preference for the mother-figure. Bowlby writes, "There is abundant evidence that almost every child habitually prefers one person, usually his mother-figure, to whom to go when distressed . . . in her absence, he will *make do* with someone else" (emphasis added).[50] Ainsworth clarifies that infants have a principal attachment figure, with other attachment figures ordered in terms of a hierarchy of whom the infant prefers.[51] Yet, this fails to account for normative multiple caregiver systems prevalent in the non-Western world.[52]

Even though the mother-child bond is the most powerful bond in nearly all human cultures, in many contexts it is buoyed by a larger caregiving network that is integral to human sociality and development. Multiple attachments can form simultaneously with a wider distribution of persons whom children expect to care for and protect them, which challenges the hegemonic universality of the infant-mother dyad as ideal for secure attachment.[53] "The dyad does not exist in isolation," argue anthropologists Courtney Meehan and Sean Hawks. "It is embedded in and influenced by the greater social network in which it resides."[54] Infants who benefit from multiple caregivers may develop greater resiliency, enhancing their sense of security that an entire community is available and reliable.[55] They have a broader and more accessible safe haven, a larger secure base, and a variety of persons attuned to their needs.

Religious reflections on friendship have often followed a dyadic pattern, focusing on a pair of friends. And yet, given Aelred's monastic context, his vision for spiritual friendship is situated in the context of a broader community.[56] For Aelred, spiritual friendship in monastic community begins in particular intimate friendships but expands to a much greater network of friends.[57] As we engage in religious reflections on friendship, it is important to account for this broader understanding by paying attention to an entire network friendship that arises within religious groups. Attachment bonds arise not merely among a pair of friends as a static or fixed relationship, but more dynamically across entire religious communities.

In his book *Spiritual Friendship,* Aelred recounts a conversation among three spiritual friends, not just a dyad. And everywhere Aelred goes within the monastery, he delights in his co-inhabitants not merely as neighbors but as beloved friends. He testifies,

> When I was walking around the monastery cloister three days ago, as the beloved crowd of brothers was sitting together in a circle, I marveled as though walking among the pleasures of paradise . . . I found not one brother in that whole multitude whom I did not love, and by whom I did not think I was loved in turn; and so I was filled with joy so great that it surpassed all the delights of this world. Indeed, I felt as though my spirit had been poured into all of them, and their affection had been transplanted into me, so that I could say with the Prophet, "Behold, how good and pleasant it is, when brothers dwell together in unity."[58]

Aelred finds that his deep affection for his brothers as spiritual friends enables him to experience the delight of friendship with God—not just one friend, but the collective unit comprised of unique individuals, so that the whole is greater than the sum of its parts.[59]

Friendship in religion, then, is not merely a one-on-one dyadic or instrumental phenomenon. It is consonant with Aelred's theology to understand spiritual friendship as having a communal orientation in a network of secure attachments as transcendent human bonds that can foster religious identity and connection in a more robust way than dyadic interpersonal relationships can. Friendship as part of the bonding dimension of religion is ideally situated within a religious community of shared beliefs, behaviors, and belonging that emerges in a secure relational network of constitutive friendships that evoke transcendent connection to others and the divine.

CONCLUSION: FROM BOUNDS
TO BONDS OF RELIGION

Moving beyond the initial bounds of believing, behaving, and belonging through which religion has frequently been conceived, the bonding dimension invites us to acknowledge friendship as an integral part of religion. In many cases, friendship is an expression of the emotional attachment intrinsic to human experience, beginning in infancy and continuing through the lifespan. When situated in the context of religious community, healthy bonds of friendship resemble what Aelred described as the attachment of spiritual friendship, which can facilitate a sense of transcendence and union with the divine. These bonds are not bound to dyadic relationships, but are dynamic as they flourish across an entire unbounded, ever-expanding interpersonal network.

This new interdisciplinary perspective draws our attention back to the important work of religious reflections on friendship and sets a course for continued inquiry. Reflecting on friendship was relevant for the Roman Catholic monastic tradition in which Aelred was located in twelfth-century England; it remains important for religious traditions across cultures. In every religious community, friendship bonds impact the human experience of religion. Not only can these bonds be analyzed in terms of attachment, but these bonds live and grow across networks of relationships. For instance, could friendship bonds be mapped for an entire religious community, and if so, how might that correlate with the quality of those members' religious experience and group identification? Two sociologists, for instance, researched emotional attachment within a Southern sorority by mapping the relational connections across the group.[60] A similar study of networked friendship bonds in religious community could be illuminating, grounded in empirical research in particular contexts.

Because the quality of relational bonds impacts human religious experience, a distinction between secure and insecure attachment is important. In positive instances, secure attachment is expressed in expansive friendship that contributes to the flourishing of individuals and communities. In negative instances, insecure attachment is expressed in restrictive friendship, as in some instances noted above by Aelred, that distort people's experiences of themselves, one another, and the divine. Several religious researchers have begun exploring the connection between attachment in religious groups and faith, though not expressly in terms of friendship.[61] In my research in the area of adolescent faith development, I investigate secure and insecure attachment relationships for adolescents in faith communities and the impact that spiritual friendship has on their faith. This intersection of attachment theory, spiritual friendship, and youth ministry has not otherwise been explored. My work is in its early stages, but it suggests a correlation between the quality of a young person's friendships within a religious group and that person's identification with that religious group and the contours of their faith in general.[62]

This chapter has been limited to exploring the importance of the human bond of friendship for religion. The bond of attachment to God or a divine being is another avenue for inquiry, already begun by the field of the psychology of religion.[63] What overlap might exist between the psychological investigation of attachment to God, and theological explorations of friendship with God? Hussam S. Timani, for instance, has recently explored the Friendship of

God in the Sufi tradition, looking at biblical figures with *walaya* status, which indicates their proximity to God on the same level of the Muslim prophets.[64] Such areas for future exploration arise when we expand the dimensions of religion to include bonding, a pursuit begun in this chapter accounting for the attachment of spiritual friendship. Imagining friendship within an attachment bond framework opens new possibilities for friendship in religious perspective, evoking our imagination for human flourishing in religious community through the networked bonds of friendship.

NOTES

1. Mordecai M. Kaplan, *Judaism as a Civilization: Toward a Reconstruction of American-Jewish Life* (Philadelphia: The Jewish Publication Society, 1934), 215–16, 516. I quote here Kaplan's summary of his argument, adding italics to highlight the concepts that correspond with behaving, belonging, and believing, respectively: "Jewish organization should embrace all the *activities* of Jews, and integrate those activities into an organic unity. To such communities will *belong* all Jews who feel physical or spiritual kinship with Jewish people, no matter what their personal *philosophy* may be" (emphasis added). With such diverse Jewish communities, ranging from the Zionist impulse for a national civilization in Palestine to autonomous subcultures within other nations, Kaplan argues it is impossible to expect universal behaviors or orthodoxy. He therefore emphasizes belonging and deemphasizes behavior and beliefs.

2. Kaplan, *Judaism as a Civilization,* 518.

3. Grace Davie, *Religion in Britain since 1945: Believing without Belonging,* (Cambridge, MA: Blackwell, 1994), 2. In her 2015 update, Davie identifies this group as the largest segment of the British population. Grace Davie, *Religion in Britain: A Persistent Paradox,* 2nd ed. (Chichester, West Sussex, UK: Wiley Blackwell, 2015), 63.

4. Alan Kreider, *The Change of Conversion and the Origin of Christendom,* Christian Mission and Modern Culture (Harrisburg, PA: Trinity Press International, 1999), 22.

5. Kreider, *Change of Conversion,* 74–75.

6. Kreider, *Change of Conversion,* 92–98. The Christendom era established common *belief* in orthodox Christianity where heresy is outlawed and unofficial alternatives live underground, religious instruction is generally rudimentary, and Christian symbols dominate society. *Belonging* envelops both civil society and the church, which are a single entity. All infants are recruited, church parishes encompass entire neighborhoods, church and state exist in symbiosis, church loyalty is required, the "world" is externalized to all non-Christendom societies, clericalism develops, social affinities are localized, and mission is deemphasized. Finally, common *behaviors* are coerced through social and financial pressures and enforced by church and state alike. These behaviors are defined by a common-sense conflation of local custom

and scriptural norms (especially, the Old Testament), and exceptionally committed Christians are set apart in the clergy or monastic orders.

7. Vassilis Saroglou, "Believing, Bonding, Behaving, and Belonging: The Big Four Religious Dimensions and Cultural Variation," *Journal of Cross-Cultural Psychology* 42, no. 8 (2011): 1323–27, https://doi.org/10.1177/0022022111412267.

8. Saroglou, "Believing, Bonding, Behaving, and Belonging," 1320.

9. Saroglou argues that dysfunctional religious contexts overemphasize one dimension above the others, as in the case of dogmatism (overemphasizing belief), neurotic religion (overemphasizing bonding), moral rigorism (overemphasizing behavior), and prejudice (overemphasizing belonging). Saroglou, "Believing, Bonding, Behaving, and Belonging," 1331.

10. Saroglou, "Believing, Bonding, Behaving, and Belonging," 1332.

11. Rievaulx, *Aelred of Rievaulx's Spiritual Friendship*, 54, 77. II.61, III.87.

12. Adele M. Fiske, *Friends and Friendship in the Monastic Tradition*, CIDOC Cuaderno 51 (Cuernavaca, Mexico: Centro Intercultural de Documentacion, 1970), 373.

13. Fiske, *Friends and Friendship*, 7.

14. Rievaulx, *Spiritual Friendship*, 32. I.19.

15. Rievaulx, *Spiritual Friendship*, 57. III.2.

16. Aelred of Rievaulx, *The Mirror of Charity*, trans. Elizabeth Connor, Cistercian Fathers Series 17 (Kalamazoo, MI: Cistercian, 1990), 241. III.11.31.

17. Rievaulx, *Mirror of Charity*, 134. I.79.

18. Rievaulx, *Spiritual Friendship*, 11.

19. Rievaulx, *Mirror of Charity*, 240. III.10.29.

20. Rievaulx, *Mirror of Charity*, 270. III.29.72.

21. Rievaulx, *Mirror of Charity*, 241. III.11.32. Aelred cites the Hebrew Bible example of Amnon, who was driven by the devil to a wicked spiritual "attachment to culpable pleasure" and raped his sister Tamar.

22. Rievaulx, *Mirror of Charity*, 242–43. III.12.33. Aelred offers the examples of admiration for the martyrs and apostles, the Hebrew Bible account of Jonathan and David's love, and Jesus' love for the wealthy man in Mark 10:21.

23. Rievaulx, *Mirror of Charity*, 259. III.24.56. For instance, Aelred cites the New Testament case of Paul and Barnabas leaving Antioch and Paul sending Timothy on a mission.

24. Rievaulx, *Mirror of Charity*, 243. III.12.34.

25. Rievaulx, *Mirror of Charity*, 243. III.12.35.

26. Rievaulx, *Mirror of Charity*, 260. III.25.58.

27. Rievaulx, *Mirror of Charity*, 244. III.14.36. Aelred lists numerous examples of this in scripture.

28. Rievaulx, *Mirror of Charity*, 246. III.15.38.

29. Fiske, *Friends and Friendship*, 331, 334.

30. Rievaulx, *Mirror of Charity*, 248–49. III.17.40.

31. Rievaulx, *Mirror of Charity*, 254. III.20.48.

32. Rievaulx, *Mirror of Charity*, 227. III.4.9.

33. Saroglou, "Believing, Bonding, Behaving, and Belonging," 1332.

34. Rievaulx, *Mirror of Charity*, 241. III.11.31.

35. Rievaulx, *Mirror of Charity*, 152. I.34.105–6.

36. Rievaulx, *Spiritual Friendship*, 68–69. III.54–8.

37. John Bowlby, *A Secure Base: Clinical Applications of Attachment Theory*, 1988 (London: Routledge, 2005), 31.

38. Mary D. Salter Ainsworth, "Attachments Beyond Infancy," *American Psychologist* 44, no. 4 (1989): 711.

39. Rievaulx, *Spiritual Friendship*, 29. I.1.

40. Rievaulx, *Spiritual Friendship*, 42. II.1.

41. Fiske, *Friends and Friendship*, 369.

42. Bowlby, *Secure Base*, 35.

43. Rievaulx, *Spiritual Friendship*, 88. III.126–7.

44. Rievaulx, *Mirror of Charity*, 234–35. III.7.21.

45. Rievaulx, *Spiritual Friendship*, 65. III.38.

46. Aristotle, *The Athenian Constitution; The Eudemian Ethics; On Virtues and Vices*, trans. H. Rackham, Loeb Classical Library 258 (Cambridge, MA: Harvard University Press, 1935), 397. EE 7.4.3.

47. Rievaulx, *Mirror of Charity*, 159. I.34.114.

48. Rievaulx, *Spiritual Friendship*, 67–68. III.51.

49. Saroglou, "Believing, Bonding, Behaving, and Belonging," 1320.

50. Bowlby, *Secure Base*, 31.

51. Mary D. Salter Ainsworth et al., *Patterns of Attachment: A Psychological Study of the Strange Situation*, Classic ed. (1978; repr., New York: Psychology Press, 2015), 265.

52. Birgitt Röttger-Rössler, "Bonding and Belonging beyond WEIRD Worlds," in *Different Faces of Attachment: Cultural Variations on a Universal Human Need*, ed. Hiltrud Otto and Heidi Keller (New York: Cambridge University Press, 2014), 147.

53. Courtney L. Meehan and Sean Hawks, "Cooperative Breeding and Attachment among the Aka Foragers," in *Attachment Reconsidered: Cultural Perspectives on a Western Theory*, ed. Naomi Quinn and Jeannette Marie Mageo, (New York: Palgrave Macmillan, 2013), 108.

54. Courtney L. Meehan and Sean Hawks, "Maternal and Allomaternal Responsiveness: The Significance of Cooperative Caregiving in Attachment Theory," in *Different Faces of Attachment: Cultural Variations on a Universal Human Need*, ed. Hiltrud Otto and Heidi Keller (New York: Cambridge University Press, 2014), 114.

55. Suzanne Gaskins, "The Puzzle of Attachment: Unscrambling Maturational and Cultural Contributions to the Development of Early Emotional Bonds," in *Attachment Reconsidered: Cultural Perspectives on a Western Theory*, ed. Naomi Quinn and Jeannette Marie Mageo, (New York: Palgrave Macmillan, 2013), 50. This provides them with greater physical, social, and emotional investment. See also Meehan and Hawks, "Cooperative Breeding and Attachment among the Aka Foragers," 86.

56. Brian Patrick McGuire, *Friendship & Community: The Monastic Experience, 350–1250* (Cistercian Studies Series 95. Kalamazoo, MI: Cistercian, 1988), xliv.

57. Marsha L. Dutton, "The Sacramentality of Community in Aelred," in *A Companion to Aelred of Rievaulx (1110–1167)*, ed. Marsha L. Dutton, vol. 76, (Boston: Brill, 2017), 255.

58. Rievaulx, *Spiritual Friendship*, 75. III.82.

59. Rievaulx, *Spiritual Friendship*, 45. II.14.

60. Pamela Paxton and James Moody, "Structure and Sentiment: Explaining Emotional Attachment to Group," *Social Psychology Quarterly* 66, no. 1, (2003), 34–47.

61. For instance, see Knabb and Pelletier's (2014) study on attachment-based functioning within church-affiliated small groups, and Freeze and DiTommaso's (2015) investigation of the extension of attachment theory to adults' attachment to church family. Joshua J. Knabb and Joseph Pelletier, "'A Cord of Three Strands is Not Easily Broken': An Empirical Investigation of Attachment-Based Small Group Functioning in the Christian Church," *Journal of Psychology and Theology* 42, no. 4 (2014): 343–58; and Tracy A. Freeze and Enrico DiTommaso, "Attachment to God and Church Family: Predictors of Spiritual and Psychological Well-Being," *Journal of Psychology and Christianity* 34, no. 1 (2015): 60–72.

62. Sarah Ann Bixler, "Networks of Belonging: Envisioning Adolescent Attachment in Congregations," PhD diss., Princeton Theological Seminary (Ann Arbor, MI: ProQuest Dissertations Publishing, 2021).

63. See, for instance, Lee A. Kirkpatrick, "An Attachment Theory Approach to the Psychology of Religion," *The International Journal for the Psychology of Religion* 20, no. 1 (1992): 3–28.

64. Hussam S. Timani, "'The Friendship of God' in Islam: Why Biblical Figures Matter" (paper presentation, American Academy of Religion, Denver, November 21, 2022).

BIBLIOGRAPHY

Ainsworth, Mary D. Salter. "Attachments Beyond Infancy." *American Psychologist* 44, no. 4 (1989): 709–16.

Ainsworth, Mary D. Salter, Mary C. Blehar, Everett Waters, and Sally N. Wall. *Patterns of Attachment: A Psychological Study of the Strange Situation*. Classic ed. 1978. Reprint, New York: Psychology Press, 2015.

Aristotle. *The Athenian Constitution; The Eudemian Ethics; On Virtues and Vices*. Translated by H. Rackham. Cambridge, MA: Harvard University Press, 1935.

Bixler, Sarah Ann. "Networks of Belonging: Envisioning Adolescent Attachment in Congregations," PhD diss., Princeton Theological Seminary. Ann Arbor, MI: ProQuest Dissertations Publishing, 2021.

Bowlby, John. *A Secure Base: Clinical Applications of Attachment Theory*. 1988. London: Routledge, 2005.

Davie, Grace. *Religion in Britain: A Persistent Paradox*. 2nd ed. Chichester, West Sussex, UK: Wiley Blackwell, 2015.

Davie, Grace. *Religion in Britain Since 1945: Believing without Belonging*. Cambridge, MA: Blackwell, 1994.

Dutton, Marsha L. "The Sacramentality of Community in Aelred." In *A Companion to Aelred of Rievaulx (1110–1167)*, edited by Marsha L. Dutton, 76:246–67. Boston: Brill, 2017.

Fiske, Adele M. *Friends and Friendship in the Monastic Tradition*. CIDOC Cuaderno 51. Cuernavaca, Mexico: Centro Intercultural de Documentacion, 1970.

Freeze, Tracy A. and Enrico DiTommaso. "Attachment to God and Church Family: Predictors of Spiritual and Psychological Well-Being." *Journal of Psychology and Christianity* 34, no. 1 (2015): 60–72.

Gaskins, Suzanne. "The Puzzle of Attachment: Unscrambling Maturational and Cultural Contributions to the Development of Early Emotional Bonds." In *Attachment Reconsidered: Cultural Perspectives on a Western Theory*, edited by Naomi Quinn and Jeannette Marie Mageo, 33–64. New York: Palgrave Macmillan, 2013.

Kaplan, Mordecai M. *Judaism as a Civilization: Toward a Reconstruction of American-Jewish Life*. Philadelphia: The Jewish Publication Society, 1934.

Kirkpatrick, Lee A. "An Attachment-Theory Approach to the Psychology of Religion." *The International Journal for the Psychology of Religion* 20, no. 1 (1992): 3–28.

Kittay, Eva Feder. "Human Dependency and Rawlsian Equality." In *Feminists Rethink the Self*, edited by Diana T. Meyers, 219–66. Feminist Theory and Politics. Boulder, CO: Westview, 1997.

Knabb, Joshua J. and Joseph Pelletier. "'A Cord of Three Strands is Not Easily Broken': An Empirical Investigation of Attachment-Based Small Group Functioning in the Christian Church." *Journal of Psychology and Theology* 42, no. 4 (2014): 343–58.

Kreider, Alan. *The Change of Conversion and the Origin of Christendom*. Christian Mission and Modern Culture. Harrisburg, PA: Trinity Press International, 1999.

McGuire, Brian Patrick. *Friendship & Community: The Monastic Experience, 350–1250*. Cistercian Studies Series 95. Kalamazoo, MI: Cistercian, 1988.

Meehan, Courtney L., and Sean Hawks. "Cooperative Breeding and Attachment among the Aka Foragers." In *Attachment Reconsidered: Cultural Perspectives on a Western Theory*, edited by Naomi Quinn and Jeannette Marie Mageo, 85–113. New York: Palgrave Macmillan, 2013.

Meehan, Courtney L., and Sean Hawks. "Maternal and Allomaternal Responsiveness: The Significance of Cooperative Caregiving in Attachment Theory." In *Different Faces of Attachment: Cultural Variations on a Universal Human Need*, edited by Hiltrud Otto and Heidi Keller, 113–40. New York: Cambridge University Press, 2014.

Paxton, Pamela, and James Moody. "Structure and Sentiment: Explaining Emotional Attachment to Group." *Social Psychology Quarterly* 66, no. 1 (2003): 34–47.

Rievaulx, Aelred of. *Aelred of Rievaulx's Spiritual Friendship: A New Translation*. Translated by Mark F. Williams. Cranbury, NJ: University of Scranton Press; Associated University Presses, 1994.

Rievaulx, Aelred of. *The Mirror of Charity*. Translated by Elizabeth Connor. Cistercian Fathers Series 17. Kalamazoo, MI: Cistercian, 1990.

Röttger-Rössler, Birgitt. "Bonding and Belonging beyond WEIRD Worlds." In *Different Faces of Attachment: Cultural Variations on a Universal Human Need*, edited by Hiltrud Otto and Heidi Keller, 141–68. New York: Cambridge University Press, 2014.

Saroglou, Vassilis. "Believing, Bonding, Behaving, and Belonging: The Big Four Religious Dimensions and Cultural Variation." *Journal of Cross-Cultural Psychology* 42, no. 8 (2011): 1320–40.

Timani, Hussam S. "A Comparative Exploration of 'the Friendship of God' in the Catholic and Sufi Traditions." Paper presentation. American Academy of Religion. Denver: November 21, 2022.

Index

Abraham, 3, 99, 126, 128, 131
accompaniment/accompanying, 5, 6, 107, 111–12, 114, 165, 210
action, 7, 15, 39, 43, 48, 82, 99, 124, 167, 192–93
adelphopoiesis (brother-making), 179, 186n43
Aelred of Rievaulx, 6, 7, 141–42, 149–51, 154n35, 155n38, 209, 212–19
affect/affect theory, 5, 107–11, 116–17, 215
affection, 42, 48, 125, 137, 143, 148, 165, 212–14, 216, 218
agape/agapē, 6, 72, 127, 138n17, 161–65, 180, 187n57, 191–92, 196–99, 202–3
agrarian communities/societies, 4, 41, 44, 45, 46, 49
Ainsworth, Mary, 215, 217
Aldred, Raymond C., 4, 77, 86, 87
Allah, 3, 93–101
Allen, Danielle, 42, 51
allegory, 78, 82
āhāb, 48
almsgiving, 152
altruism/altruistic, 125–26, 170n51
Ambrose, 127–28, 129, 132–34
animality, 108, 111, 116, 117

animals, 14, 107, 108–9, 110–17, 117–18n9, 119n31, 120n38
anthropocentrism, 115
anthropology, 116, 163
anthropomorphism, 114–15
Aotearoa, New Zealand, 2, 18, 51–52, 57n100
Apocrypha/apocryphal books, 126
apophatism/apophatic/apophatic theological traditions, 107, 113–14
Aquinas, Thomas, 6, 141–42, 151–53, 155nn52–53, 160–62, 164, 167, 198
Arendt, Hannah, 192, 193–94, 196
Aristotle, 2, 14, 42, 71, 125, 141, 147, 159, 116, 168, 193, 194, 198–99, 205n8, 216
ascesis, 179–80, 183
attachment, 7, 35, 110, 184n5, 209, 212–20
attachment theory, 7, 209, 215, 217, 219
Augustine, 6, 132, 134–36, 141–49, 153, 160, 161, 164, 170n48, 205n8
awliya', 95, 96

Balthasar, Hans Urs von, 183
Bargh, Maria, 49
Barzakh (point of mediation), 97–98
Beaman, Lori, 4, 27, 31, 32–36
Beardy, Isaiah, 17

About the Editors and Contributors

Anne-Marie Ellithorpe is Research Associate at the Vancouver School of Theology and adjunct faculty at Corpus Christi College. She holds a Ph.D. from the University of Queensland in Brisbane, Australia and is engaged in research and consultancy work in Canada and Aotearoa on various projects, including Indigenous themes and theologies. Dr. Ellithorpe's research is primarily friendship-focused, including personal, civic, theological, and spiritual dimensions of friendship. She authored *Towards Friendship-Shaped Communities: A Practical Theology of Friendship*, published in April 2022, is co-editor of *Visions of the End Times: Revelations of Hope and Challenge* (2022), and has published in the *Journal of Moral Theology* and several conference volumes. Anne-Marie co-chairs the Religious Reflections on Friendship unit of the American Academy of Religion.

Rabbi Dr. Laura Duhan-Kaplan is Director of Interreligious Studies and Professor of Jewish Studies at the Vancouver School of Theology, and Rabbi Emerita of Or Shalom Synagogue. She holds a Ph.D. in Philosophy and Education from Claremont Graduate University. Over the years, Dr. Duhan-Kaplan has received five professional awards for her teaching of philosophy and religion. Her recent books include *Mouth of the Donkey: Re-imagining Biblical Animals* (2021) and *Shechinah, Bring Me Home: Kabbalah and the Omer in Real Life* (2022). Recent co-edited books include *Visions of the End Times: Revelations of Hope and Challenge* (2022), *Encountering the Other: Christian and Multi-faith Perspectives* (2020), and *Spirit of Reconciliation: A Multi-faith Resource* (2020).

Hussam S. Timani is Professor of Philosophy and Religion and Co-Director of the Middle East and North Africa Studies Program at Christopher Newport University. He is co-editor of *Strangers in this World: Multireligious Reflections on Immigration* (Fortress Press, 2015) and *Post-Christian Interreligious Liberation Theology* (2019). Dr. Timani is the recipient of the 2017 *National Association for the Advancement of the Colored People (NAACP) Award* for leadership and service as interfaith guidepost in the Commonwealth of Virginia and the 2009 *Rumi Forum Education Award* for service, leadership, and dedication to the cause of dialogue, peace, tolerance, community service, and understanding.

* * *

Rev. Dr. Raymond C. Aldred is a member of the Cree Nation (Swan River Band) from Alberta, Treaty 8. He is the director of the Indigenous Studies Program at the Vancouver School of Theology. Its mission is to partner with the Indigenous Church around theological education. Dr. Aldred, a communications trainer, holds a Doctor of Theology from Wycliffe College, Toronto School of Theology, and is ordained with the Anglican Church of Canada. Co-edited projects include *Spirit of Reconciliation: A Multi-faith Resource* (2020) and *Our Home and Treaty Land: Walking Our Creation Story* (2022).

Rev. Sarah Ann Bixler (Ph.D., Princeton Theological Seminary) is Assistant Professor of Formation and Practical Theology and Associate Dean of the Seminary at Eastern Mennonite University in Harrisonburg, Virginia. With a career in ministry, teaching, and administration at Anabaptist Mennonite institutions, she engages in theological reflection on the formative practices of Christian communities. Her publications include "The Self Unveiled: The Dis-Integration of Mennonite Women's Head Coverings" in *Resistance: Confronting Violence, Power, and Abuse within Peace Churches*, ed. Cameron Altaras and Carol Penner (2022) and editor of the *Collected Essays of Richard R. Osmer* (2022).

Rev. Dr. Liz Carmichael MBE is an Emeritus Research Fellow at St John's College, Oxford. As a medical doctor, she worked one year in Newfoundland/Labrador, Canada, then seven years in Soweto, South Africa (1975–1981). Back in Oxford Dr. Carmichael completed a second BA in Theology, and a doctorate on the language of friendship in Christian theology which became the book *Friendship: Interpreting Christian Love* (2004). Working 1991–1996 in the Anglican Diocese of Johannesburg, Dr. Carmichael was ordained in 1992 and served on the peace committees during South Africa's transition to democracy. She was Chaplain and Tutor in Theology at St John's College 1996–2011, and subsequently wrote *Peacemaking and Peacebuilding in South Africa: The National Peace Accord 1991–1994* (2022).

Brandy Daniels is Assistant Professor of Theology and Gender & Women's Studies at the University of Portland. She has published over 14 peer-reviewed essays, on wide-ranging topics including Bonhoeffer and Foucault on racial identity; poststructuralism and liberation theology; Eastern Orthodox apophatic theology; and Lacanian psychoanalytic theory. She is working on her first monograph, entitled *How (Not) to Be Christian*. Dr. Daniels co-chairs the Queer Studies in Religion unit of the American Academy of Religion, the LGBTQIA+ Working Group of the Society of Christian Ethics, and is on the executive committee for the Political Theology Network. She is an ordained Disciples of Christ minister and a part of Portland Interfaith Clergy Resistance.

Dorothy Dean is Assistant Professor of Religion at Hastings College in Hastings, Nebraska, and holds a Ph.D. in Theology from Vanderbilt University. She has published articles on ecofeminist theology and "human nonexceptionalism" in the Anthropocene, and on the implications of feminist aesthetics for biodiversity. She is currently writing about secular spirituality and climate grief. Dr. Dean has been a member of the American Academy of Religion since 2009 and is on the steering committees for the Feminist Theory and Religious Reflection Unit and the Religious Reflections on Friendship Seminar.

Allen G. Jorgenson is Assistant Dean, Professor of Systematic Theology, and holds the Willam D. Huras Chair in Ecclesiology and Church History at Martin Luther University College, Wilfrid Laurier University. His most recent publications include *Indigenous and Christian Perspectives in Dialogue: Kairotic Place and Borders* (Lexington, 2021) and a translation with Iain G. Nicol of collection of Schleiermacher's sermons entitled *Jesus' Life in Dying: Friedrich Schleiermacher's Pre-Easter Reflections to the Community of the Redeemer* (2020).

Dr. Jeffery D. Long, the Carl W. Zeigler Professor of Religion, Philosophy, and Asian Studies at Elizabethtown College in Pennsylvania, specializes in the religions and philosophies of India. He is the author of several books and numerous articles, as well as the editor of the series "Explorations in Indic Traditions" for Lexington Books. In 2020, he received Elizabethtown College's Ranck Award for Excellence in Research, and in 2022, his book, *Hinduism in America: A Convergence of Worlds*, received the Rajinder and Jyoti Gandhi Book Award for Excellence in Theology, Philosophy, and Critical Reflection from the Dharma Academy of North America. Dr. Long has spoken in numerous venues, both national and international, including Princeton University, Yale University, the University of Chicago, Jawaharlal Nehru University, and Delhi University, and has also given three talks at the United Nations.

Marcus Mescher is Associate Professor of Christian Ethics at Xavier University. He holds a Ph.D. from Boston College and specializes in Catholic social teaching and moral formation. His research and writing concentrate in the following areas: human dignity and rights; social/environmental justice for the global common good; how moral agency is impacted by cultural context and digital technology; sexual justice and the ethics of marriage and family life; and how to heal social divisions and unjust inequalities in pursuit of inclusive solidarity. Dr. Mescher has contributed book chapters to several edited volumes and has published articles in the *Journal of Moral Theology*, the *Journal of Catholic Social Thought*, *Jesuit Higher Education*, and *Praxis: An Interdisciplinary Journal of Faith and Justice*. He is the author of *The Ethics of Encounter: Christian Neighbor Love as a Practice of Solidarity* (2020) and *Fratelli Tutti Study Guide* (2021). His current research and writing focus on moral injury caused by clergy sexual abuse and its concealment by church officials.

Shelly Penton is a Ph.D. Candidate in Modern and Contemporary Religious Thought at the University of Virginia. Her research lies at the intersections of religious studies, memory studies, and media studies. More specifically, her work grapples with narrations of race and history in contemporary film, turning to cultural memory studies and the Jewish and Christian traditions to rethink epistemological questions and categories. Penton holds an MDiv from Vanderbilt University and an MA in Religion, Literature, and Visual Culture from the University of Chicago.

John M. Thompson is Professor of Philosophy and Religion at Christopher Newport University in Newport News, Virginia. He earned his Ph.D. in the historical and cultural study of religions from the Graduate Theological Union in Berkeley, California. Although he specializes in Buddhism and Chinese traditions, Dr. Thompson has broad interests in the fields of religion, theology, philosophy, and Asian Studies. He has published three books and over 50 scholarly and popular articles, including several specifically focusing on issues of religion and violence. John has been an active member of the American Academy of Religion for over 20 years, presenting numerous papers and serving on the steering committee of the Mysticism Group twice, and was recently elected to the steering committee of AAR's Comparative Approaches to Religion and Violence unit.

Adam Tietje is a Th.D. Candidate at Duke Divinity School in Theology and Ethics. He previously served as an active duty U.S. Army chaplain for nine years and continues to serve in the U.S. Army Reserve. His scholarly interests include theological ethics, political theology, war ethics, the ethics and the care of moral injury and trauma, and military chaplains at the intersection of church and state. He is the author of *Toward a Pastoral Theology of Holy Saturday: Providing Spiritual Care for War Wounded Souls* and several other publications, including book chapters and articles in the *Journal of Church and State*, *Pastoral Psychology*, and *Pro Ecclesia*. He is an ordained minister in the United Church of Christ.

Paul J. Wadell is Professor Emeritus of Theology and Religious Studies, St. Norbert College, De Pere, Wisconsin. From 2000 to 2010, Paul Wadell was coordinator for faculty and staff development of St. Norbert's Faith, Learning & Vocation program. Previously, Dr. Wadell taught for many years at Catholic Theological Union. His principal areas of scholarly interest include virtue ethics, the role of friendship in the moral life, and theological and ethical dimensions of vocation. He is the author of a number of books, including *Living Vocationally: The Journey of the Called Life*, co-authored with Charles R. Pinches (2021), *Happiness and the Christian Moral Life: An Introduction to Christian Ethics* (2008), *Becoming Friends: Worship, Justice, and the Practice of Christian Friendship* (2002), and *Friendship and the Moral Life* (1989). Dr. Wadell also contributed chapters to several volumes on theology and ethics and has written numerous articles for both scholarly and popular theological journals. Dr. Wadell earned a Ph.D. in theology from the University of Notre Dame.